COLLECTED POEMS

COLLECTED POEMS

BY

ALFRED NOYES

VOL. III.

THE LORD OF MISRULE
TALES OF THE MERMAID TAVERN
THE WINE-PRESS
THE SEARCH-LIGHTS
A BELGIAN CHRISTMAS EVE
A SALUTE FROM THE FLEET

William Blackwood & Sons
Edinburgh and London
1920

CONTENTS OF VOL. III.

CONTENTS.

COLLECTED POEMS.

THE LORD OF MISRULE
AND OTHER POEMS.

THE MAY-TREE.

THE May-tree on the hill
 Stands in the night
So fragrant and so still
 So dusky white,

That, stealing from the wood
 In that sweet air,
You'd think Diana stood
 Before you there.

If it be so, her bloom
 Trembles with bliss.
She waits across the gloom
 Her shepherd's kiss.

Touch her.   A bird will start
 From those pure snows,—
The dark and fluttering heart
 Endymion knows.

THE WAGGON.

CRIMSON and black on the sky, a waggon of clover
   Slowly goes rumbling, over the white chalk road;
And I lie in the golden grass there, wondering why
      So little a thing
     As the jingle and ring of the harness,
      The hot creak of leather,
      The peace of the plodding,
    Should suddenly, stabbingly, make it
      Dreadful to die.

Only, perhaps, in the same blue summer weather,
   Hundreds of years ago, in this field where I lie,
Cædmon, the Saxon, was caught by the self-same thing:
   The serf lying, black with the sun, on his beautiful
     wain-load,
       The jingle and clink of the harness,
       The hot creak of leather,
       The peace of the plodding;
     And wondered, O terribly wondered,
       That men must die.

OLD GREY SQUIRREL.

A GREAT while ago, there was a school-boy.
  He lived in a cottage by the sea.
And the very first thing he could remember
  Was the rigging of the schooners by the quay.

He could watch them, when he woke, from his window,
  With the tall cranes hoisting out the freight.
And he used to think of shipping as a sea-cook,
  And sailing to the Golden Gate.

For he used to buy the yellow penny dreadfuls,
  And read them where he fished for conger-eels,
And listened to the lapping of the water,
  The green and oily water round the keels.

There were trawlers with their shark-mouthed flat-fish,
  And red nets hanging out to dry,
And the skate the skipper kept because he liked 'em,
  And landsmen never knew the fish to fry.

There were brigantines with timber out of Norroway,
  Oozing with the syrups of the pine.
There were rusty dusty schooners out of Sunderland,
  And ships of the Blue Cross line.

And to tumble down a hatch into the cabin
  Was better than the best of broken rules;
For the smell of 'em was like a Christmas dinner,
  And the feel of 'em was like a box of tools.

And, before he went to sleep in the evening,
   The very last thing that he could see
Was the sailor-men a-dancing in the moonlight
   By the capstan that stood upon the quay.

He is perched upon a high stool in London.
   The Golden Gate is very far away.
They caught him, and they caged him, like a squirrel.
   He is totting up accounts, and going grey.

He will never, never, never sail to 'Frisco.
   But the very last thing that he will see
Will be sailor-men a-dancing in the sunrise
   By the capstan that stands upon the quay. . . .

To the tune of an old concertina,
   By the capstan that stands upon the quay.

THE LORD OF MISRULE.

"On May-days the wild heads of the parish would choose a Lord of Misrule, whom they would follow even into the church, though the minister were at prayer or preaching, dancing and swinging their may-boughs about like devils incarnate."—*Old Puritan Writer.*

ALL on a fresh May morning, I took my love to church,
To see if Parson Primrose were safely on his perch.
He scarce had won to *Thirdly*, or squire begun to snore,
        When, like a sun-lit sea-wave,
            A green and crimson sea-wave,
A frolic of madcap May-folk came whooping through the
    door :—

        Come up, come in with streamers !
            Come in with boughs of may !
        Come up and thump the sexton,
            And carry the clerk away.
        Now skip like rams, ye mountains,
            Ye little hills, like sheep !
        Come up and wake the people
            That parson puts to sleep.

They tickled their nut-brown tabors. Their garlands flew
    in showers,
And lasses and lads came after them, with feet like dancing
    flowers.
Their queen had torn her green gown, and bared a shoulder
    as white,
        O, white as the may that crowned her,
            While all the minstrels round her
Tilted back their crimson hats and sang for sheer delight :

Come up, come in with streamers!
  Come in, with boughs of may!
Now by the gold upon your toe
  You walked the primrose way.
Come up, with white and crimson!
  O, shake your bells and sing;
Let the porch bend, the pillars bow,
  Before our Lord, the Spring!

The dusty velvet hassocks were dabbled with fragrant
    dew.
The font grew white with hawthorn, it frothed in every pew.
Three petals clung to the sexton's beard as he mopped and
      mowed at the clerk,
          And "Take that sexton away," they cried;
            "Did Nebuchadnezzar eat may?" they cried.
"Nay, that was a prize from Betty," they cried, "for kissing
    her in the dark."

        Come up, come in with streamers!
          Come in, with boughs of may!
        Who knows but old Methuselah
          May hobble the green-wood way?
        If Betty could kiss the sexton,
          If Kitty could kiss the clerk,
        Who knows how Parson Primrose
          Might blossom in the dark?

The congregation spluttered.   The squire grew purple
    and all,
And every little chorister bestrode his carven stall.
The parson flapped like a magpie, but none could hear his
    prayers;
          For Tom Fool flourished his tabor,
            Flourished his nut-brown tabor,
Bashed the head of the sexton, and stormed the pulpit
    stairs.

High in the old oak pulpit
    This Lord of all mis-rule—
I think it was Will Summers
    That once was Shakespeare's fool—
Held up his hand for silence,
    And all the church grew still:
"And are you snoring yet," he said,
    "Or have you slept your fill?

"Your God still walks in Eden, between the ancient
    trees,
Where Youth and Love go wading through pools of prim-
    roses.
And this is the sign we bring you, before the darkness fall,
    That Spring is risen, is risen again,
    That Life is risen, is risen again,
That Love is risen, is risen again, and Love is Lord of all.

At Paske began our morrice
    And ere Pentecost our May;
Because, albeit your words be true,
    You know not what you say.
You chatter in church like jackdaws,
    Words that would wake the dead,
Were there one breath of life in you,
    One drop of blood, he said.

He died and He went down to hell! You know not what
    you mean.
Our rafters were of green fir. Also our beds were green.
But out of the mouth of a fool, a fool, before the darkness
    fall,
    We tell you He is risen again,
    The Lord of Life is risen again,
The boughs put forth their tender buds, and Love is Lord
    of all!

He bowed his head.   He stood so still,
  They bowed their heads as well.
And softly from the organ-loft
  The song began to swell.
Come up with blood-red streamers,
  The reeds began the strain.
The *vox humana* pealed on high,
    The spring is risen again !

The *vox angelica* replied—*The shadows flee away !*
Our house-beams were of cedar.   Come in, with boughs of may !
The *diapason* deepened it—*Before the darkness fall,*
      We tell you He is risen again !
        Our God hath burst his prison again !
The Lord of Life is risen again ; and Love is Lord of all.

CRIMSON SAILS.

WHEN Salomon sailed from Ophir . . .
  The clouds of Sussex thyme
That crown the cliffs in mid-July
Were all we needed—you and I—
But Salomon sailed from Ophir,
  And broken bits of rhyme
Blew to us on the white chalk coast
  From O, what elfin clime?

A peacock butterfly flaunted
  Its four great crimson wings,
As over the edge of the chalk it flew
Black as a ship on the Channel blue . . .
When Salomon sailed from Ophir,—
  He brought, as the high sun brings,
Honey and spice to the Queen of the South,
Sussex or Saba, a song for her mouth,
Sweet as the dawn-wind over the downs
And the tall white cliffs that the wild thyme crowns,
  A song that the whole sky sings :—

When Salomon sailed from Ophir,
  With Olliphants and gold,
The kings went up, the kings went down,
Trying to match King Salomon's crown,

But Salomon sacked the sunset,
   Wherever his black ships rolled.
He rolled it up like a crimson cloth,
   And crammed it into his hold.

Chorus : Salomon sacked the sunset!
      Salomon sacked the sunset!
     He rolled it up like a crimson cloth,
      And crammed it into his hold.

His masts were Lebanon cedars,
   His sheets were singing blue,
But that was never the reason why
He stuffed his hold with the sunset sky!
The kings could cut their cedars,
   And sail from Ophir, too ;
But Salomon packed his heart with dreams,
   And all the dreams were true.

Chorus : The kings could cut their cedars,
      Cut their Lebanon cedars ;
     But Salomon packed his heart with dreams,
      And all the dreams were true.

When Salomon sailed from Ophir,
   He sailed not as a king.
The kings—they weltered to and fro,
Tossed wherever the winds could blow ;
But Salomon's tawny seamen
   Could lift their heads and sing,
Till all their crowded clouds of sail
   Grew sweeter than the Spring.

Chorus : Their singing sheets grew sweeter,
      Their crowded clouds grew sweeter,
     For Salomon's tawny seamen, sirs,
      Could lift their heads and sing :

When Salomon sailed from Ophir
    With crimson sails so tall,
The kings went up, the kings went down,
Trying to match King Salomon's crown ;
But Salomon brought the sunset,
    To hang on his Temple wall ;
He rolled it up like a crimson cloth,
    So his was better than all.

Chorus : Salomon gat the sunset,
        Salomon gat the sunset ;
    He carried it like a crimson cloth
        To hang on his Temple wall.

THE HILL-FLOWERS.

I.

Moving through the dew, moving through the dew,
Ere I waken in the city—Life, thy dawn makes all things
*   new !*
And up a fir-clad glen, far from all the haunts of men,
Up a glen among the mountains, O, my feet are wings again !

Moving through the dew, moving through the dew,
O mountains of my boyhood, I come again to you,
By the little path I know, with the sea far below,
And above, the great cloud-galleons with their sails of rose
    and snow ;

As of old, when all was young, and the earth a song unsung,
And the heather through the crimson dawn its Eden incense
    flung
From the mountain-heights of joy, for a careless-hearted
    boy,
And the lav'rocks rose like fountain sprays of bliss that
    ne'er could cloy,

From their little beds of bloom, from the golden gorse and
    broom,
With a song to God the Giver, o'er that waste of wild
    perfume ;
Blowing from height to height, in a glory of great light,
While the cottage-clustered valleys held the lilac last of
    night,

So, when dawn is in the skies, in a dream, a dream, I rise,
And I follow my lost boyhood to the heights of Paradise.
Life, thy dawn makes all things new!   Hills of Youth, I
      come to you,
Moving through the dew, moving through the dew.

II.

Moving through the dew, moving through the dew,
Floats a brother's face to meet me! Is it you? Is it you?
For the night I leave behind keeps these dazzled eyes still
      blind!
But O, the little hill-flowers, their scent is wise and kind;

And I shall not lose the way from the darkness to the day,
While dust can cling as their scent clings to memory for
      aye;
And the least link in the chain can recall the whole again,
And heaven at last resume its far-flung harvests, grain by
      grain.

To the hill-flowers clings my dust, and tho' eyeless Death
      may thrust
All else into the darkness, in their heaven I put my trust;
And a dawn shall bid me climb to the little spread of
      thyme
Where first I heard the ripple of the fountain-heads of
      rhyme.

And a fir-wood that I know, from dawn to sunset glow,
Shall whisper to a lonely sea, that swings far, far below.
Death, thy dawn makes all things new.   Hills of Youth, I
      come to you,
Moving through the dew, moving through the dew.

BEYOND DEATH.

I.

In lonely bays
Where Love runs wild,
  All among the flowering grasses,
Where light, light, light, as a sea-bird's wing
  The chuckle of the child-god passes,
O, to awake, to shake away the night
  And find you dreaming there,
On the other side of death, with the sea-wind blowing
      round you,
  And the scent of the thyme in your hair.

II.

Tho' beauty perish,
Perish like a flower,
  And song be an idle breath,
Tho' heaven be a dream, and youth for but an hour,
  And life much less than death,
And the Maker less than that He made,
  And hope less than despair,
If Death have shores where Love runs wild,
  I think you might be there.

III.

Re-born, re-born
From the splendid sea,
  There should you awake and sing,
With every supple sweet from the head to the feet
  Modelled like a wood-dove's wing,—

O, to awake, to shake away the night,
    And find you happy there,
On the other side of death, with the sea-wind blowing
        round you,
    And the scent of the thyme in your hair,

THE PSYCHE OF OUR DAY.

As constant lovers may rejoice
    With seas between, with worlds between,
Because a fragrance and a voice
    Are round them everywhere :
So let me travel to the grave,
    Believing still—for I have seen—
That Love's triumphant banners wave
    Beyond my own despair.

I have no trust in my own worth ;
    Yet have I faith, O love, for you,
That every beauty in bloom or leaf,
    That even age and wrong
May touch, may hurt you, on this earth,
    But only, only as kisses do ;
Or as the fretted string of grief
    Completes the bliss of song.

That you shall see, on any grave
    The snow fall, like that unseen hand
Which O, so often, pressed your hair
    To cherish and console :
That seas may roar and winds rave,
    But you shall feel and understand
What vast caresses everywhere
    Convey you to the goal.

So was it always in the years
    When Love began, when Love began
With eyes that were not touched of tears
    And lips that still could sing—

And all around us, in the May,
   The child-god with his laughter ran,
And every bloom, on every spray,
   Betrayed his fluttering wing.

So hold it, keep it, count it, sweet,
   Until the end, until the end.
It is not cruelty, but bliss
   That pains and is so fond :
Crush life like thyme beneath your feet,
   And O, my love, when that strange friend,
The Shadow of Wings, which men call Death
   Shall close your eyes, with that last kiss,
Ask not His name.   A rosier breath
   Shall waken you—beyond.

THE RIVER OF STARS.

(A TALE OF NIAGARA.)

THE lights of a hundred cities are fed by its midnight power.
Their wheels are moved by its thunder. But they, too, have
    their hour.
The tale of the Indian lovers, a cry from the years that are
    flown,
        While the river of stars is rolling,
        Rolling away to the darkness,
Abides with the power in the midnight, where love may find
    its own.

She watched from the Huron tents, till the first star shook
    in the air.
The sweet-pine scented her fawn-skins, and breathed from
    her braided hair.
Her crown was of milk-white blood-root, because of the
    tryst she would keep,
        Beyond the river of beauty
        That drifted away in the darkness
Drawing the sunset thro' lilies, with eyes like stars, to the
    deep.

He watched, like a tall young wood-god, from the red pine
    that she named ;
But not for the peril behind him, where the eyes of the
    Mohawks flamed.

Eagle-plumed he stood.   But his heart was hunting afar
    Where the river of longing whispered . . .
        And one swift shaft from the darkness
Felled him, her name in his death-cry, his eyes on the
    sunset star.
.   .   .   .

She stole from the river and listened.   The moon on her
    wet skin shone.
As a silver birch in a pine-wood, her beauty flashed and
    was gone.
There was no wave in the forest.   The dark arms closed
    her round.
        But the river of life went flowing,
            Flowing away to the darkness,
For her breast grew red with his heart's blood, in a night
    where the stars are drowned.

Teach me, O my lover, as you taught me of love in a day,
Teach me of death, and for ever, and set my feet on the way,
To the land of the happy shadows, the land where you are
    flown.
        —And the river of death went weeping,
            Weeping away to the darkness.—
Is the hunting good, my lover, so good that you hunt alone?

She rose to her feet like a shadow.   She sent a cry thro'
    the night,
Sa-sa-kuon, the death-whoop, that tells of triumph in fight.
It broke from the bell of her mouth like the cry of a
    wounded bird,
        But the river of agony swelled it
            And swept it along to the darkness,
And the Mohawks, couched in the darkness, leapt to their
    feet as they heard.

Close as the ring of the clouds that menace the moon with
    death,
At once they circled her round.   Her bright breast panted
    for breath.

With only her own wild glory keeping the wolves at bay,
     While the river of parting whispered,
       Whispered away to the darkness,
She looked in their eyes for a moment, and strove for a
    word to say.

Teach me, O my lover! — She set her foot on the
    dead.
She laughed on the painted faces with their rings of yellow
    and red,—
*I thank you, wolves of the Mohawk, for a woman's hands
    might fail.—*
     —And the river of vengeance chuckled,
       Chuckled away to the darkness,—
*But ye have killed where I hunted.   I have come to the end
    of my trail.*

*I thank you, braves of the Mohawk, who laid this thief at
    my feet.*
He tore my heart out living, and tossed it his dogs to eat.
*Ye have taught him of death in a moment, as he taught me
    of love in a day.*
     —And the river of passion deepened,
       Deepened and rushed to the darkness.—
*And yet may a woman requite you, and set your feet on the
    way.*

*For the woman that spits in my face, and the shaven heads
    that gibe,*
*This night shall a woman show you the tents of the Huron
    tribe.*
*They are lodged in a deep valley.   With all things good it
    abounds.*
      Where the red-eyed, green-mooned river
       Glides like a snake to the darkness,
*I will show you a valley, Mohawks, like the Happy Hunting
    Grounds.*

Follow! They chuckled, and followed like wolves to the
    glittering stream.
Shadows obeying a shadow, they launched their canoes in
    a dream.
Alone, in the first, with the blood on her breast, and her
    milk-white crown,
        She stood. She smiled at them, *Follow*,
          Then urged her canoe to the darkness,
And, silently flashing their paddles, the Mohawks followed
    her down.

.   .   .   .

And now—as they slid thro' the pine-woods with their
    peaks of midnight blue,
She heard, in the broadening distance, the deep sound that
    she knew,
A mutter of steady thunder that grew as they glanced
    along ;
        But ever she glanced before them
          And danced away to the darkness,
And or ever they heard it rightly, she raised her voice in a
    song :—

The wind from the Isles of the Blessèd, it blows across the
    foam.
It sings in the flowing maples of the land that was my home.
Where the moose is a morning's hunt, and the buffalo feeds
    from the hand.—
        And the river of mockery broadened,
          Broadened and rolled to the darkness—
And the green maize lifts its feathers, and laughs the snow
    from the land.

The river broadened and quickened. There was nought
    but river and sky.
The shores were lost in the darkness. She laughed and
    lifted a cry :

Follow me !   Sa-sa-kuon ! Swifter and swifter they swirled—
    And the flood of their doom went flying,
        Flying away to the darkness,
Follow me, follow me, Mohawks, ye are shooting the edge of
    the world.

They struggled like snakes to return.   Like straws they
    were whirled on her track.
For the whole flood swooped to that edge where the un-
    plumbed night dropt black,
The whole flood dropt to a thunder in an unplumbed hell
    beneath,
        And over the gulf of the thunder
           A mountain of spray from the darkness
Rose and stood in the heavens, like a shrouded image of
    death.

She rushed like a star before them.   The moon on her
    glorying shone.
Teach me, O my lover,—her cry flashed out and was gone.
A moment they battled behind her.   They lashed with
    their paddles and lunged ;
        Then the Mohawks, turning their faces
           Like a blood-stained cloud to the darkness,
Over the edge of Niagara swept together and plunged.

And the lights of a hundred cities are fed by the ancient
    power ;
But a cry returns with the midnight ; for they, too, have
    their hour.
Teach me, O my lover, as you taught me of love in a day,
    — While the river of stars is rolling,
        Rolling away to the darkness,—
Teach me of death, and for ever, and set my feet on the way !

THE DAY OF REMEMBRANCE.

DAZZLE of the sea, azure of the sky, glitter of the dew on
    the grass,
        Pass to Oblivion
        In the darkness
    With all that ever is or ever was.

Yet, O flocks of cloud with your violet shadows, O white
    may crowding o'er the lane,
        The Shepherd that drives you
        To the darkness
    Shall lead you thro' the crimson dawn again.

Bear your load of beauty to the sunset, and the golden
    gates of death.
        The Eternal shall remember
        In the darkness
    And recall you at a word, at a breath.

Even as the mind of a man may remember his lost and
    linkless hours,
        This world that is scattered
        To the darkness,
    Dismembered and dis-petalled, clouds and flowers,

Cities, suns, and systems, as He said of old, they sleep!
        Not a bird, not a leaf shall pass by,
        But on the day of remembrance
        In the darkness,
    In a moment, in the twinkling of an eye,

They shall flash to their places, in the music of the whole,
    even as our fathers said !
  For a Power shall remember
    In the darkness,
 And the universal sea give up her dead.

THE STRANGE GUEST.

You cannot leave a new house
    With any open door,
But a strange guest will enter it
    And never leave it more.

Build it on a waste land,
    Dreary as a sin.
Leave her but a broken gate,
    And Beauty will come in.

Build it all of scarlet brick.
    Work your wicked will.
Dump it on an ash-heap,
    Then—O then, be still.

Sit and watch your new house
    Leave an open door.
A strange guest will enter it
    And never leave it more.

She will make your raw wood
    Mellower than gold.
She will take your new lamps
    And sell them for old.

She will crumble all your pride,
    Break your folly down.
Much that you rejected
    She will bless and crown.

She will rust your naked roof,
　Split your pavement through,
Dip her brush in sun and moon
　And colour it anew.

Leave her but a window
　Wide to wind and rain,
You shall find her footsteps
　When you come again.

Though she keep you waiting
　Many months or years,
She shall stain and make it
　Beautiful with tears.

She shall hurt and heal it,
　Soften it and save,
Blessing it, until it stand
　Stronger than the grave.

You cannot leave a new house
　With any open door,
But a strange guest will enter it
　And never leave it more.

GHOSTS.

O TO creep in by candle-light,
   When all the world is fast asleep,
Out of the cold winds, out of the night,
   Where the nettles wave and the rains weep!
O, to creep in, lifting the latch
   So quietly that no soul could hear,
And, at those embers in the gloom,
   Quietly light one careful match—
You should not hear it, have no fear—
   And light the candle and look round
The old familiar room;
   To see the old books upon the wall
And lovingly take one down again,
   And hear—O, strange to those that lay
So patiently underground—
   The ticking of the clock, the sound
Of clicking embers . . .
               watch the play
Of shadows . . .
           till the implacable call
Of morning turn our faces grey;
   And, or ever we go, we lift and kiss
Some idle thing that your hands may touch,
   Some paper or book that your hands let fall,
And we never—when living—had cared so much
   As to glance upon twice . . .
              But now, O bliss
To kiss and to cherish it, moaning our pain,
   Ere we creep to the silence again.

AFTER RAIN.

LISTEN! On sweetening air
 The blackbird growing bold
Flings out, where green boughs glisten,
 Three splashes of wild gold.

Daughter of April, hear!
 And sing, O barefoot boy!
That carol of wild sweet water
 Has washed the world with joy.

Glisten, O fragrant earth,
 Assoiled by heaven anew,
And O, ye lovers listen,
 With eyes that glisten, too.

TO A FRIEND OF BOYHOOD,
LOST AT SEA.

O WARM blue sky and dazzling sea,
Where have you hid my friend from me?
   The white chalk coast, the leagues of surf
Laugh in the sun-light now as then,
   And violets in the short sweet turf
Make fragmentary heavens again,
    And sea-born wings of rustling snow
    Pass and re-pass, as long ago.

Old friend, do you remember yet
The days when secretly we met
   In that old harbour, years a-back,
Where I admired your billowing walk ;
   Or in that perilous fishing-smack
What tarry oaths perfumed your talk,
    The sails we set, the ropes we spliced,
    The raw potato that we sliced,

For mackerel-bait—and how it shines
Far down, at end of the taut lines !—
   And the great catch we made that day
Loading our boat with rainbows, quick
   And quivering, while you smoked your clay,
And I took home your *Deadwood Dick*
    In yellow and red, when day was done,
    And you took home my Stevenson?

Not leagues, as when you sailed the deep,
But only some frail bars of sleep
    Divide us now !   Methinks you still
Recall, as I, in dreams, the quay,
    The little port below the hill ;
And all the changes of the sea,
    Like some great music, can but roll
    Our lives still nearer to the goal.

THE CRAGS.

(IN MEMORY OF THOMAS BAILEY ALDRICH.)

HAD I the right Falernian, friend,
A mellower thanks than this I'd send
     For all those golden days
     Among your creeks and bays;

Where, founded on a rock, your house
Between the pines' unfading boughs
     Watches through sun and rain
     That lonelier coast of Maine;

And the Atlantic's mounded blue
Breaks on your crags the summer through,
     A long pine's length below,
     In rainbow-tinted snow.

While on your railed verandah there
As on a deck you sail through air,
     And sea and cloud and sky
     Go softly streaming by.

Like delicate oils, at set of sun,
Smoothing the waves the colours run
     Around the enchanted hull,
     Anchored and beautiful;

Restoring to that sun-dried star
You brought from coral isles afar,
    With shells that mock the moon,
    The tints of their lagoon ;

Till, from within, your lamps declare
Your harbours by the colours there,
    An Indian god, a fan
    Painted in Old Japan.

Then, best of all, I think, at night
The moon that makes a road of light
    Across the whispering sea,
    A road—for memory ;

When the blue dusk has filled the pane,
And the great pine-logs burn again,
    And books are good to read.
    —For his were books indeed !

Their silken shadows, rustling, dim,
May sing no more of Spain for him ;
    No shadows of old France
    Renew their courtly dance.

He walks no more where shadows are
But left their ivory gates ajar,
    That shadows might prolong
    The dance, the tale, the song.

His was no narrow test or rule,
He chose the best of every school,—
    Stendhal and Keats and Donne,
    Balzac and Stevenson ;

Wordsworth and Flaubert filled their place.
Dumas met Hawthorne face to face.
    There were both new and old
    In his good realm of gold.

Our modern Vergil builded there
A Camelot of more lustrous air,
    And there, too, found a home
    The Tennyson of Rome.

The title-pages bore his name;
And, nightly, by the dancing flame,
    Following him, I found
    That all was haunted ground;

Until a friendlier shadow fell
Upon the leaves he loved so well,
    And I no longer read,
    But talked with him instead.

THE SONG-TREE.

GROW, my song, like a tree,
　　As thou hast ever grown,
Since first, a wondering child,
　　Long since, I cherished thee.
It was at break of day,
　　Well I remember it,—
The first note that I heard,
　　A magical undertone,
Sweeter than any bird
　　—Or so it seemed to me—
And my tears ran wild.
　　This tale, this tale is true.
The light was growing gray ;
　　And the rhymes ran so sweet
(For I was only a child)
　　That I knelt down to pray.

Grow, my song, like a tree.
　　Since then I have forgot
　　A thousand dreams, but not
The song that set me free,
　　So that to thee I gave
My hopes and my despairs,
　　My boyhood's ecstasy,
My manhood's prayers.
　　In dreams I have watched thee grow,
A ladder of sweet boughs,
　　Where angels come and go,

And birds keep house.
    In dreams, I have seen thee wave
Over a distant land,
    And watched thy roots expand,
And given my life to thee,
    As I would give my grave.

Grow, my song, like a tree,
    And when I am grown old,
Let me die under thee,
    Die to enrich thy mould;
Die at thy roots, and so
    Help thee to grow.
Make of this body and blood
    Thy sempiternal food.
Then let some little child,
    Some friend I shall not see,
When the great dawn is gray,
    Some lover I have not known,
In summers far away,
    Sit listening under thee.
And in thy rustling hear
    That mystical undertone,
Which made my tears run wild,
    And made thee, O, how dear.

In the great years to be?
    I am proud then?   Ah, not so.
I have lived and died for thee.
    Be patient.   Grow.

Grow, my song, like a tree.

A SPELL.

(AN EXCELLENT WAY TO GET A FAIRY.)

GATHER, first, in your left hand
  (This must be at fall of day)
Forty grains of wild sea-sand
  Where you think a mermaid lay.
I have heard that it is best
  If you gather it, warm and sweet,
Out of the dint of her left breast
  Where you see her heart has beat.

    Out of the dint in that sweet sand
      Gather forty grains, I say ;
    Yet—if it fail you—understand,
      There remains a better way.

Out of this you melt your glass
  While the veils of night are drawn,
Whispering, till the shadows pass,
  " *Nixie—pixie—leprechaun !* "
Then you blow your magic vial,
  Shape it like a crescent moon,
Set it up and make your trial,
  Singing, " *Elaby, ah, come soon !* "

    Round the cloudy crescent go,
      On the hill-top, in the dawn,
    Singing softly, on tip-toe,
      " *Elaby Gathon ! Elaby Gathon !*
    Nixie—pixie—leprechaun ! "

Bring the blood of a white hen
    Slaughtered at the break of day,
While the cock, in the fairy glen,
    Thrusts his gold neck every way,
Over the brambles, peering, calling,
    Under the ferns, with a sudden fear,
Far and wide—as the dews are falling—
    Clamouring, calling, everywhere.

> *Round the crimson vial go,*
>   *On the hill-top, in the dawn,*
> *Singing softly, on tip-toe*
>   *" Nixie—pixie—leprechaun !"*
> *If this fail, at break of day,*
> *I can show you a better way.*

Bring the buds of the hazel-copse,
    Where two lovers kissed at noon ;
Bring the crushed red wild-thyme tops
    Where they murmured under the moon.
Bring the four-leaved clover also,
    One of the white, and one of the red,
Bring the flakes of the May that fall so
    Lightly over their bridal bed.

> *Drop them into the vial—so—*
>   *On the hill-top, in the dawn,*
> *Singing softly, on tip-toe,*
>   *" Nixie—pixie—leprechaun !"*
> *And, if once will not suffice,*
>   *Do it thrice !*
> *If this fail, at break of day,*
>   *There remains a better way.*

Bring an old and crippled child
    —*Ah, tread softly, on tip-toe !*—
Tattered, tearless, wonder-wild,
    From that under-world below,

Bring a wizened child of seven
   Reeking from the City slime,
Out of hell into your heaven,
   Set her knee-deep in the thyme.

    Feed her—clothe her—even so!
      Set her on a fairy-throne.
    When her eyes begin to glow,
      Leave her for an hour—alone.

You shall need no spells or charms,
   On that hill-top, in that dawn.
Where she lifts her wasted arms,
   You shall see a veil withdrawn.
There shall be no veil between them,
   Though her head be old and wise!
You shall know that she has seen them
   By the glory in her eyes.

    Round her irons on that hill
      Earth has tossed a fairy fire:
    Watch, and listen, and be still,
      Lest you baulk your own desire.

When she sees four azure wings
   Light upon her claw-like hand;
When she lifts her head and sings,
   You shall hear and understand:
You shall hear a bugle calling
   Wildly over the dew-dashed down;
And a sound as of the falling
   Ramparts of a conquered town.

    You shall hear a sound like thunder;
      And a veil shall be withdrawn,
    When her eyes grow wide with wonder
      On that hill-top, in that dawn.

BLIND MOONE OF LONDON.

"Dispersed through Shakespeare's plays are innumerable little fragments of ballads, the entire copies of which could not be recovered.
Many of these are of the most beautiful and pathetic simplicity."

BLIND MOONE of London
   He fiddled up and down,
Thrice for an angel,
   And twice for a crown.
He fiddled at the *Green Man,*
   He fiddled at the *Rose;*
And where they have buried him
   Not a soul knows.

All his tunes are dead and gone, dead as yesterday.
   And his lanthorn flits no more
   Round the *Devil Tavern* door,
Waiting till the gallants come, singing from the play;
   Waiting in the wet and cold!
   All his Whitsun tales are told.
He is dead and gone, sirs, very far away.

   He would not give a silver groat
      For good or evil weather.
   He carried in his white cap
      A long red feather.
   He wore a long coat
      Of the Reading-tawny kind,
   And darned white hosen
      With a blue patch behind.

So—one night—he shuffled past, in his buckled shoon.
        We shall never see his face,
        Twisted to that queer grimace,
Waiting in the wind and rain, till we called his tune ;
        Very whimsical and white,
        Waiting on a blue Twelfth Night !
He is grown too proud at last—old blind Moone.

        Yet when May was at the door,
          And Moone was wont to sing,
        Many a maid and bachelor
          Whirled into the ring :
        Standing on a tilted wain
          He played so sweet and loud,
        The Mayor forgot his golden chain
          And jigged it with the crowd.

Old blind Moone, his fiddle scattered flowers along the
    street ;
        Into the dust of Brookfield Fair
        Carried a shining primrose air,
Crooning like a poor mad maid, O, very low and sweet,
        Drew us close, and held us bound,
        Then—to the tune of *Pedlar's Pound*,
Caught us up, and whirled us round, a thousand frolic feet.

        Master Shakespeare was his host.
          The tribe of Benjamin
        Used to call him Merlin's Ghost
          At the Mermaid Inn.
        He was only a crowder,
          Fiddling at the door.
        Death has made him prouder,—
          We shall not see him more.

Only—if you listen, please—through the master's themes,
      You shall hear a wizard strain,
      Blind and bright as wind and rain
Shaken out of willow-trees, and shot with elfin gleams.
      How should I your true love know?
      Scraps and snatches—even so!
That is old blind Moone again, fiddling in your dreams.

      Once, when Will had called for sack
        And bidden him up and play,
      Old blind Moone, he turned his back,
        Growled, and walked away,—
      Sailed into a thunder-cloud,
        Snapped his fiddle-string,
      And hobbled from *The Mermaid*
        Sulky as a king.

Only from the darkness now, steals the strain we knew :
      No one even knows his grave!
      Only here and there a stave,
Out of all his hedgerow flock, be-drips the may with dew.
      And I know not what wild bird
      Carried us his parting word :—
Master Shakespeare needn't take the crowder's fiddle, too.

      Will has wealth and wealth to spare :
        Give him back his own.
      At his head a grass-green turf,
        At his heels a stone.
      See his little lanthorn-spark.
        Hear his ghostly tune,
      Glimmering past you, in the dark,
        Old blind Moone!

All the little crazy brooks, where love and sorrow run
        Crowned with sedge and singing wild,
        Like a sky-lark—or a child !—
Old blind Moone he knew their springs, and played 'em
    every one ;
        Stood there, in the darkness, blind,
        And sung them into Shakespeare's mind. . . .

Old blind Moone of London, O now his songs are done,
The light upon his lost white face, they say it was the sun !

The light upon his poor old face, they say it was the sun !

TALES OF THE MERMAID TAVERN.

DEDICATED TO EDMUND GOSSE.

I.—A KNIGHT OF THE OCEAN-SEA.

UNDER that foggy sunset London glowed
Like one huge cob-webbed flagon of old wine.
And, as I walked down Fleet Street, the soft sky
Flowed thro' the roaring thoroughfares, transfused
Their hard sharp outlines, blurred the throngs of black
On either pavement, blurred the rolling stream
Of red and yellow busses, till the town
Turned to a golden suburb of the clouds.
And, round that mighty bubble of St Paul's,
Over the up-turned faces of the street,
An air-ship slowly sailed, with whirring fans,
A voyager in the new-found realms of gold,
A shadowy silken chrysalis whence should break
What radiant wings in centuries to be.

So, wandering on, while all the shores of Time
Softened into Eternity, it seemed
A dead man touched me with his living hand,
A flaming legend passed me in the streets

Of London—laugh who will—that City of Clouds,
Where what a dreamer yet, in spite of all,
Is man, that splendid visionary child
Who sent his fairy beacon through the dusk,
On a blue bus before the moon was risen,—
This Night, at eight, the Tempest!

                         Dreaming thus,
(Small wonder that my footsteps went astray!)
I found myself within a narrow street,
Alone.   There was no rumour, near or far,
Of the long tides of traffic.   In my doubt
I turned and knocked upon an old inn-door,
Hard by, an ancient inn of mullioned panes,
And crazy beams and over-hanging eaves :
And, as I knocked, the slowly changing west
Seemed to change all the world with it and leave
Only that old inn steadfast and unchanged,
A rock in the rich-coloured tides of time.

And, suddenly, as a song that wholly escapes
Remembrance, at one note, wholly returns,
There, as I knocked, memory returned to me.
I knew it all—the little twisted street,
The rough wet cobbles gleaming, far away,
Like opals, where it ended on the sky ;
And, overhead, the darkly smiling face
Of that old wizard inn ; I knew by rote
The smooth sun-bubbles in the worn green paint
Upon the doors and shutters.

                        There was one
Myself had idly scratched away one dawn,
One mad May-dawn, three hundred years ago,
When out of the woods we came with hawthorn boughs
And found the doors locked, as they seemed to-night.
Three hundred years ago—nay, Time was dead !
No need to scan the sign-board any more
Where that white-breasted siren of the sea
Curled her moon-silvered tail among such rocks

As never in the merriest seaman's tale
Broke the blue bliss of fabulous lagoons
Beyond the Spanish Main.

                      And, through the dream,
Even as I stood and listened, came a sound
Of clashing wine-cups: then a deep-voiced song
Made the old timbers of the Mermaid Inn
Shake as a galleon shakes in a gale of wind
When she rolls glorying through the Ocean-sea.

SONG.

I.

Marchaunt Adventurers, chaunting at the windlass,
    Early in the morning, we slipped from Plymouth Sound,
All for Adventure in the great New Regions,
    All for Eldorado and to sail the world around!
Sing! the red of sun-rise ripples round the bows again!
    Marchaunt Adventurers, O sing, we're outward bound,
All to stuff the sunset in our old black galleon,
    All to seek the merchandize that no man ever found.
Chorus: Marchaunt Adventurers,
                Marchaunt Adventurers,
    Marchaunt Adventurers, O, whither are ye bound?—
All for Eldorado and the great new Sky-line,
    All to seek the merchandize that no man ever found!

II.

Marchaunt Adventurers, O, what'ull ye bring home again?—
    Woonders and works and the thunder of the sea!
Whom will ye traffic with?—The King of the Sunset!
    What shall be your pilot then?—A wind from *Galilee!*
Nay, but ye be marchaunts, will ye come back empty-
    handed?—
    Ay, we be marchaunts, though our gain we ne'er shall
    see!

Cast we now our bread upon the waste wild waters!
  After many days, it shall return with usury!
Chorus: Marchaunt Adventurers!
                 Marchaunt Adventurers!
  What shall be your profit in the mighty days to be?—
Englande!—Englande!—Englande!—Englande!
  Glory everlasting and the lordship of the sea!

        And there, framed in the lilac patch of sky
        That ended the steep street, dark on its light,
        And standing on those glistering cobble-stones
        Just where they took the sunset's kiss, I saw
        A figure like foot-feathered Mercury,
        Tall, straight and splendid as a sunset cloud,
        Clad in a crimson doublet and trunk-hose,
        A rapier at his side; and, as he paused,
        His long fantastic shadow swayed and swept
        Against my feet.
                    A moment he looked back,
        Then swaggered down as if he owned a world
        Which had forgotten—did I wake or dream?—
        Even his gracious ghost!
                         Over his arm
        He swung a gorgeous murrey-coloured cloak
        As on the day when—did I dream or wake?
        And had not all this happened once before?—
        When he had laid that cloak before the feet
        Of Gloriana!   By that Ciprus cloak,
        'Twas he!   Our Ocean-Shepherd!   Walter Raleigh!
        He brushed me passing, and with one vigorous thrust
        Opened the door and entered.   At his heels
        I followed—into the Mermaid!—through three yards
        Of pitch-black gloom, then into an old inn-parlour
        Swimming with faces in a mist of smoke
        That up-curled, blue, from long Winchester pipes,
        While—like some rare old picture, in a dream
        Recalled—quietly listening, laughing, watching,
        Pale on that old black oaken wainscot floated

One bearded oval face, young, with deep eyes,
Whom Raleigh hailed as " Will ! "
                              But as I stared
A sudden buffet from a brawny hand
Made all my senses swim, and the room rang
With laughter as upon the rush-strewn floor
My feet slipped and I fell.   Then a gruff voice
Growled over me—" Get up now, John-a-dreams,
Or else mine host must find another drawer !
Hast thou not heard us calling all this while ? "
And, as I scrambled up, the rafters rang
With cries of " Sack !   Bring me a cup of sack !
Canary !   Sack !   Malmsey ! and Muscadel ! "
I understood and flew.   I was awake,
A leather-jerkined pot-boy to these gods,
A prentice Ganymede to the Mermaid Inn !

There, flitting to and fro with cups of wine
I heard them toss the song-enchanted names
From mouth to mouth—Lyly and Peele and Lodge,
Kit Marlowe, Michael Drayton, and the rest,
With Ben, rare Ben, brick-layer Ben, who rolled
Like a great galleon on his ingle-bench.
Some twenty years of age he seemed ; and yet
This young Gargantua with the bull-dog jaws,
The T for Tyburn branded on his thumb,
And grim pock-pitted face was growling tales
To Dekker that would fright a buccaneer,—
How, soldiering in Flanders, he had killed
His man, and won that scar on his bronzed fist ;
Was taken prisoner and turned Catholick ;
And now returned to London, was resolved
To blast away the vapours of the town
With Boreas-throated plays of thunderous mirth.
" I'll thwack their Tribulation-Wholesomes, lad,
Their yellow-faced Envies and lean Thorns-i'-the Flesh,
At the *Blackfriars Theatre*, or *The Rose*,
Or else *The Curtain*.   Failing these, I'll find

Some good square inn-yard with wide galleries
And windows level with the stage. 'Twill serve
My Comedy of Vapours ; though, I grant,
For Tragedy a private House is best,
Or just as Burbage tip-toes to a deed
Of blood, or, over your stable's black half-door,
Marked *Battlements* in white chalk, your breathless David
Glowers at the whiter Bathsheba within,
Some humorous coach-horse neighs a 'hallelujah
And the pit splits its doublets. Over goes
The whole damned apple-barrel, and the yard
Is all one rough and tumble, scramble and scratch
Of prentices, green madams, and cut-purses
For half-chewed Norfolk pippins. Never mind !
We'll build the perfect stage in Shoreditch yet.
And Will, there, hath half promised I shall write
A piece for his own company ! What d'ye think
Of *Venus and Adonis*, his first heir,
Printed last week ? A bouncing boy, my lad !
And he's at work on a *Midsummer's Dream*
That turns the world to fairy-land ! "

                                           All these
And many more were there, and all were young.
There, as I brimmed their cups, I heard the voice
Of Raleigh ringing across the smoke-wreathed room,—
" Ben, could you put a frigate on the stage,
I've found a tragedy for you. Have you heard
The true tale of Sir Humphrey Gilbert ? "

                                           " No ! "

" Why, Ben, of all the tragical affairs
Of the Ocean-sea, and of that other Ocean
Where all men sail so blindly, and misjudge
Their friends, their charts, their storms, their stars, their God,
If there be truth in the blind crowder's song
I bought in Bread Street for a penny, this
Is the brief type and chronicle of them all.
Listen ! " Then Raleigh sent these rugged rhymes
Of some blind crowder rolling in great waves

Of passion across the gloom.   At each refrain
His voice dropped to a broad deep undertone,
As if the distant roar of breaking surf
Or the low thunder of eternal tides
Filled up the pauses of the nearer storm,
Storm against storm, a soul against the sea :—

A KNIGHT OF THE OCEAN-SEA.

Sir Humphrey Gilbert, hard of hand,
   Knight-in-chief of the Ocean-sea,
Gazed from the rocks of his New Found Land
   And thought of the home where his heart would be.

He gazed across the wintry waste
   That weltered and hissed like molten lead,—
" He saileth twice who saileth in haste!
   I'll wait the favour of Spring," he said.

Ever the more, ever the more,
He heard the winds and the waves roar!
Thunder on thunder shook the shore.

The yellow clots of foam went by
   Like shavings that curl from a ship-wright's plane,
Clinging and flying, afar and nigh,
   Shuddering, flying and clinging again.

A thousand bubbles in every one
   Shifted and shimmered with rainbow gleams;
But—had they been planets and stars that spun,
   He had let them drift by his feet like dreams :

Heavy of heart was our Admirall,
 For, out of his ships,—and they were but three!—
He had lost the fairest and most tall,
 And—he was a Knight of the Ocean-sea.

   Ever the more, ever the more,
   He heard the winds and the waves roar!
   Thunder on thunder shook the shore.

Heavy of heart, heavy of heart,
 For she was a galleon mighty as May,
And the storm that ripped her glory apart
 Had stripped his soul for the winter's way;

And he was aware of a whisper blown
 From foc'sle to poop, from windward to lee,
That the fault was his, and his alone,
 And—he was a Knight of the Ocean-sea.

"Had he done that!   Had he done this!"
 And yet his mariners loved him well;
But an idle word is hard to miss,
 And the foam hides more than the deep can tell.

And the deep had buried his best-loved books,
 With many a hard-won chart and plan:
And a king that is conquered must see strange looks,
 So bitter a thing is the heart of man!

And—"Whom will you find to pay your debt?
 For a venture like this is a costly thing!
Will they stake yet more, tho' your heart be set
 On the mightier voyage you planned for the spring?"

He raised his head like a Viking crowned,—
  " I'll take my old flag to her Majestie,
And She will lend me ten thousand pound
    To make her Queen of the Ocean-sea ! "

        Ever the more, ever the more,
        He heard the winds and the waves roar !
        Thunder on thunder shook the shore.

Outside—they heard the great winds blow !
    Outside—the blustering surf they heard,
And the bravest there would ha' flinched to know
    That they must be taken at their own word.

For the great grim waves were as molten lead
    —And he had two ships who sailed with three !—
" And I sail not home till the spring," he said,
    " They are all too frail for the Ocean-sea."

But the trumpeter thought of an ale-house bench,
    And the cabin-boy longed for a Devonshire lane,
And the gunner remembered a green-gowned wench,
    And the foc'sle whisper went round again,—

" Sir Humphrey Gilbert is hard of hand,
    But his courage went down with the ship, may-be,
And we wait for the Spring in a desert land,
    For—*he is afraid of the Ocean-sea.*"

        Ever the more, ever the more,
        He heard the winds and the waves roar !
        Thunder on thunder shook the shore.

He knew, he knew how the whisper went !
    He knew he must master it, last or first !
He knew not how much or how little it meant ;
    But his heart was heavy and like to burst.

"Up with your sails, my sea-dogs all!
    The wind has veered!   And my ships," quoth he,
"They will serve for a British Admirall
    Who is Knight-in-chief of the Ocean-sea!"

His will was like a North-east wind
    That swept along our helmless crew;
But he would nct stay on the *Golden Hind*,
    For that was the stronger ship of the two.

"My little ship's company, lads, hath passed
    Perils and storms a-many with me!
Would ye have me forsake them at the last?
    They'll need a Knight of the Ocean-sea!"

> *Ever the more, ever the more,*
> *We heard the winds and the waves roar!*
> *Thunder on thunder shook the shore.*

Beyond Cape Race, the pale sun splashed
    The grim grey waves with silver light
Where, ever in front, his frigate crashed
    Eastward, for England and the night.

And still as the dark began to fall,
    Ever in front of us, running free,
We saw the sails of our Admirall
    Leading us home through the Ocean-sea.

> *Ever the more, ever the more,*
> *We heard the winds and the waves roar!*
> *But he sailed on, sailed on before.*

On Monday at noon of the third fierce day
    A-board our *Golden Hind* he came,
With a trail of blood, marking his way
    On the salt wet decks as he walked half-lame.

For a rusty nail thro' his foot had pierced.
  "Come, master-surgeon, mend it for me;
Though I would it were changed for the nails that amerced
  The dying thief upon Calvary."

The surgeon bathed and bound his foot,
  And the master entreated him sore to stay;
But roughly he pulled on his great sea-boot
  With—"The wind is rising and I must away!"

I know not why so little a thing,
  When into his pinnace we helped him down,
Should make our eye-lids prick and sting
  As the salt spray were into them blown;

But he called as he went—"Keep watch and steer
  By my lanthorn at night!"   Then he waved his hand
With a kinglier watch-word, "We are as near
  To heaven, my lads, by sea as by land!"

      Ever the more, ever the more,
      We heard the gathering tempest roar!
      But he sailed on, sailed on before.

Three hundred leagues on our homeward road,
  We strove to signal him, swooping nigh,
That he would ease his decks of their load
  Of nettings and fights and artillery.

And dark and dark that night 'gan fall,
  And high the muttering breakers swelled,
Till that strange fire which seamen call
  "Castor and Pollux," we beheld,

An evil sign of peril and death,
  Burning pale on the high main-mast;
But calm with the might of Gennesareth
  Our Admirall's voice went ringing past,

Clear thro' the thunders, far and clear,
    Mighty to counsel, clear to command,
Joyfully ringing, "We are as near
    To heaven, my lads, by sea as by land!"

        Ever the more, ever the more,
        We heard the rising hurricane roar!
        But he sailed on, sailed on before.

And over us fled the fleet of the stars,
    And, ever in front of us, far or nigh,
The lanthorn on his cross-tree spars
    Dipped to the Pit or soared to the Sky!

'Twould sweep to the lights of Charles's Wain,
    As the hills of the deep 'ud mount and flee,
Then swoop down vanishing cliffs again
    To the thundering gulfs of the Ocean-sea.

We saw it shine as it swooped from the height,
    With ruining breakers on every hand,
Then—a cry came out of the black mid-night,
    As near to heaven by sea as by land!

And the light was out!   Like a wind-blown spark,
    All in a moment!   And we—and we—
Prayed for his soul as we swept thro' the dark;
    For he was a Knight of the Ocean-sea.

        Over our fleets for evermore
        The winds 'ull triumph and the waves roar!
        But he sails on, sails on before!

Silence a moment held the Mermaid Inn,
Then Michael Drayton, raising a cup of wine,
Stood up and said,—"Since many have obtained
Absolute glory that have done great deeds,

But fortune is not in the power of man,
So they that, truly attempting, nobly fail,
Deserve great honour of the common-wealth.
Such honour did the Greeks and Romans give
To those that in great enterprises fell
Seeking the true commodity of their country
And profit to all mankind ; for, though they failed,
Being by war, death, or some other chance,
Hindered, their images were set up in brass,
Marble and silver, gold and ivory,
In glorious temples and great palace-halls,
No less to make men emulate their virtues
Than to give honour to their just deserts.
God, from the time that He first made the world,
Hath kept the knowledge of His Ocean-sea
And the huge Æquinoctiall Continents
Reserved unto this day.   Wherefore I think
No high exploit of Greece and Rome but seems
A little thing to these Discoveries
Which our adventurous captains even now
Are making, out there, Westward, in the night,
Captains most worthy of commendacion,
Hugh Willoughby—God send him home again
Safe to the Mermaid !—and Dick Chauncellor,
That excellent pilot.   Doubtless this man, too,
Sir Humphrey Gilbert, was worthy to be made
Knight of the Ocean-sea.   I bid you all
Stand up, and drink to his immortal fame !"

II.—A COINER OF ANGELS.

Some three nights later, thro' the thick brown fog
A link-boy, dropping flakes of crimson fire,
Flared to the door and, through its glowing frame,
Ben Jonson and Kit Marlowe, arm in arm,
Swaggered into the Mermaid Inn, and called
For red-deer pies.
              There, as they supped, I caught
Scraps of ambrosial talk concerning Will,
His *Venus and Adonis.*
                 "Gabriel thought
'Twas wrong to change the old writers and create
A cold Adonis."
              "Laws were made for Will,
Not Will for laws, since first he stole a buck
In Charlecote woods."
              "Where never a buck chewed fern,"
Laughed Kit, "unless it chewed the fern-seed too,
And walked invisible."
              "Bring me some wine," called Ben,
And, with his knife thrumming upon the board,
He chanted, while his comrade munched and smiled.

I.

Will Shakespeare's out like Robin Hood
   With his merry men all in green,
To steal a deer in Charlecote wood
   Where never a deer was seen.

II.

He's hunted all a night of June,
    He's followed a phantom horn,
He's killed a buck by the light of the moon,
    Under a fairy thorn.

III.

He's carried it home with his April-hearted band.
    There never was haunch so fine;
For this buck was born in Elfin-land
    And fed upon sops-in-wine.

IV.

This buck had browsed on elfin boughs
    Of rose-marie and bay,
And he's carried it home to the little white house
    Of sweet Anne Hathaway.

V.

"The dawn above your thatch is red!
    Slip out of your bed, sweet Anne!
I have stolen a fairy buck," he said,
    "The first since the world began.

VI.

"Roast it on a golden spit,
    And see that it do not burn;
For we never shall feather the like of it
    Out of the fairy fern."

VII.

She scarce had donned her long white gown
    And given him kisses four,
When the surly Sheriff of Stratford-town
    Knocked at the little green door.

VIII.

They have gaoled sweet Will for a poacher ;
    But squarely he fronts the squire,
With "When did *you* hear in your woods of a deer ?
    Was it under a fairy briar ? "

IX.

Sir Thomas he puffs,—" If God thought good
    My water-butt ran with wine,
Or He dropt me a buck in Charlecote wood,
    I wot it is mine, not thine ! "

X.

" If *you* would eat of elfin meat,"
    Says Will, "you must blow up your horn !
Take your bow, and feather the doe
    That's under the fairy thorn !

XI.

" If *you* would feast on elfin food,
    You've only the way to learn !
Take your bow and feather the doe
    That's under the fairy fern ! "

XII.

They're hunting high, they're hunting low,
    They're all away, away,
With horse and hound to feather the doe
    That's under the fairy spray!

XIII.

Sir Thomas he raged!   Sir Thomas he swore!
    But all and all in vain,
For there never was deer in his woods before,
    And there never would be again!

And, as I brought the wine—" This is my grace,"
Laughed Kit, " Diana grant the jolly buck
That Shakespeare stole were toothsome as this pie."
He suddenly sank his voice,—" Hist, who comes here?
Look—Richard Bame, the Puritan!   O, Ben, Ben,
Your Mermaid Inn's the study for the stage,
Your only teacher of exits, entrances,
And all the shifting comedy.   Be grave!
Bame is the godliest hypocrite on earth!
Remember I'm an atheist, black as coal.
He has called me Wormall in an anagram.
Help me to bait him; but be very grave.
We'll talk of Venus."
                        As he whispered thus,
A long white face with small black-beaded eyes
Peered at him through the doorway.   All too well,
Afterwards, I recalled that scene, when Bame,
Out of revenge for this same night, I guessed,
Penned his foul tract on Marlowe's tragic fate;
And, twelve months later, I watched our Puritan
Riding to Tyburn in the hangman's cart
For thieving from an old bed-ridden dame
With whom he prayed, at supper-time on Sundays.

Like a conspirator he sidled in,
Clasping a little pamphlet to his breast,
While, feigning not to see him, Ben began :—

"Will's *Venus and Adonis*, Kit, is great,
A round, sound, full-blown piece of thorough work,
On a great canvas, coloured like one I saw
In Italy, by one—Titian!   None of the toys
Of artistry your lank-haired losels turn,
Your Phyllida—Love-lies-bleeding—Kiss-me-Quicks,
Your fluttering Sighs and Mark how-I-break-my-beats,
Begotten like this, whenever and how you list,
Your Moths of verse that shrivel in every taper
But a sound piece of craftsmanship to last
Until the stars are out.   'Tis twice the length
Of Vergil's books—he's listening!   Nay, don't look!—
Two hundred solid stanzas, think of that;
But each a square celestial brick of gold
Laid level and splendid.   I've laid bricks and know
What thorough work is.   If a storm should shake
The Tower of London down, Will's house would stand.
Look at his picture of the stallion,
Nostril to croup, that's thorough finished work!

Think of that kiss of Venus!   Deep, sweet, slow,
As the dawn breaking to its perfect flower
And golden noon of bliss, then slow, sweet, deep,
Like a great honeyed sunset it dissolves
Away!"
                  A hollow groan, like a bass viol,
Resounded thro' the room.   Up started Kit
In feigned alarm—"What, Master Richard Bame,
Quick, Ben, the good man's ill.   Bring him some wine!
Red wine for Master Bame, the blood of Venus
That stained the rose!"
                              "White wine for Master Bame,"
Ben echoed, "Juno's cream that" . . . Both at once
They thrust a wine-cup to the sallow lips.

"Sirs, you mistake!" coughed Bame, waving his hands
And struggling to his feet.
     "Sirs, I have brought
A message from a youth who walked with you
In wantonness, aforetime, and is now
Groaning in sulphurous fires!"
       "Kit, that means hell!"
"Yea, sirs, a pamphlet from the pit of hell,
Written by Robert Greene before he died.
Mark what he styles it—*A Groatsworth of Wit
Bought with a Million of Repentance!*"
       "Ah,
Poor Rob was all his life-time either drunk,
Wenching, or penitent, Ben! Poor lad, he died
Young. Let me see now, Master Bame, you say
Rob Greene wrote this on earth before he died,
And then you printed it yourself in hell!"
"Stay, sir, I came not to this haunt of sin
To make mirth for Beëlzebub!"
      "O, Ben,
That's you!"
    "'Swounds, sir, am I Beëlzebub?
Ogs gogs!" roared Ben, his hand upon his hilt!
"Nay, sir, I signified the god of flies!
I spake out of the scriptures!" snuffled Bame
With deprecating eye.
      "I come to save
A brand that has been kindled at this Inn,
But not yet charred, not yet so far consumed,
One Richard Cholmeley, who declares to all
He was persuaded to turn Atheist
By Marlowe's reasoning. I have wrestled with him,
But find him still so constant to your words
That only you can save him from the pit."
"Why, Master Bame," said Kit, "had I the keys
To hell, the damned should all come out and dance
A morrice round the Mermaid Inn to-night."
"Nay, sir, the damned are damned!"

                              " Come sit you down !
Take some more wine !   You'd have them all be damned
Except Dick Cholmeley.   What must I unsay
To save him ? "   A quick eye-lid dropt at Ben.
" Now tell me, Master Bame ! "

                              " Sir, he derides
The books of Moses ! "

                              " Bame, do you believe ?—
There's none to hear us but Beëlzebub—
Do you believe that we must taste of death
Because God set a foolish naked wench
Too near an apple-tree, how long ago ?
Five thousand years ?   But there were men on earth
Long before that ! "   " Come, come, sir, if you read
The books of Moses . . ."   " Moses was a juggler ! "
" A juggler, sir, how, what ! "   " Nay, sir, be calm !
Take some more wine—the white, if that's too red,—
And talk of Moses quietly.   Help yourself
To red-deer pie.   Good !   All the miracles
You say that he performed—why, what are they ?
I know one Heriots, lives in Friday Street,
Can do much more than Moses !   Eat your pie
In patience, friend, the mouth of man performs
One good work at a time.   What says he, Ben ?
The red deer stops his—what ?   Sticks in his gizzard ?
O—*led them through the wilderness !*   No doubt
He did—for forty years, and might have made
The journey in six months.   Believe me, sir,
That is no miracle.   Moses gulled the Jews !
Versed in the sly tricks of the Egyptians,
Only one art betrayed him.   Sir, his books
Are filthily written.   I would undertake—
If I were put to write a new religion—
A method far more admirable.   Eh, what ?
Gruel in the vestibule ?   Interpret, Ben.
His mouth's too full.   O, *the New Testament !*
Why, there, consider, were not all the Apostles
Fishermen and base fellows, without wit

Or worth? The Apostle Paul alone had wit,
And he was a timorous fellow in bidding men
Subject themselves to worldly magistrates
Against their conscience. I shall fry for this?
I fear no bug-bears or hob-goblins, sir,
And would have all men not to be afraid
Of roasting, toasting, pitch-forks, or the threats
Of earthly ministers, tho' their mouths be stuffed
With curses or with crusts of red-deer pie!
One thing I will confess—if I must choose—
Give me the Papists that can serve their God
Not with your scraps, but solemn ceremonies,
Organs, and singing men, and shaven crowns.
Your protestant is a hypocritical ass!"

"Profligate! You blaspheme!" Up started Bame,
A little unsteady now upon his feet,
And shaking his crumpled pamphlet over his head:

"Nay—if your pie be done, you shall partake
A second course. Be seated, sir, I pray.
We atheists will pay the reckoning.
I had forgotten that a Puritan
Will swallow Moses like a red-deer pie
Yet choke at a wax-candle! Let me read
Your pamphlet. What, 'tis half addressed to me!
Ogs-gogs! Ben! Hark to this—the Testament
Of poor Rob Greene will cut Will Shakespeare off
With less than his own Groatsworth. Hark to this."

And there, unseen by them, a quiet figure
Entered the room and beckoning me for wine
Seated himself to listen, Will himself,
While Marlowe read aloud with knitted brows.
"'Trust them not; for there is an upstart crow
Beautified with our feathers!'
                                        —O, he bids
All green eyes open!—'And being an absolute

Johannes fac-totum is in his own conceit
The only Shake-scene in a country.'"

                                 " Feathers ! "
Exploded Ben, "Why, come to that, he pouched
Your eagle's feather of blank verse, and lit
His Friar Bacon's little magic lamp
At the Promethean fire of Faustus.   Jove,
It was a faëry buck, indeed, that Will
Poached in that green-wood."
                            " Ben, see that you walk
Like Adam, naked !   Nay, in nakedness
Adam was first.   Trust me, you'll not escape
This calumny !   Vergil is damned—he wears
A hen-coop round his waist, nicked in the night
From Homer !   Plato is branded for a thief,
Why, he wrote Greek !   And old Prometheus, too,
Who stole his fire from heaven ! "
                                " Who printed it ? "

" Chettle !   I know not why, unless he too
Be one of these same dwarfs that find the world
Too narrow for their jealousies.   Ben, Ben,
I tell thee 'tis the dwarfs that find no world
Wide enough for their jostling, while the giants,
The gods themselves, can in one tavern find
Room wide enough to swallow the wide heaven
With all its crowded solitary stars."

"Ah, but the Mermaid, then, must swallow this,"
The voice of Shakespeare quietly broke in,
As laying a hand on either shoulder of Kit
He stood behind him in the gloom and smiled
Across the table at Ben, whose eyes still blazed
With boyhood's generous wrath.   "Rob was a poet.
And had I known . . . no matter !   I am sorry
He thought I wronged him.   His heart's blood beats in this.
Look, where he says he dies forsaken, Kit ! "

"Died drunk, more like," growled Ben.   "And if he
        did,"
Will answered, "none was there to help him home,
Had not a poor old cobbler chanced upon him
Dying in the streets, and taken him to his house,
And let him break his heart on his own bed.
Read his last words.   You know he left his wife
And played the moth at tavern tapers, burnt
His wings and dropt into the mud.   Read here,
His dying words to his forsaken wife,
Written in blood, Ben, blood.   Read it.   *I charge thee,
Doll, by the love of our youth, by my soul's rest,
See this man paid!   Had he not succoured me
I had died in the streets.'*   How young he was to call
Thus on their poor dead youth, this withered shadow
That once was Robin Greene.   He left a child—
See—in its face he prays her not to find
The father's, but her own.   *'He is yet green
And may grow straight,'* so flickers his last jest,
Then out for ever.   At the last he begged
A penny-pott of malmsey.   In the bill,
All's printed now for crows and daws to peck,
You'll find four shillings for his winding-sheet.
He had the poet's heart, and God help all
Who have that heart and somehow lose their way
For lack of helm, souls that are blown abroad
By the great winds of passion, without power
To sway them, chartless captains.   Multitudes ply
Trimly enough from bank to bank of Thames
Like shallow wherries, while tall galleons,
Out of their very beauty driven to dare
The uncompassed sea, founder in starless nights,
And all that we can say is—'They died drunk!'"
"I have it from veracious witnesses,"
Bame snuffled, "that the death of Robert Greene
Was caused by a surfeit, sir, of Rhenish wine
And pickled herrings.   Also, sir, that his shirt
Was very foul, and while it was at wash

He lay i' the cobbler's old blue smock, sir!"
                                        "Gods,"
The voice of Raleigh muttered nigh mine ear,
" I had a dirty cloak, once, on my arm ;
But, a Queen's feet had trodden it. . . .
                              Drawer, take
Yon pamphlet, have it fried in cod-fish oil
And bring it hither.   Bring a candle, too,
And sealing·wax ! Be quick.   The rogue shall eat it,
And then I'll seal his lips."
                        "No—not to-night,"
Kit whispered, laughing, " I've a prettier plan
For Master Bame."
                        "As for that scrap of paper,"
The voice of Shakespeare quietly resumed,
" Why, which of us could send his heart and soul
Thro' Caxton's wooden press and hope to find
The pretty pair unmangled.   I'll not trust
The spoken word, no, not of my own lips,
Before the Judgment Throne, against myself
Or on my own defence ; and I'll not trust
The printed word to mirror Robert Greene.
See—here's another Testament, in ink,
Written, not printed, for the Mermaid Inn.
Rob sent it from his death-bed straight to me,
Read it.   'Tis for the Mermaid Inn alone ;
And when 'tis read, we'll burn it, as he asks."
Then, from the hands of Shakespeare, Marlowe took
A little scroll, and while the winds without
Rattled the shutters with their ghostly hands
And wailed among the chimney-tops, he read :—

          Greeting to all the Mermaid Inn
          From their old Vice and Slip of Sin,
          Greeting, Ben, to you, and you
          Will Shakespeare and Kit Marlowe, too.
          Greeting from your Might-have-been,
          Your broken sapling, Robert Greene.

Read my letter—'tis my last,
Then let Memory blot me out,
I would not make my maudlin past
A trough for every swinish snout.
First, I leave a debt unpaid.
It's all chalked up, not much all told,
For Bread and Sack.   When I am cold,
Doll can pawn my Spanish blade
And pay mine host.   She'll pay mine host!
But . . . I have chalked up other scores
In your own hearts, behind the doors,
Not to be paid so quickly.   Yet,
O, if you would not have my ghost
Creeping in at dead of night,
Out of the cold wind, out of the wet,
With weeping face and helpless fingers
Trying to wipe the marks away,
Read what I can write, still write,
While this life within them lingers.
Let me pay, lads, let me pay.
Item, for a peacock phrase,
Flung out in a sudden blaze,
Flung out at his friend Shake-scene,
By this ragged Might-have-been,
This poor Jackdaw, Robert Greene.

Will, I knew it all the while!
And you know it—and you smile!
My quill was but a Jackdaw's feather,
While the quill that Ben, there, wields,
Fluttered down thro' azure fields,
From an eagle in the sun;
And yours, Will, yours, no earth-born thing,
A plume of rainbow-tinctured grain,
Dropt out of an angel's wing.
Only a Jackdaw's feather mine,
And mine ran ink, and Ben's ran wine,
And yours the pure Pierian streams.

But I had dreams, O, I had dreams!
Dreams, you understand me, Will;
And I fretted at the tether
That bound me to the lowly plain,
Gnawed my heart out, for I knew
Once, tho' that was long ago,
I might have risen with Ben and you
Somewhere near that Holy Hill
Whence the living rivers flow.
Let it pass.   I did not know
One bitter phrase could ever fly
So far through that immortal sky
—Seeing all my songs had flown so low—
One envious phrase that cannot die
From century to century.

Kit Marlowe ceased a moment, and the wind,
As if indeed the night were all one ghost,
Wailed round the Mermaid Inn, then sent once more
Its desolate passion through the reader's voice :—

Some truth there was in what I said.
Kit Marlowe taught you half your trade;
And something of the rest you learned
From me,—but all you took you earned.
You took the best I had to give,
You took my clay and made it live;
And that—why, that's what God must do !—
My music made for mortal ears
You flung to all the listening spheres.
You took my dreams and made them true.
And, if I claimed them, the blank air
Might claim the breath I shape to prayer.
I do not claim it !   Let the earth
Claim the thrones she brings to birth.
Let the first shapers of our tongue
Claim whate'er is said or sung,
Till the doom repeal that debt

And cancel the first alphabet.
Yet, when like a god, you scaled
The shining crags where my foot failed;
When I saw my fruit of the vine
Foam in the Olympian cup,
Or in that broader chalice shine
Blood-red, a sacramental drink,
With stars for bubbles, lifted up,
Through the universal night,
Up to the celestial brink,
Up to that quintessential Light
Where God acclaimed you for the wine
Crushed from those poor grapes of mine;
O, you'll understand, no doubt,
How the poor vine-dresser fell,
How a pin-prick can let out
All the bannered hosts of hell.
Nay, a knife-thrust, the sharp truth—
I had spilt my wine of youth,
The Temple was not mine to build.
My place in the world's march was filled.

Yet—through all the years to come—
Men to whom my songs are dumb
Will remember them and me
For that one cry of jealousy,
That curse where I had come to bless,
That harsh voice of unhappiness.
They'll note the curse, but not the pang,
Not the torment whence it sprang.
They'll note the blow at my friend's back,
But not the soul stretched on the rack.
They'll note the weak convulsive sting,
Not the crushed body and broken wing.

Item,—for my thirty years,
Dashed with sun and splashed with tears,

Wan with revel, red with wine,
This Jack-o'-lanthorn life of mine.
Other wiser, happier men,
Take the full three-score-and-ten,
Climb slow, and seek the sun.
Dancing down is soon done.
Golden boys, beware, beware,—
The ambiguous oracles declare
Loving gods for those that die
Young, as old men may; but I,
Quick as was my pilgrimage,
Wither in mine April age.

Item,—one groatsworth of wit,
Bought at an exceeding price,
Ay, a million of repentance,
Let me pay the whole of it.
Lying here these deadly nights,
Lads, for me the Mermaid lights
Gleam as for a castaway
Swept along a midnight sea
The harbour-lanthorns, each a spark,
A pin-prick in the solid dark,
That lets trickle through a ray
Glorious out of Paradise,
To stab him with new agony.
Let me pay, lads, let me pay!
Let the Mermaid pass the sentence:
I am pleading guilty now,
A dead leaf on the laurel-bough,
And the storm whirls me away.

Kit Marlowe ceased; but not the wailing wind
That round and round the silent Mermaid Inn
Wandered, with helpless fingers trying the doors,
Like a most desolate ghost.
                                        A sudden throng

Of players bustled in, shaking the rain
From their plumed hats.   " Veracious witnesses,"
The snuffle of Bame arose anew, "declare
It was a surfeit killed him, Rhenish wine
And pickled herrings.   His shirt was very foul.
He had but one.   His doublet, too, was frayed,
And his boots broken . . ."

                       " What ! Gonzago, you ! "
A short fat player called in a deep voice
Across the room and, throwing aside his cloak
To show the woman's robe he wore beneath,
Minced up to Bame and bellowed—"'Tis such men
As you, that tempt us women to our fall,"
And all the throng of players rocked and roared,
Till at a nod and wink from Kit a hush
Held them again.

             " Look to the door," he said,
" Is any listening ? "   The young player crept,
A mask of mystery, to the door and peeped.
" All's well !   The coast is clear ! "

                   " Then shall we tell
Our plan to Master Bame ? "

                  Round the hushed room
Went Kit, a pen and paper in his hand,
Whispering each to read, digest, and sign,
While Ben re-filled the glass of Master Bame.
" And now," said Kit aloud, " what think you, lads ?
Shall he be told ? "   Solemnly one or two
'Gan shake their heads with " Safety, safety, Kit ! "
" O, Bame can keep a secret.   Come, we'll tell him.
He can advise us how a righteous man
Should act.   We'll let him share an he approve.
Now, Master Bame,—come closer—my good friend,
Ben Jonson here, hath lately found a way
Of—hush !   Come closer—coining money, Bame."
" Coining ! "   " Ay, hush, now !   Hearken !   A certain, sure,
And indiscoverable method, sir.
He is acquainted with one Poole, a felon

Lately released from Newgate, hath great skill
In mixture of metals—hush!—and, by the help
Of a right cunning maker of stamps, we mean
To coin French crowns, rose-nobles, pistolettes,
Angels and English shillings."

                              For one breath,
Bame stared at him with bulging beetle-eyes,
Then murmured shyly as a country maid
In her first wooing, "Is't not against the law?"
"Why, sir, who makes the law?   Why should not Bame
Coin his own crowns like Queen Elizabeth?
She is but mortal!   And consider, too,
The good works it should prosper in your hands,
Without regard to red-deer pies and wine
White as the Milky Way.   Such secrets, Bame,
Were not good for the general; but a few
Discreet and righteous palms, your own, my friend,
And mine,—what think you?"

                          With a hesitant glance
Of well-nigh child-like cunning, screwing his eyes,
Bame laughed a little huskily and looked round
At that grave ring of anxious faces, all
Holding their breath and thrilling his blunt nerves
With their stage - practice.   "And no risk?" breathed
     Bame,
"No risk at all?"   "O, sir, no risk at all!
We make the very coins.   Besides, that part
Touches not you.   Yours is the honest face,
That's all we want."

                       "Why, sir, if you are sure
There is no risk . . ."

                            "You'll help to spend it.   Good!
We'll talk anon of this, and you shall carry
More angels in your pocket, master Bame,
Than ever you'll meet in heaven.   Hand on seal
To this now, master Bame, to prove your faith.
Come, all have signed it.   Here's the quill, dip, write.

Good!"
            And Kit, pocketing the paper, bowed
The gull to the inn door, saying as he went,—
"You shall hear further when the plan's complete.
But there's one great condition—not one word,
One breath of scandal more on Robert Greene.
He's dead; but he was one of us.   The day
You air his shirt, I air this paper, too."
No gleam of understanding, even then,
Illumed that lanthorn face: no stage, indeed,
Has known such acting as the Mermaid Inn
That night, and Bame but sniggered, "Why, of course,
There's good in all men; and the best of us
Will make mistakes."
                    "But no mistake in this,"
Said Kit, "or all together we shall swing
At Tyburn—who knows what may leap to light?—
You understand?   No scandal!"   "Not a breath!"
So, in dead silence, master Richard Bame
Went out into the darkness and the night,
To ask, as I have heard, for many a moon,
The price of malmsey-butts and silken hose,
And doublets slashed with satin.
                                As the door
Slammed on his back, the pent-up laughter burst
With echo and re-echo round the room,
But ceased as Will tossed on the glowing hearth
The last poor Testament of Robert Greene.
All watched it burn.   The black wind wailed and moaned
Around the Mermaid as the sparks flew up.
"God, what a night for ships upon the sea,"
Said Raleigh, peering thro' the wet black panes.
"Well, we may thank Him for the Little Red Ring!"
"The Little Red Ring!" cried Kit, "the Little Red Ring!"
Then up stood Dekker on the old black settle.
"Give it a thumping chorus, lads," he called,
And sang this brave song of the Mermaid Inn :—

I.

Seven wise men on an old black settle,
    Seven wise men of the Mermaid Inn,
Ringing blades of the one right metal,
    What is the best that a blade can win?
Bread and cheese, and a few small kisses?
    Ha! ha! ha!   Would you take them—you?
—Ay, if Dame Venus would add to her blisses
    A roaring fire and a friend or two!

Chorus: Up now, answer me, tell me true!
            —Ay, if the hussy would add to her blisses
                A roaring fire and a friend or two!

II.

What will you say when the world is dying?
    What, when the last wild midnight falls
Dark, too dark for the bat to be flying
    Round the ruins of old St Paul's?
What will be last of the lights to perish?
    —What but the little red ring we knew,
Lighting the hands and the hearts that cherish
    A fire, a fire, and a friend or two!

Chorus: Up now, answer me, tell me true!
            What will be last of the stars to perish?
                The fire that lighteth a friend or two!

III.

Up now, answer me, on your mettle,
    Wisest man of the Mermaid Inn,
Soberest man on the old black settle,
    Out with the truth!   It was never a sin.—

Well, if God saved me alone of the seven,
  Telling me *you* must be damned, or *you*,
"This," I would say, "this is hell, not heaven!
  Give me the fire and a friend or two!"

Chorus: Steel was never so ringing true:
     "God," we would say, "this is hell, not heaven!
      Give us the fire, and a friend or two!"

III.—BLACK BILL'S HONEY-MOON.

THE garlands of a Whitsun Ale were strewn
About our rushes, the night that Raleigh brought
Bacon to sup with us.   There, on that night
I saw the singer of the *Faërie Queen*
Quietly spreading out his latest cantos
For Shakespeare's eye, like white sheets in the sun.
Marlowe, our morning star, and Michael Drayton
Talked in that ingle-nook.   And Ben was there,
Humming a song upon that old black settle:
           " Or leave a kiss but in the cup
                And I'll not ask for wine."
But, meanwhile, he drank malmsey.
                                    Francis Bacon
Straddled before the fire ; and, all at once,
He said to Shakespeare, in a voice that gripped
The Mermaid Tavern like an arctic frost:
" *There are no poets in this age of ours,*
Not to compare with Plautus.   They are all
Dead, the men that were famous in old days."
" Why—so they are," said Will.   The humming stopped.
I saw poor Spenser, a shy gentle soul,
With haunted eyes like star-lit forest pools,
Smuggling his cantos under his cloak again.
" There's verse enough, no doubt," Bacon resumed,
" But English is no language for the Muse.
Whom would you call our best ?   There's Gabriel Harvey,
And Edward, Earl of Oxford.   Then there's Dyer,
And Dr Golding ; while, for tragedy,
Thomas, Lord Buckhurst, hath a lofty vein.

And, in a lighter prettier vein, why, Will,
There is *thyself!* But where's Euripides?"
"Dead," echoed Ben, in a deep ghost-like voice.
And drip—drip—drip—outside, we heard the rain
Miserably dropping round the Mermaid Inn.

"Thy Summer's Night—eh, Will? Midsummer's Night?—
That's a quaint fancy," Bacon droned anew,
"But—Athens was an error, Will! Not Athens!
Titania knew not Athens! Those wild elves
Of thy Midsummer's Dream—eh? Midnight's Dream?—
Are English all. Thy woods, too, smack of England;
They never grew round Athens. Bottom, too,
He is not Greek!"
                              "Greek?" Will said, with a chuckle,
"Bottom a Greek? Why, no, he was the son
Of Marian Hacket, the fat wife that kept
An ale-house, Wincot-way. I lodged with her,
Coming from Stratford. You have never walked
Along that countryside? By Burton Heath?
Ah well, you would not know my fairy-lands.
It warms my blood to let my home-spuns play
Around your cold white Athens. There's a joy
In jumping time and space."
                              But as he took
The cup of sack I proffered, solemnly
The lawyer shook his head. "Will, couldst thou use
Thy talents with discretion and obey
Classic examples, thou mightst match old Plautus,
In all except priority of the tongue.
This English tongue is only for an age,
But Latin for all time. So I propose
To embalm in Latin my philosophies.
Well—seize your hour! But, ere you die, you'll sail
A British galleon to the golden courts
Of Cleopatra."
                              "Sail it!" Marlowe roared,
Mimicking in a fit of thunderous glee

The drums and trumpets of his Tamburlaine:
" And let her buccaneers bestride the Sphinx,
And play at bowls with Pharaoh's pyramids,
And hale white Egypt with their tarry hands
Home to the Mermaid!   Lift the good old song
That Rob Greene loved.   Gods, how the lad would shout
      it!
Stand up and sing, John Davis!"

                              "Up," called Raleigh,
" Lift the Chanty of Black Bill's Honey-moon, Jack!
We'll keep the chorus going!"

                              "Silence, all!"
Ben Jonson echoed, rolling on his bench:
" This gentle lawyer hath a longing, lads,
To hear a right Homeric hymn.   Now, Jack!
But wet your whistle, first!   A cup of sack
For the first canto!   Muscadel, the next!
Canary for the last!"   I brought the cup.
John Davis emptied it at one mighty draught,
Leapt on a table, stamped with either foot,
And straight began to troll this mad sea-tale:

BLACK BILL'S HONEY-MOON.

CANTO THE FIRST.

Let old Blind Moone at the hawthorn-tide
    Prattle in Devonshire lanes!
Let all his pedlar poets beside
    Rattle their gallows chains.
A tale like mine they never shall tell
    Or a merrier ballad sing,
Till the Man in the Moon pipe up the tune
    And the stars play Kiss-in-the-Ring!

Chorus: Till Philip of Spain in England reign
            And the stars play Kiss-in-the-Ring!

All in the gorgeous dawn of day
   From grey old Plymouth Sound
Our galleon crashed thro' the crimson spray
   To sail the world around:
Cloud i' the Sun was her white-scrolled name,—
   There was never a lovelier lass
For sailing in state after pieces of eight
   With her bombards all of brass.

Chorus: Culverins, robinets, iron may-be;
          But her bombards all of brass!

Now, they that go down to the sea in ships,
   Though piracy be their trade,
For all that they pray not much with their lips
   They know where the storms are made:
With the stars above and the sharks below,
   They need not parson or clerk;
But our bo'sun Bill was an atheist still,
   Except—sometimes—in the dark!

Chorus: Now let Kit Marlowe mark!
       Our bo'sun Bill was an atheist still,
          Except—sometimes—in the dark!

All we adventured for, who shall say,
   Nor yet what our port might be?—
A magical city of old Cathay,
   Or a castle of Muscovy,
With our atheist bo'sun, Bill, Black Bill,
   Under the swinging Bear,
Whistling at night for a seaman to light
   His little poop-lanthorns there.

Chorus: On the deep, in the night, for a seaman to light
        His little lost lanthorns there.

But, as over the Ocean-sea we swept,
    We chanced on a strange new land
Where a valley of tall white lilies slept
    With a forest on either hand;
A valley of white in a purple wood
    And, behind it, faint and far,
Breathless and bright o'er the last rich height,
    Floated the sunset-star.

Chorus: Fair and bright o'er the rose-red height,
            Venus, the sunset-star.

'Twas a marvel to see, as we beached our boat,
    Black Bill, in that peach-bloom air,
With the great white lilies that reached to his throat
    Like a stained-glass bo'sun there,
And our little ship's chaplain, puffing and red,
    A-starn as we onward stole,
With the disk of a lily behind his head
    Like a cherubin's aureole.

Chorus: He was round and red, and behind his head
          He'd a cherubin's aureole.

"Hyrcania, land of honey and bees,
    We have found thee at last," he said,
"Where the honey-comb swells in the hollow trees,"
    (O, the lily behind his head!)
"The honey-comb swells in the purple wood!
    'Tis the swette which the heavens distil,
Saith Pliny himself, on my little book-shelf!
    Is the world not sweet to thee, Bill?"

Chorus: Saith Pliny himself, on my little book-shelf!
          Is the world not sweet to thee, Bill?"

Now a man may taste of the devil's hot spice,
    And yet if his mind run back
To the honey of childhood's Paradise
    His heart is not wholly black;

And Bill, Black Bill, from the days of his youth,
  Tho' his chest was broad as an oak,
Had cherished one innocent little sweet tooth,
  And it itched as our chaplain spoke.

Chorus: He had kept one perilous little sweet tooth,
      And it itched as our chaplain spoke.

All around was a mutter of bees,
  And Bill 'gan muttering too,—
"If the honey-comb swells in the hollow trees,
  (What else can a Didymus do?)
I'll steer to the purple woods myself
  And see if this thing be so,
Which the chaplain found on his little book-shelf,
  For Pliny lived long ago."

Chorus: There's a platter of delf on his little book-shelf,
      And Pliny lived long ago.

Scarce had he spoken when, out of the wood,
  And buffeting all around,
Rooting our sea-boots where we stood,
  There rumbled a marvellous sound,
As a mountain of honey were crumbling asunder,
  Or a sunset-avalanche hurled
Honey-comb boulders of golden thunder
  To smother the old black world.

Chorus: Honey-comb boulders of musical thunder
      To mellow this old black world.

And the chaplain he whispered—"This honey, one
      saith,
  On my camphired cabin-shelf,
None may harvest on pain of death;
  For the bee would eat it himself!

None walketh those woods but him whose voice
   In the dingles you then did hear!"
"A VOICE?" growls Bill! "Ay, Bill, r-r-rejoice!
   'Twas the great Hyrcanian Bear!"

Chorus: Give thanks! *Re-*joice! 'Twas the glor-
        r-r-ious Voice
        Of the great Hyrcanian Bear!

But, marking that Bill looked bitter indeed,
   For his sweet tooth hungered sore,
"Consider," he saith, "that the Sweet hath need
   Of the Sour, as the Sea of the Shore!
As the night to the day is our grief to our joy,
   And each for its brother prepares
A banquet, Bill, that would otherwise cloy.
   .Thus is it with honey and bears."

Chorus: Roses and honey and laughter would cloy!
        Give us thorns, too, and sorrow and bears!

"Consider," he saith, "how by fretting a string
   The lutanist maketh sweet moan,
And a bird ere it fly must have air for its wing
   To buffet or fall like a stone:
Tho' you blacken like Pluto you make but more white
   These blooms which not Enna could yield!
Consider, Black Bill, ere the coming of night,
   The lilies," he saith, "of the field."

Chorus: "Consider, Black Bill, in this beautiful light,
        The lilies," he saith, "of the field."

"Consider the claws of a Bear," said Bill,
   "That can rip off the flesh from your bones,
While his belly could cabin the skipper and still
   Accommodate Timothy Jones!

Why, that's where a seaman who cares for his grog
    Perspires how this world isn't square !
If there's *cause* for a *cow*, if there's *use* for a *dog*,
    By Pope John, there's no *Sense* in a *Bear !*"

    Chorus : Cause for a cow, use for a dog,
             By'r Lakin, no *Sense* in a *Bear !*

But our little ship's chaplain—"Sense," quoth he,
    "Hath the Bear tho' his making have none ;
For, my little book saith, by the sting of this bee
    Would Ursus be wholly foredone ;
But, or ever the hive he adventureth nigh
    And its crisp gold-crusted dome,
He lardeth his nose and he greaseth his eye
    With a piece of an honey-comb."

Chorus : His velvety nose and his sensitive eye
          With a piece of an honey-comb.

Black Bill at the word of that golden crust
    —For his ears had forgotten the roar,
And his eyes grew soft with their innocent lust—
    'Gan licking his lips once more :
"Be it bound like a missal and printed as fair,
    With capitals blue and red,
'Tis a lie ; for what honey could comfort a bear
    Till the bear win the honey?" he said.

Chorus : "Ay, *whence* the first honey wherewith the first
        bear
        First larded his nose?" he said.

"Thou first metaphysical bo'sun, Bill,"
    Our chaplain quizzingly cried,
"Wilt thou riddle me redes of a dumpling still
    With thy 'how came the apple inside'?"

"Nay," answered Bill, "but I quest for truth,
    And I find it not on your shelf!
I will face your Hyrcanian Bear, forsooth,
    And look at his nose myself."

Chorus: For truth, for truth, or a little sweet tooth—
        I will into the woods myself.

Breast-high thro' that foam-white ocean of bloom
    With its wonderful spokes of gold,
Our sun-burnt crew in the rose-red gloom
    Like buccaneer galleons rolled:
Breast-high, breast-high in the lilies we stood,
    And before we could say "good-night,"
Out of the valley and into the wood
    He plunged thro' the last rich light.

Chorus: Out of the lilies and into the wood,
        Where the Great Bear walks all night!

And our little ship's chaplain he piped thro' the trees
    As the moon rose, white and still,
"Hylas, return to thy Heracles!"
    And we helped him with "Come back, Bill!"
Thrice he piped it, thrice we halloo'd,
    And thrice we were dumb to hark;
But never an answer came from the wood,
    So—we turned to our ship in the dark.

Chorus: Good-bye, Bill! you're a Didymus still;
        But—you're all alone in the dark.

"This honey now"—as the first canto ceased,
Sir Francis Bacon pompously began—
"Which Pliny calleth, as it were, the swette
Of heaven, or spettle of the stars, is found
In Muscovy. Now . . ."   "Bring the muscadel,"
Ben Jonson roared—"'Tis a more purple drink,
And suits with the next canto!"

                              At one draught
John Davis drained the cup, and with one hand
Beating the measure, rapidly trolled again.

BLACK BILL'S HONEY-MOON.

CANTO THE SECOND.

Now, Rabelais, art thou quite foredone,
Dan Chaucer, Drayton, Every One!
Leave we aboard our *Cloud i' the Sun*
    This crew of pirates dreaming—
Of Angels, minted in the blue
Like golden moons, Rose-nobles, too,
As under the silver-sliding dew
    Our emerald creek lay gleaming!

Chorus : Under the stars lay gleaming!

And mailed with scales of gold and green
The high star-lilied banks between,
Nosing our old black hulk unseen,
    Great alligators shimmered:
Blood-red jaws i' the blue-black ooze,
Where all the long warm day they snooze,
Chewing old cuds of pirate·crews,
    Around us grimly glimmered.

Chorus : Their eyes like rubies glimmered.

Let us now sing of Bill, good sirs!
Follow him, all green forestères,
Fearless of Hyrcanian bears
    As of these ghostly lilies!
For O, not Drayton there could sing
Of wild Pigwiggen and his King
So merry a jest, so jolly a thing
    As this my tale of Bill is.

Chorus : Into the woods where Bill is!

Now starts he as a white owl hoots,
And now he stumbles over roots,
And now beneath his big sea-boots
     In yon deep glade he crunches
Black cakes of honey-comb that were
So elfin-sweet, perchance, last year ;
But neither Bo'sun, now, nor Bear
     At that dark banquet munches.

Chorus : Onward still he crunches !

Black cakes of honey-comb he sees
Above him in the forks of trees
Filled by stars instead of bees
     With brimming silver glisten :
But ah, such food of gnome and fay
Could neither Bear nor Bill delay
Till where yon ferns and moon-beams play
     He starts and stands to listen !

Chorus : What melody doth he listen ?

Is it the Night-wind as it comes
Through the wood and softly thrums
Silvery tabors, purple drums,
     To speed some wild-wood revel ?
Nay, Didymus, what faint sweet din
Of viol and flute and violin
Makes all the forest round thee spin,
     The Night-wind or the Devil ?

Chorus : No doubt at all—the Devil !

He stares, with naked knife in hand,
This buccaneer in fairyland !
Dancing in a saraband
     The red ferns reel about him !

Dancing in a morrice-ring
The green ferns curtsey, kiss and cling!
Their Marions flirt, their Robins fling
    Their feathery heels to flout him!

Chorus: The whole wood reels about him.

Dance, ye shadows! O'er the glade,
Bill, the Bo'sun, undismayed,
Pigeon-toes with glittering blade!
    Drake was never bolder!
Devil or Spaniard, what cares he
Whence your eerie music be?
Till—lo, against yon old oak-tree
    He leans his brawny shoulder!

Chorus: He lists and leans his shoulder!

Ah, what melody doth he hear
As to that gnarled old tree-trunk there
He lays his wind-bit brass-ringed ear,
    And steals his arm about it?
What Dryad could this Bo'sun win
To that slow-rippling amorous grin?—
'Twas full of singing bees within!
    Not Didymus could doubt it!

Chorus: So loud they buzzed about it!

Straight, o'er a bough one leg he throws,
And up that oaken main-mast goes
With reckless red unlarded nose
    And goose-berry eyes of wonder!
Till now, as in a galleon's hold,
Below, he sees great cells of gold
Whence all the hollow trunk up-rolled
    A low melodious thunder.

Chorus: A sweet and perilous thunder!

Ay, there, within that hollow tree,
Will Shakespeare, might'st thou truly see
The Imperial City of the Bee,
    In Chrysomelan splendour!
And, in the midst, one eight-foot dome
Swells o'er that Titan honey-comb
Where the Bee-Empress hath her home,
    With such as do attend her.

Chorus : Weaponed with stings attend her!

But now her singing sentinels
Have turned to sleep in waxen cells,
And Bill leans down his face and smells
    The whole sweet summer's cargo—
In one deep breath, the whole year's bloom,
Lily and thyme and rose and broom,
One Golden Fleece of flower-perfume
    In that old oaken Argo.

Chorus : That green and golden Argo!

And now he hangs with dangling feet
Over that dark abyss of sweet,
Striving to reach such wild gold meat
    As none could buy for money :
His left hand grips a swinging branch
When—crack!   Our Bo'sun, stout and stanch,
Falls like an Alpine avalanche,
    Feet first into the honey!

Chorus : Up to his ears in honey!

And now his red un-larded nose
And bulging eyes are all that shows
Above it, as he puffs and blows!
    And now—to 'scape the scathing

Of that black host of furious bees
His nose and eyes he fain would grease,
And bobs below those golden seas
    Like an old woman bathing.

Chorus : Old Mother Hubbard bathing !

And now he struggles, all in vain,
To reach some little bough again ;
But, though he heaves with might and main,
    This honey holds his ribs, sirs,
So tight, a barque might sooner try
To steer a cargo through the sky
Than Bill, thus honey-logged, to fly
    By flopping of his jib, sirs !

Chorus : His tops'l and his jib, sirs !

Like Oberon in the hive his beard
With wax and honey all besmeared
Would make the crescent moon afeard
    That now is sailing brightly
Right o'er his leafy donjon-keep !
But that she knows him sunken deep,
And that his tower is straight and steep,
    She would not smile so lightly.

Chorus : Look down and smile so lightly.

She smiles in that small heavenly space,
Ringed with the tree-trunk's leafy grace,
While upward grins his ghastly face
    As if some wild-wood Satyr,
Some gnomish Ptolemy should dare
Up that dark optic tube to stare,
As all unveiled she floated there,
    Poor maiden moon, straight at her !

Chorus : The buccaneering Satyr !

But there, till some one help him out,
Black Bill must stay, without a doubt.
Help ! Help ! he gives a muffled shout !
    None but the white owls hear it !
Who ? Whoo ? they cried : Bill answers " ME !
I am stuck fast in this great tree !
Bring me a rope, good Timothy !
    There's honey, lads, we'll share it !"

Chorus : Ay, now he wants to share it.

Then, thinking help may come with morn,
He sinks, half-famished and out-worn,
And scarce his nose exalts its horn
    Above that sea of glory !
But, even as he owns defeat,
His belly saith, " A man must eat,
And since there is none other meat,
Come, lap this mess before 'ee ! "

Chorus : This glorious mess before 'ee.

Then Dian sees a right strange sight
As, bidding him a fond good-night,
She flings a silvery kiss to light
    In that deep oak-tree hollow,
And finds that gold and crimson nose
A moving, munching, ravenous rose
That up and down unceasing goes,
    Save when he stops to swallow !

Chorus : He finds it hard to swallow !

Ay, now his best becomes his worst,
For honey cannot quench his thirst,
Though he should eat until he burst ;
    But, ah, the skies are kindly,

And from their tender depths of blue
They send their silver-sliding dew.
So Bill thrusts out his tongue anew
 And waits to catch it—blindly!

Chorus: For ah, the stars are kindly!

And sometimes, with a shower of rain,
They strive to ease their prisoner's pain:
Then Bill thrusts out his tongue again
 With never a grace, the sinner!
And day and night and day goes by,
And never a comrade comes anigh,
And still the honey swells as high
 For supper, breakfast, dinner!

Chorus: Yet Bill has grown no thinner!

The young moon grows to full and throws
Her buxom kiss upon his nose,
As nightly over the tree she goes,
 And peeps and smiles and passes,
Then with her fickle silver flecks
Our old black galleon's dreaming decks;
And then her face, with nods and becks,
 In midmost ocean glasses.

Chorus: 'Twas ever the way with lasses!

Ah, Didymus, hast thou won indeed
That Paradise which is thy meed?
(Thy tale not all that run may read!)
 Thy sweet hath now no leaven!
Now, like an onion in a cup
Of mead, thou liest for Jove to sup,
Could Polyphemus lift thee up
 With Titan hands to heaven!

Chorus: This great oak-cup to heaven!

The second canto ceased ; and, as they raised
Their wine-cups with the last triumphant note,
Bacon, undaunted, raised his grating voice—
" This honey which, in some sort, may be styled
The Spettle of the Stars . . ."   " Bring the Canary ! "
Ben Jonson roared.   " It is a moral wine
And suits the third, last canto ! "   At one draught
John Davis drained it and began anew.

BLACK BILL'S HONEY-MOON.

CANTO THE THIRD.

A month went by.   We were hoisting sail !
    We had lost all hope of Bill ;
Though, laugh as you may at a seaman's tale,
    He was fast in his honey-comb still !
And often he thinks of the chaplain's word
    In the days he shall see no more,—
How the Sweet, indeed, of the Sour hath need ;
    And the Sea, likewise, of the Shore.

Chorus :   The Chaplain's word of the Air and a Bird ;
            Of the Sea, likewise, and the Shore !

" O, had I the wings of a dove, I would fly
    To a heaven, of aloes and gall !
I have honeyed," he yammers, " my nose and mine eye,
    And the bees cannot sting me at all !
And it's O, for the sting of a little brown bee,
    Or to blister my hands on a rope,
Or to buffet a thundering broad-side sea
    On a deck like a mountain-slope ! "

Chorus : With her mast snapt short, and a list to port
            And a deck like a mountain-slope.

But alas, and he thinks of the chaplain's voice
    When that roar from the woods out-brake—
R-r-re-joice!   R-r-re-joice!   Now wherefore rejoice
    In the music a bear could make?
'Tis a judgment, may-be, that I stick in this tree;
    Yet in this I out-argued him fair!
Though I live, though I die, in this honey-comb pie,
    By Pope Joan, there's no sense in a bear!

Chorus: Notes in a nightingale, plums in a pie,
        By'r Lakin, no *Sense* in a *Bear!*

He knew not our anchor was heaved from the mud:
    He was growling it over again,
When—a strange sound suddenly froze his blood
    And curdled his big slow brain!—
A marvellous sound, as of great steel claws
    Gripping the bark of his tree,
Softly ascended!   Like lightning ended
    His honey-comb reverie!

Chorus: The honey-comb quivered!   The little leaves
        shivered!
        Something was climbing the tree!

Something that breathed like a fat sea-cook,
    Or a pirate of fourteen ton!
But it clomb like a cat (tho' the whole tree shook)
    Stealthily tow'rds the sun,
Till, as Black Bill gapes at the little blue ring
    Overhead, which he calls the sky,
It is clean blotted out by a monstrous Thing
    Which—*hath larded its nose and its eye.*

Chorus: O, well for thee, Bill, that this monstrous Thing
        Hath blinkered its little red eye.

Still as a mouse lies Bill with his face
    Low down in the dark sweet gold,
While this monster turns round in the leaf-fringed space!
    Then—taking a good firm hold,
As the skipper descending the cabin-stair,
    Tail-first, with a vast slow tread,
Solemnly, softly, cometh this Bear
    Straight down o'er the Bo'sun's head.

Chorus: Solemnly—slowly—cometh this Bear,
        Tail-first o'er the Bo'sun's head.

Nearer—nearer—then all Bill's breath
    Out-bursts in one leap and yell!
And this Bear thinks, "Now am I gripped from beneath
    By a roaring devil from hell!"
And madly Bill clutches his brown bow-legs,
    And madly this Bear doth hale,
With his little red eyes fear-mad for the skies
    And Bill's teeth fast in his tail.

Chorus: Small wonder a bear should quail!
        To have larded his nose, to have greased his
           eyes,
        And be stung at the last in his tail.

Pull, Bo'sun! Pull, Bear! In the hot sweet gloom,
    Pull Bruin, pull Bill, for the skies!
Pull—out of their gold with a bombard's boom
    Come Black Bill's honeyed thighs!
Pull! Up! Up! Up! with a scuffle and scramble,
    To that little blue ring of bliss,
This Bear doth go with our Bo'sun in tow
    Stinging his tail, I wis.

Chorus: And this Bear thinks—"Many great bees I know,
        But there never was Bee like this!"

.   .   .   .

All in the gorgeous death of day
   We had slipped from our emerald creek,
And our *Cloud i' the Sun* was careening away
   With the old gay flag at the peak,
When suddenly, out of the purple wood,
   Breast-high thro' the lilies there danced
A tall lean figure, black as a nigger,
   That shouted and waved and pranced!

Chorus: A gold-greased figure, but black as a nigger,
         Waving his shirt as he pranced!

" 'Tis Hylas! 'Tis Hylas!" our chaplain flutes,
   And our skipper he looses a shout!
" 'Tis Bill! Black Bill, in his old sea-boots!
   Stand by to bring her about!
Har-r-rd a-starboard!" And round we came,
   With a lurch and a dip and a roll,
And a banging boom thro' the rose-red gloom
   For our old Black Bo'sun's soul!

Chorus: Alive! Not dead! Tho' behind his head
         He'd a seraphin's aureole!

.   .   .   .   .   .

And our chaplain he sniffs, as Bill finished his tale,
   (With the honey still scenting his hair!)
O'er a plate of salt beef and a mug of old ale—
   "By Pope John, there's no sense in a bear!"
And we laughed, but our Bo'sun he solemnly growls—
   "Till the sails of yon heavens be furled,
It taketh—now, mark!—all the beasts in the Ark,
   Teeth and claws, too, to make a good world!"

Chorus: Till the great—blue—sails—be—furled,
        It taketh—now, mark!—all the beasts in the Ark,
   Teeth and claws, too, to make a good world!

"Sack! Sack! Canary! Malmsey! Muscadel!"
As the last canto ceased, the Mermaid Inn
Chorussed.   I flew from laughing voice to voice;
But, over all the hubbub, rose the drone
Of Francis Bacon,—"Now, this Muscovy
Is a cold clime, not favourable to bees
(Or love, which is a weakness of the south)
As well might be supposed.   Yet, as hot lands
Gender hot fruits and odoriferous spice,
In this case we may think that honey and flowers
Are comparable with the light airs of May
And a more temperate region.   Also we see,
As Pliny saith, this honey being a swette
Of heaven, a certain spettle of the stars,
Which, gathering unclean vapours as it falls,
Hangs as a fat dew on the boughs, the bees
Obtain it partly thus, and afterwards
Corrupt it in their stomaches, and at last
Expel it through their mouths and harvest it
In hives; yet, of its heavenly source it keeps
A great part.   Thus, by various principles
Of natural philosophy we observe——"
      And, as he leaned to Drayton, droning thus,
I saw a light gleam of celestial mirth
Flit o'er the face of Shakespeare—scarce a smile—
A swift irradiation from within
As of a cloud that softly veils the sun.

IV.—THE SIGN OF THE GOLDEN SHOE.

PART I.

A BRAZIER smouldered in the door to keep
The Plague away.   The Mermaid reeked with smoke
Of scented woods.   Nash crept into the room
Shivering like a fragment of the night,
His face yellow as parchment, and his eyes
Burning.
        "The Plague!   He has taken it !" voices cried.
"That's not the Plague!   The old carrion crow is drunk ;
But stand away.   What ails you, Nash, my lad ?"
Then, through the clamour, as through a storm at sea,
The master's voice, the voice of Ben, rang out,
"Nash!"
        Ben leapt to his feet, and like a ship
Shouldering the waves, he shouldered the throng aside.
"What ails you, man?   What's that upon your breast ?
Blood !"
        "Marlowe is dead," said Nash,
And stunned the room to silence. . . .
                " Marlowe—dead !"
Ben caught him by the shoulders.   "Nash!   Awake!
What do you mean?   Marlowe?   Kit Marlowe ?   Dead ?
I supped with him—why—not three nights ago !
You are drunk !   You are dazed !   There's blood upon
      your coat !"
"That's—where he died," said Nash, and suddenly sank
Sidelong across a bench, bowing his head
Between his hands. . . .

Wept, I believe.   Then, like a whip of steel,
His lean black figure sprang erect again.
"Marlowe!" he cried, "Kit Marlowe, killed for a punk,
A taffeta petticoat!   Killed by an apple-squire!
Drunk?   I was drunk; but I am sober now,
Sober enough, by God!   Poor Kit is dead."

.   .   .   .

The Mermaid Inn was thronged for many a night
With startled faces.   Voices rose and fell,
As I recall them, in a great vague dream,
Curious, pitiful, angry, thrashing out
The tragic truth.   Then, all along the Cheape,
The ballad-mongers waved their sheets of rhyme,
Croaking: *Come buy!   Come buy!   The bloody death
Of Wormall, writ by Master Richard Bame!
Come buy!   Come buy!   The Atheist's Tragedy.*
And, even in Bread Street, at our very door,
The crowder to his cracked old fiddle sang:—

> " *He was a poet of proud repute
>   And wrote full many a play,
> Now strutting in a silken suit,
>   Now begging by the way.*"

Then, out of the hubbub and the clash of tongues,
The bawdy tales and scraps of balladry,
(As out of chaos rose the slow round world)
At last, though for the Mermaid Inn alone,
Emerged some tragic semblance of a soul,
Some semblance of the rounded truth, a world
Glimpsed only through great mists of blood and tears,
Yet smitten, here and there, with dreadful light,
As I believe, from heaven.
                              Strangely enough,
(Though Ben forgot his pipe and Will's deep eyes
Deepened and softened, when they spoke of Kit,
For many a month thereafter) it was Nash
That took the blow like steel into his heart.
Nash, our " Piers Penniless," whom Rob Greene had called

"Young Juvenal," the first satirist of our age,
Nash, of the biting tongue and subtle sneer,
Brooded upon it, till his grief became
Sharp as a rapier, ready to lunge in hate
At all the lies of shallower hearts.

                                    One night,
The night he raised the mists from that wild world,
He talked with Chapman in the Mermaid Inn
Of Marlowe's poem that was left half-sung,
His *Hero and Leander*.

                        "Kit desired,
If he died first, that you should finish it,"
Said Nash.

                A loaded silence filled the room
As with the imminent spirit of the dead
Listening.   And long that picture haunted me:
Nash, like a lithe young Mephistopheles
Leaning between the silver candle-sticks,
Across the oak table, with his keen white face,
Dark smouldering eyes, and black, dishevelled hair;
Chapman, with something of the steady strength
That helms our ships, and something of the Greek,
The cool clear passion of Platonic thought
Behind the fringe of his Olympian beard
And broad Homeric brows, confronting him
Gravely.

                There was a burden of mystery
Brooding on all that night; and, when at last
Chapman replied, I knew he felt it, too.
The curious pedantry of his wonted speech
Was charged with living undertones, like truths
Too strange and too tremendous to be breathed
Save thro' a mask.   And though, in lines that flamed
Once with strange rivalry, Shakespeare himself defied
Chapman, that spirit "by spirits taught to write
Above a mortal pitch," Will's nimbler sense
Was quick to breathings from beyond our world
And could not hold them lightly.

"Ah, then Kit,"
Said Chapman, "had some prescience of his end,
Like many another dreamer.   What strange hints
Of things past, present, and to come, there lie
Sealed in the magic pages of that music
Which, laying strong hold on universal laws,
Ranges beyond these mud-walls of the flesh,
Though dull wits fail to follow.   It was this
That made men find an oracle in the books
Of Vergil, and an everlasting fount
Of science in the prophets."

Once again
That haunted silence filled the shadowy room;
And, far away up Bread Street, we could hear
The crowder, piping of black Wormall still :—

> "*He had a friend, once gay and green,*
>   *Who died of want alone,*
>   *In whose black fate he might have seen*
>   *The warning of his own.*"

"Strange he should ask a hod-man like myself
To crown that miracle of his April age,"
Said Chapman, murmuring softly under breath,
"*Amorous Leander, beautiful and young* . . .
Why, Nash, had I been only charged to raise
Out of his grave in the green Hellespont
The body of that boy,
To make him sparkle and leap thro' the cold waves
And fold young Hero to his heart again,
The task were scarce as hard.

But . . . stranger still,"—
And his next words, although I hardly knew
All that he meant, went tingling through my flesh—
"Before you spoke, before I knew his wish,
I had begun to write!

I knew and loved
His work.   Himself I hardly knew at all ;
And yet—I know him now !   I have heard him now,

And, since he pledged me in so rare a cup,
I'll lift and drink to him, though lightnings fall
From envious gods to scourge me.   I will lift
This cup in darkness to the soul that reigns
In light on Helicon.   Who knows how near?
For I have thought, sometimes, when I have tried
To work his will, the hand that moved my pen
Was mine, and yet—not mine.   The bodily mask
Is mine, and sometimes, dull as clay, it sleeps
With old Musæus.   Then strange flashes come,
Oracular glories, visionary gleams,
And the mask moves, not of itself, and sings."
   "I know that thought," said Nash.   "A mighty ship,
A lightning-shattered wreck, out in that night,
Unseen, has foundered thundering.   We sit here
Snug on the shore, and feel the wash of it,
The widening circles running to our feet.
Can such a soul go down to glut the sharks
Without one ripple?   Here comes one sprinkle of spray.
Listen!"   And through that night, quick and intense,
And hushed for thunder, tingled once again,
Like a thin wire, the crowder's distant tune :—

   "*Had he been prenticed to the trade
      His father followed still,
   This exit he had never made,
      Nor played a part so ill.*"

" Here is another," said Nash, "I know not why ;
But like a weed in the long wash, I too
Was moved, not of myself, to a tune like this.
O, I can play the crowder, fiddle a song
On a dead friend, with any the best of you,
Lie and kick heels in the sun on a dead man's grave.
And yet—God knows—it is the best we can ;
And better than the world's way, to forget."
So saying, like one that murmurs happy words
To torture his own grief, half in self-scorn,
He breathed a scrap of balladry that raised

The mists a moment from that Paradise,
That primal world of innocence, where Kit
In childhood played, outside his father's shop,
Under the sign of the *Golden Shoe*, as thus :—

A cobbler lived in Canterbury
—He is dead now, poor soul !—
He sat at his door and stitched in the sun,
Nodding and smiling at everyone ;
For St Hugh makes all good cobblers merry,
And often he sang as the pilgrims passed,
" I can hammer a soldier's boot,
And daintily glove a dainty foot.
Many a sandal from my hand
Has walked the road to Holy Land.
Knights may fight for me, priests may pray for me,
Pilgrims walk the pilgrim's way for me,
I have a work in the world to do !
—*Trowl the bowl, the nut-brown bowl,*
        To good St Hugh !—
The cobbler must stick to his last."

    And anon he would cry
" Kit ! Kit ! Kit !" to his little son,
" Look at the pilgrims riding by !
Dance down, hop down, after them, run !
Then, like an unfledged linnet, out
Would tumble the brave little lad,
With a piping shout,—
" O, look at them, look at them, look at them, Dad !
Priest and prioress, abbot and friar,
Soldier and seaman, knight and squire !
How many countries have they seen ?
Is there a king there, is there a queen ?
Dad, one day,
Thou and I must ride like this,
All along the Pilgrim's Way,
By Glastonbury and Samarcand,
El Dorado and Cathay,

London and Persepolis,
All the way to Holy Land!"

   Then, shaking his head as if he knew,
Under the sign of the *Golden Shoe*,
Touched by the glow of the setting sun,
While the pilgrims passed,
The little cobbler would laugh and say:
"When you are old you will understand
'Tis a very long way
To Samarcand!
Why, largely to exaggerate
Befits not men of small estate;
But—I should say, yes, I should say,
'Tis a hundred miles from where you stand;
And a hundred more, my little son,
A hundred more, to Holy Land! . . .
I have a work in the world to do
—*Trowl the bowl, the nut-brown bowl,*
     To good St Hugh!—
The cobbler must stick to his last."
"Which last," said Nash, breaking his rhyme off short,
"The crowder, after his kind, would seem to approve.
Well—all the waves from that great wreck out there
Break, and are lost in one with-drawing sigh:

          The little lad that used to play
               Around the cobbler's door,
          Kit Marlowe, Kit Marlowe,
               We shall not see him more.

But—could I tell you how that galleon sank,
Could I but bring you to that hollow whirl,
The black gulf in mid-ocean, where that wreck
Went thundering down, and round it hell still roars,
That were a tale to snap all fiddle-strings."
"Tell me," said Chapman.
                              "Ah, you wondered why,"
Said Nash, "you wondered why he asked your help

To crown that work of his.   Why, Chapman, think,
Think of the cobbler's awl—there's a stout lance
To couch at London, there's a conquering point
To carry in triumph through Persepolis!
I tell you Kit was nothing but a child,
When some rich patron of the *Golden Shoe*
Beheld him riding into Samarcand
Upon a broken chair, the which he said
Was a white steed, splashed with the blood of kings.
    When, on that patron's bounty, he did ride
So far as Cambridge, he was a brave lad,
Untamed, adventurous, but still innocent,
O, innocent as the cobbler's little self!
He brought to London just a bundle and stick,
A slender purse, an Ovid, a few scraps
Of song, and all unshielded, all unarmed,
A child's heart, packed with splendid hopes and dreams.
I say a child's heart, Chapman, and that phrase
Crowns, not dis-crowns, his manhood.
                                    Well—he turned
An honest penny, taking some small part
In plays at the *Red Bull.*   And, all the while,
Beyond the paint and tinsel of the stage,
Beyond the greasy cock-pit with its reek
Of orange-peel and civet, as all of these
Were but the clay churned by the glorious rush
Of his white chariots and his burning steeds,
Nay, as the clay were a shadow, his great dreams,
Like bannered legions on some proud crusade,
Empurpling all the deserts of the world,
Swept on in triumph to the glittering towers
Of his abiding City.
                        Then—he met
That damned blood-sucking cockatrice, the pug
Of some fine strutting mummer, one of those plagues
Bred by our stage, a puff-ball on the hill
Of Helicon.   As for his wench—she too
Had played so many parts that she forgot

The cue for truth.   King Puff had taught her well.
He was the vainer and more foolish thing,
She the more poisonous.
                          One dark day, to spite
Archer, her latest paramour, a friend
And apple-squire to Puff, she set her eyes
On Marlowe . . . feigned a joy in his young art,
Murmured his songs, used all her London tricks
To coney-catch the country green-horn.   Man,
Kit never even *saw* her painted face !
He pored on books by candle-light and saw
Everything thro' a mist.   O, I could laugh
To think of it, only—his up-turned skull
There, in the dark, now that the flesh drops off,
Has laughed enough, a horrible silent laugh,
To think his Angel of Light was, after all,
Only the red-lipped Angel of the Plague.
He was no better than the rest of us,
No worse.   He felt the heat.   He felt the cold.
He took her down to Deptford to escape
Contagion, and the crashing of sexton's spades
On dead men's bones in every churchyard round ;
The jangling bell and the cry, *Bring out your dead*.
And there she told him of her luckless life,
Wedded, deserted, both against her will,
A luckless Eve that never knew the snake.
True and half-true she mixed in one wild lie,
And then—she caught him by the hand and wept.
No death-cart passed to warn him with its bell.
Her eyes, her perfumed hair, and her red mouth,
Her warm white breast, her civet-scented skin,
Swimming before him, in a piteous mist,
Made the lad drunk, and—she was in his arms ;
And all that God had meant to wake one day
Under the Sun of Love, suddenly woke
By candle-light and cried 'The Sun !   The Sun !'
And he believed it, Chapman, he believed it !
He was a cobbler's son, and he believed

In Love!   Blind, through that mist he caught at Love,
The everlasting King of all this world.

Kit was not clever.   Clever men—like Pomp—
Might jest.   And fools might laugh.   But when a man,
Simple as all great elemental things,
Makes his whole heart a sacrificial fire
To one whose love is in her supple skin,
There comes a laughter in which jests break up
Like icebergs in a sea of burning marl.
Then dreamers turn to murderers in an hour.
Then topless towers are burnt, and the Ocean-sea
Tramples the proud fleet, down, into the dark,
And sweeps over it, laughing.   Come and see,
The heart now of this darkness—no more waves,
But the black central hollow where that wreck
Went down for ever.
                              How should Piers Penniless
Brand that wild picture on the world's black heart?–
Last night I tried the way of the Florentine,
And bruised myself; but we are friends together
Mourning a dead friend, none will ever know!—
Kit, do you smile at poor Piers Penniless,
Measuring it out?   Ah, boy, it is my best!
Since hearts must beat, let it be *terza rima*,
A ladder of rhyme that two sad friends alone
May let down, thus, to the last circle of hell."

So saying, and motionless as a man in trance,
Nash breathed the words that raised the veil anew,
Strange intervolving words which, as he spake them,
Moved like the huge slow whirlpool of that pit
Where the wreck sank, the serpentine slow folds
Of the lewd Kraken that sucked it, shuddering, down:—

This is the Deptford Inn.   Climb the dark stair.
   Come, come and see Kit Marlowe lying dead!
See, on the table, by that broken chair,

The little phials of paint—the white and red.
  A cut-lawn kerchief hangs behind the door,
Left by his punk, even as the tapster said.

There is the gold-fringed taffeta gown she wore,
  And, on that wine-stained bed, as is most meet,
He lies alone, never to waken more.

O, still as chiselled marble, the frayed sheet
  Folds the still form on that sepulchral bed,
Hides the dead face, and peaks the rigid feet.

Come, come and see Kit Marlowe lying dead!
  Draw back the sheet, ah, tenderly lay bare
The splendour of that Apollonian head ;

The gloriole of his flame-coloured hair ;
  The lean athletic body, deftly planned
To carry that swift soul of fire and air ;

The long thin flanks, the broad breast, and the grand
  Heroic shoulders ! Look, what lost dreams lie
Cold in the fingers of that delicate hand ;

And, shut within those lyric lips, what cry
  Of unborn beauty, sunk in utter night,
Lost worlds of song, sealed in an unknown sky,

Never to be brought forth, clothed on with light.
  Was this, then, this the secret of his song ?—
Who ever loved that loved not at first sight?

It was not Love, not Love, that wrought this wrong ;
  And yet—what evil shadow of this dark town
Could quench a soul so flame-like clean and strong,

Strike the young glory of his manhood down,
  Dead, like a dog, dead in a drunken brawl,
Dead for a phial of paint, a taffeta gown ?

What if his blood were hot ?   High over all
    He heard, as in his song the world still hears,
Those angels on the burning heavenly wall

Who chant the thunder-music of the spheres.
    Yet—through the glory of his own young dream
Here did he meet that face, wet with strange tears,

Andromeda, with piteous face astream,
    Hailing him, Perseus.   In her treacherous eyes
As in dark pools the mirrored stars will gleam,

Here did he see his own eternal skies ;
    And here—she laughed, nor found the dream amiss ;
But bade him pluck and eat—in Paradise.

Here did she hold him, broken up with bliss,
    Here, like a supple snake, around him coiled,
Here did she pluck his heart out with a kiss ;

Here were the wings clipped and the glory soiled,
    Here adders coupled in the pure white shrine,
Here was the Wine spilt, and the Shew-bread spoiled.

Black was that feast, though he who poured the Wine
    Dreamed that he poured it in high sacrament.
Deep in her eyes he saw his own eyes shine,

Beheld Love's god-head and was well content.
    Subtly her hand struck the pure silver note,
The throbbing chord of passion that God meant

To swell the bliss of heaven.   Round his young throat
    She wound her swarthy tresses ; then, with eyes
Half mad to see their power, half mad to gloat,

Half mad to batten on their own devilries,
    And mark what heaven-born splendours they could quell,
She held him quivering in a mesh of lies,

And in soft broken speech began to tell—
   There, as against her heart, throbbing he lay—
The truth that hurled his soul from heaven to hell.

Quivering, she watched the subtle whip-lash flay
   The white flesh of the dreams of his pure youth ;
Then sucked the blood and left them cold as clay.

Luxuriously she lashed him with the truth.
   Against his mouth her subtle mouth she set
To show, as through a mask, O, without ruth,

As through a cold clay mask (brackish and wet
   With what strange tears !) it was not his, not his,
The kiss that through his quivering lips she met.

Kissing him, " *thus*," she whispered, " *did he kiss.*
   Ah, is the sweetness like a sword, then, sweet?
Last night—ah, kiss again—aching with bliss,

Thus was I made his own, from head to feet."
   —A sudden agony thro' his body swept
Tempestuously.—" *Our wedded pulses beat*

Like this and this ; and then, at dawn, he slept."
   She laughed, pouting her lips against his cheek
To drink ; and, as in answer, Marlowe wept.

As a dead man in dreams, he heard her speak.
   Clasped in the bitter grave of that sweet clay,
Wedded and one with it, he moaned.   Too weak

Even to lift his head, sobbing, he lay.
   Then, slowly, as their breathings rose and fell,
He felt the storm of passion, far away,

Gather.   The shuddering waves began to swell,
   And, through the menace of the thunder-roll,
The thin quick lightnings, thrilling through his hell,

Lightnings that hell itself could not control
  (Even while she strove to bow his neck anew)
Woke the great slumbering legions of his soul.

Sharp was that severance of the false and true,
  Sharp as a sword drawn from a shuddering wound.
But they, that were one flesh, were cloven in two.

Flesh leapt from clasping flesh, without a sound.
  He plucked his body from her white embrace,
And cast him down, and grovelled on the ground.

Yet, ere he went, he strove once more to trace,
  Deep in her eyes, the loveliness he knew;
Then—spat his hatred into her smiling face.

She clung to him—He flung her off.   He drew
  His dagger, thumbed the blade, and laughed—"Poor
    punk!
What?   Would you make me your own murderer, too?"

    "That was the day of our great feast," said Nash,
  "Aboard the *Golden Hind*.   The grand old hulk
Was drawn up for the citizens' wonderment
At Deptford.   Ay, Piers Penniless was there!
Soaked and besotted as I was, I saw
Everything.   On her poop the minstrels played;
And round her sea-worn keel, like meadow-sweet
Curtseying round a lightning-blackened oak,
Prentices and their sweethearts, heel and toe,
Danced the brave English dances, clean and fresh
As May.
        But in her broad gun-guarded waist
Once red with British blood, long tables groaned
For revellers not so worthy.   Where her guns
Had raked the seas, barrels of ale were sprung,

Bestrid by roaring tipplers.   Where at night
The storm-beat crew silently bowed their heads
With Drake before the King of Life and Death,
A strumpet wrestled with a mountebank
For pence, a loose-limbed Lais with a clown
Of Cherry Hilton.   Leering at their lewd twists,
Cross-legged upon the deck, sluggish with sack,
Like a squat toad sat Puff . . .
Propped up against the bulwarks, at his side,
Archer, his apple-squire, hiccoughed a bawdy song.

Suddenly, through that orgie, with wild eyes,
Yet with her customary smile, O, there
I saw in day-light what Kit Marlowe saw
Through blinding mists, the face of his first love.
She stood before her paramour on the deck,
Cocking her painted head to right and left,
Her white teeth smiling, but her voice a hiss:
'Quickly,' she said to Archer, 'come away,
Or there'll be blood spilt!'

                                    'Better blood than wine,'
Said Archer, struggling to his feet, 'but who,
Who would spill blood?'

                                    'Marlowe!' she said.

                                                    Then Puff
Reeled to his feet.   'What, Kit, the cobbler's son?
The lad that broke his leg at the *Red Bull*,
Tamburlaine-Marlowe, he that would chain kings
To's chariot-wheel?   What, is he rushing hither?
He would spill blood for Gloriana, hey?
O, my Belphœbe, you will crack my sides!
Was this the wench that shipped a thousand squires?
O, ho!   But here he comes.   Now, solemnly, lads,—
Now walk the angels on the walls of heaven
To entertain divine Zenocrate!'

And there stood Kit, high on the storm-scarred poop,
Against the sky, bare-headed.   I saw his face,

Pale, innocent, just the clear face of that boy
Who walked to Cambridge with a bundle and stick,—
The little cobbler's son.   Yet—there I caught
My only glimpse of how the sun-god looked,
And only for one moment.

                When he saw
His mistress, his face whitened, and he shook.
Down to the deck he came, a poor weak man;
And yet—by God—the only man that day
In all our drunken crew.

                'Come along, Kit,'
Cried Puff, 'we'll all be friends now, all take hands,
And dance—ha! ha!—the shaking of the sheets!'
Then Archer, shuffling a step, raised his cracked voice
In Kit's own song to a falsetto tune,
Snapping one hand, thus, over his head as he danced:—

    ' Come, live with me, and be my love,
       And we will all the pleasures prove!' . . .

Puff reeled between, laughing. 'Damn you,' cried Kit,
And, catching the fat swine by his round soft throat,
Hurled him headlong, crashing across the tables,
To lie and groan in the red bilge of wine
That washed the scuppers.

                Kit gave him not one glance.
'Archer,' he said in a whisper.

                Instantly
A long thin rapier flashed in Archer's hand.
The ship was one wild uproar.   Women screamed
And huddled together.   A drunken clamorous ring
Seethed around Marlowe and his enemy.
Kit drew his dagger, slowly, and I knew
Blood would be spilt.

                'Here, take my rapier, Kit!'
I cried across the crowd, seeing the lad
Was armed so slightly.   But he did not hear.
I could not reach him.

                All at once he leapt

Like a wounded tiger, past the rapier point
Straight at his enemy's throat.   I saw his hand
Up-raised to strike !   I heard a harlot's scream,
And, in mid-air, the hand stayed, quivering, white,
A frozen menace.
                           I saw a yellow claw
Twisting the dagger out of that frozen hand ;
I saw his own steel in that yellow grip,
His own lost lightning raised to strike at him !
I saw it flash !   I heard the driving grunt
Of him that struck !   Then, with a shout, the crowd
Sundered, and through the gap, a blank red thing
Streaming with blood, came the blind face of Kit,
Reeling, to me !   And I, poor drunken I,
Held my arms wide for him.   Here, on my breast,
With one great sob, he burst his heart and died."
.   .   .   .

Nash ceased.   And, far away down Friday Street,
The crowder with his fiddle wailed again :

> " *Blaspheming Tambolin must die*
> *And Faustus meet his end.*
> *Repent, repent, or presentlie*
> *To hell ye must descend.*"

And, as in answer, Chapman slowly breathed
Those mightiest lines of Marlowe's own despair :

> " *Think'st thou that I who saw the face of God,*
> *And tasted the eternal joys of heaven,*
> *Am not tormented with ten thousand hells ?* "

"Ah, you have said it," said Nash, "and there you know
Why Kit desired your hand to crown his work.
He reverenced you as one whose temperate eyes,
Austere and grave, could look him through and through,
One whose firm hand could grasp the reins of law
And guide those furious horses of the sun,

As Ben and Will can guide them, where you will.
His were, perchance, the noblest steeds of all,
And from their nostrils blew a fierier dawn
Above the world.   That glory is his own ;
But where he fell, he fell.   Before his hand
Had learned to quell them, he was dashed to the earth.
'Tis yours to show that good men honoured him.
For, mark this, Chapman, since Kit Marlowe fell,
There will be fools that, in the name of Art,
Will wallow in the mire, crying ' I fall,
I fall from heaven !'—fools that have only heard
From earth, the rumour of those golden hooves
Far, far above them.   Ay, you know the kind.
I am stained and tainted, Chapman, I am no saint,
I am shaken through and through with all the sins,
And yet, out of the muck wherein I lie,
Could I lift up my head, I'd tell such men
That muck's a narrow world, even for me ;
And that there's something in the seraphim,
A range of thought, even a passion or two,
Which God denied to maggots.   Could you say it,
The fools would scorn you for your lack of fire,
Because you quelled the storms they never knew
And rode so far above them,—fools of Art
That skip and vex like little vicious fleas
Their only Helicon, some green madam's breast,
In one wild night with whom, they find more ' Art '
Than in the love that wellnigh makes them spew,
A life-long love, and an eternal truth.
Art ! Art !   O, God, that I could send my soul,
In one last wave, from that night-hidden wreck,
Across the shores of all the years to be ;
O, God, that like a crowder I might shake
Their blind dark casements with the pity of it,
Piers Penniless his ballad, a poor scrap,
That but for lack of time, and hope, and pence,
He might have bettered !   For a dead man's sake,
Thus would the wave break, thus the crowder cry :—

Dead like a dog upon the road;
  Dead, for a harlot's kiss;
The Apollonian throat and brow,
The lyric lips, so silent now,
The flaming wings that heaven bestowed
  For loftier airs than this!

The sun-like eyes whose light and life
  Had gazed an angel's down,
That burning heart of honey and fire,
Quenched and dead for an apple-squire,
Quenched at the thrust of a mummer's knife,
  Dead—for a taffeta gown!

The wine that God had set apart,
  The noblest wine of all,
Wine of the grapes that angels trod,
The vintage of the glory of God,
The crimson wine of that rich heart,
  Spilt in a drunken brawl;

Poured out to make a steaming bath
  That night in the Devil's Inn,
A steaming bath of living wine
Poured out for Circe and her swine,
A bath of blood for a harlot
  To supple and sleek her skin.

And many a fool that finds it sweet
  Through all the years to be,
Crowning a lie with Marlowe's fame,
Will ape the sin, will ape the shame,
Will ape our captain in defeat;
  But—not in victory;

Till Art become a leaping-house,
    And Death be crowned as Life,
And one wild night out-shine the soul
Of Truth . . . O, fools, is this your goal?
You are not our Kit Marlowe,
    But the drunkard with the knife;

Not Marlowe, but the Jack-o'-Lent
    That lured him o'er the fen!
O, ay, the tavern is in its place,
And the punk's painted smiling face,
But where is our Kit Marlowe
    The man, the king of men?

Passion?   You kiss the painted mouth,
    The hand that clipped his wings,
The hand that into his heart she thrust
And tuned him to her whimpering lust,
And played upon his quivering youth
    As a crowder plucks the strings.

But he who dared the thunder-roll,
    Whose eagle-wings could soar,
Buffeting down the clouds of night,
To beat against the Light of Light,
That great God-blinded eagle-soul,
    We shall not see him more."

V.—THE COMPANION OF A MILE.

THWACK ! *Thwack !* One early dawn, upon our door
I heard the bladder of some motley fool
Bouncing, and all the dusk of London shook
With bells ! I leapt from bed,—had I forgotten ?—
I flung my casement wide and craned my neck
Over the painted Mermaid. There he stood,
His right leg yellow and his left leg blue,
With jingling cap, a sheep-bell at his tail,
Wielding his eel-skin bladder,—*bang ! thwack ! bang !*—
Catching a comrade's head with the recoil
And skipping away ! All Bread Street dimly burned
Like a reflected sky, green, red and white
With littered branches, ferns and hawthorn-clouds ;
For, round Sir Fool, a frolic morrice-troop
Of players, poets, prentices, mad-cap queans,
Robins and Marians, coloured like the dawn,
And sparkling like the green-wood whence they came
With their fresh boughs all dewy from the dark,
Clamoured, *Come down ! Come down, and let us in !*
High over these, I suddenly saw Sir Fool
Leap to a sign-board, swing to a conduit-head,
And perch there, gorgeous on the morning sky,
Tossing his crimson cocks-comb to the blue
And crowing like Chanticleer, *Give them a rouse !*
Tickle it, tabourer ! Nimbly, lasses, nimbly !
Tuck up your russet petticoats and dance !
Let the Cheap know it is the first of May !

And as I seized shirt, doublet and trunk-hose,
I saw the hobby-horse come cantering down,
A paste-board steed, dappled a rosy white
Like peach-bloom, bridled with purple, bitted with gold,
A crimson foot-cloth on his royal flanks,
And, riding him, His Majesty of the May!
Round him the whole crowd frolicked with a shout,
And as I stumbled down the crooked stair
I heard them break into a dance and sing:—

SONG.

I.

Into the woods we'll trip and go,
Up and down and to and fro,
Under the moon to fetch in May,
And two by two till break of day,
        A-maying,
        A-playing,
For Love knows no gain-saying!
Wisdom trips not? Even so—
Come, young lovers, trip and go,
        Trip and go.

II.

Out of the woods we'll dance and sing
Under the morning-star of Spring,
Into the town with our fresh boughs
And knock at every sleeping house,
        Not sighing,
        Or crying,
Though Love knows no denying!
Then, round your summer queen and king,
Come, young lovers, dance and sing,
        Dance and sing!

" *Chorus*," the great Fool tossed his gorgeous crest,
And lustily crew against the deepening dawn,
" *Chorus*," till all the Cheap caught the refrain,
And, with a double thunder of frolic feet,
Its ancient nut-brown tabors woke the Strand :—

A-maying,
A-playing,
For Love knows no gain-saying !
Wisdom trips not ?   Even so,—
Come, young lovers, trip and go,
Trip and go.

Into the Mermaid with a shout they rushed
As I shot back the bolts, and *bang, thwack, bang*,
The bladder bounced about me.   What cared I ?
This was all England's holy-day !   " Come in,
My yellow-hammers," roared the Friar Tuck
Of this mad morrice, " come you into church,
My nightingales, my scraps of Lincoln green,
And hear my sermon ! "   On a window-seat
He stood, against the diamonded rich panes
In the old oak parlour, and, throwing back his hood,
Who should it be but Ben, rare Ben himself ?
The wild troop laughed around him, some a-sprawl
On tables, kicking parti-coloured heels,
Some with their Marians jigging on their knees,
And, in the front of all, the motley fool
Cross-legged upon the rushes.
                              O, I knew him,—
Will Kemp, the player, who danced from London town
To Norwich in nine days and was proclaimed
Freeman of Marchaunt Venturers and hedge-king
Of English morrice-dancery for ever !
His nine-days' wonder through the country-side
Was hawked by every ballad-monger.   Kemp
Raged at their shake-rag Muses.   None but I
Guessed ever for what reason, since he chose
His anticks for himself and, in his games,

Was more than most May-fools fantastical.
I watched his thin face, as he rocked and crooned,
Shaking the squirrel's tails around his ears ;
And, out of all the players I had seen,
His face was quickest through its clay to flash
The passing mood.   Though not a muscle stirred,
The very skin of it seemed to flicker and gleam
With little summer lightnings of the soul
At every fleeting fancy.   For a man
So quick to bleed at a pin-prick or to leap
Laughing through hell to save a butterfly,
This world was difficult ; and perchance he found
In his fantastic games that open road
Which even Will Shakespeare only found at last
In motley and with some wild straws in his hair.

But "Drawer! drawer!" bellowed Friar Ben,
"Make ready a righteous breakfast while I preach ;—
Tankards of nut-brown ale, and cold roast beef,
Cracknels, old cheese, flaunes, tarts and clotted cream,
Hath any a wish not circumscribed by these?"

"A white-pot custard, for my white-pot queen,"
Cried Kemp, waving his bauble, "mark this, boy,
A white-pot custard for my queen of May,—
She is not here, but that concerns not thee!—
A white-pot Mermaid custard, with a crust,
Lashings of cream, eggs, apple-pulse and spice,
A little sugar and manchet bread.   Away!
Be swift!"
                    And as I bustled to and fro,
The Friar raised his big brown fist again
And preached in mockery of the Puritans
Who thought to strip the moonshine wings from Mab,
Tear down the May-poles, rout our English games,
And drive all beauty back into the sea.

Then laughter and chatter and clashing tankards drowned
All but their May-day jollity a-while.
But, as their breakfast ended, and I sank
Gasping upon a bench, there came still more
Poets and players crowding into the room ;
And one—I only knew him as Sir John—
Waved a great ballad at Will Kemp and laughed,
"Atonement, Will, atonement !"
                              "What," groaned Kemp,
"Another penny poet?   How many lies
Does *this* rogue tell?   Sir, I have suffered much
From these Melpomenes and strawberry quills,
And think them better at their bloody lines
On *The Blue Lady*.   Sir, they set to work
At seven o'clock in the morning, the same hour
That I, myself, that's *Cavaliero* Kemp,
With heels of feather and heart of cork, began
Frolickly footing, from the great Lord Mayor
Of London, tow'rds the worshipful Master Mayor
Of Norwich."
                  "Nay, Kemp, this is a May-day tune,
A morrice of country rhymes, made by a poet
Who thought it shame so worthy an act as thine
Should wither in oblivion if the Muse
With her Castalian showers could keep it green.
And while the fool nid-nodded all in time,
Sir John, in swinging measure, trolled this tale :—

                              I.

With Georgie Sprat, my overseer, and Thomas Slye, my
        tabourer,
    And William Bee, my courier, when dawn emblazed the
        skies,
I met a tall young butcher as I danced by little Sudbury,
    Head-master o' morrice dancers all, high head-borough
        of hyes?

By Sudbury, by Sudbury, by little red-roofed Sudbury,
  He wished to dance a mile with me !   I made a courtly
    bow :
I fitted him with morrice-bells, with treble, bass, and tenor
    bells,
  And " *Tickle your tabor, Tom*," I cried, "*we're going to
    market now.*"

And rollicking down the lanes we dashed, and frolicking up
    the hills we clashed,
  And like a sail behind me flapped his great white frock
    a-while,
Till with a gasp, he sank and swore that he could dance
    with me no more ;
  And—over the hedge a milk-maid laughed, *Not dance
    with him a mile ?*

" You lout ! " she laughed, " I'll leave my pail, and dance
    with him for cakes and ale !
  I'll dance a mile for love," she laughed, " and win my
    wager, too.
Your feet are shod and mine are bare ; but when could
    leather dance on air ?
  A milk-maid's feet can fall as fair and light as falling
    dew."

I fitted her with morrice-bells, with treble, bass, and tenor
    bells :
  The fore-bells, as I linked them at her throat, how soft
    they sang !
Green linnets in a golden nest, they chirped and trembled
    on her breast,
  And, faint as elfin blue-bells, at her nut-brown ankles
    rang.

I fitted her with morrice-bells that sweetened into wood-
    bine bells,
  And trembled as I hung them there and crowned her
    sunny brow :

"Strike up," she laughed, "my summer king!" And all
    her bells began to ring,
  And "*Tickle your tabor, Tom*," I cried, "*we're going to
    Sherwood now !*"

When cocks were crowing, and light was growing, and horns
    were blowing, and milk-pails flowing,
  We swam thro' waves of emerald gloom along a chestnut
    aisle,
Then, up a shining hawthorn-lane, we sailed into the sun
    again,
  Will Kemp and his companion, his companion of a mile.

"Truer than most," snarled Kemp, "but mostly lies!
And why does he forget the miry lanes
By Brainford with thick woods on either side,
And the deep holes, where I could find no ease
But skipped up to my waist?" A crackling laugh
Broke from his lips which, if he had not worn
The cap and bells, would scarce have roused the mirth
Of good Sir John, who roundly echoed it,
Then waved his hand and said, "Nay, but he treats
Your morrice in the spirit of Lucian, Will,
Who thought that dancing was no mushroom growth,
But sprung from the beginning of the world
When Love persuaded earth, air, water, fire,
And all the jarring elements to move
In measure. Right to the heart of it, my lad,
The song goes, though the skin mislike you so."
"Nay, an there's more of it, I'll sing it, too!
'Tis a fine tale, Sir John, I have it by heart,
Although 'tis lies throughout." Up leapt Will Kemp,
And crouched and swayed, and swung his bauble round,
Marking the measure as they trolled the tale,
Chanting alternately, each answering each.

II.

The Fool.

The tabor fainted far away behind us, but her feet that day
    They beat a rosier morrice o'er the fairy-circled green.

Sir John.

And o'er a field of buttercups, a field of lambs and butter-
    cups,
    We danced along a cloth of gold, a summer king and
       queen!

The Fool.

And straying we went, and swaying we went, with lambkins
    round us playing we went;
    Her face uplift to drink the sun, and not for me her
       smile.
We danced, a king and queen of May, upon a fleeting
    holy-day,
    But O, she'd won her wager, my companion of a mile!

Sir John.

Her rosy lips they never spoke, though every rosy foot-fall
    broke
    The dust, the dust to Eden-bloom; and, past the
       throbbing blue,
All ordered to her rhythmic feet, the stars were dancing
    with my sweet,
    And all the world a morrice-dance!

The Fool.

                  She knew not; but I knew!
Love, like Amphion with his lyre, made all the elements
    conspire
    To build his world of music.   All in rhythmic rank
       and file,

I saw them in their cosmic dance, catch hands across, retire, advance,
  For me and my companion, my companion of a mile !

Sir John.

The little leaves on every tree, the rivers winding to the sea,
  The swinging tides, the wheeling winds, the rolling heavens above,
Around the May-pole Igdrasil, they worked the Morrice-master's will,
  Persuaded into measure by the all-creative Love.

That hour I saw, from depth to height, this wildering universe unite !
  The lambs of God around us and His passion in every flower !

The Fool.

His grandeur in the dust, His dust a blaze of blinding majesty,
  And all His immortality in one poor mortal hour.

And Death was but a change of key in Life the golden melody,
  And Time became Eternity, and Heaven a fleeting smile ;
For all was each and each was all, and all a wedded unity,
  Her heart in mine, and mine in my companion of a mile.

Thwack !   *Thwack !* He whirled his bauble round about,
"This fellow beats them all," he cried, "the worst
Those others wrote was that I hopped from York
To Paris with a mortar on my head.
This fellow sends me leaping through the clouds

To buss the moon!   The best is yet to come.
Strike up, Sir John!   Ha! ha!   You know no more?"
Kemp leapt upon a table.   "Clear the way,"
He cried, and with a great stamp of his foot
And a wild crackling laugh, drew all to hark.
          "With hey and ho, through thick and thin,
                The hobby-horse is forgotten.
          But I must finish what I begin,
                Tho' all the roads be rotten,
     "By all those twenty thousand chariots, Ben,
Hear this true tale they shall!   Now, let me see,
Where was Will Kemp?   Bussing the moon's pale mouth?
Ah, yes!"   He crouched above the listening throng,—
"*Good as a play*," I heard one whispering quean,—
And, waving his bauble, shuffling with his feet
In a dance that marked the time, he sank his voice
As if to breathe great secrets, and so sang :—

                          III.

At Melford town, at Melford town, at little grey-roofed
          Melford town,
     A long mile from Sudbury, upon the village green,
We danced into a merry rout of country-folk that skipt
          about
     A hobby-horse, a May-pole, and a laughing white-pot
          queen.

They thronged about us as we stayed, and there I gave my
          sunshine maid
     An English crown for cakes and ale—her dancing was
          so true!
And "Nay," she said, "I danced my mile for love!"
          I answered with a smile,
     "'Tis but a silver token, lass, thou'st won that wager,
          too."

I took my leash of morrice-bells, my treble, bass, and tenor
bells.
   They pealed like distant marriage-bells!   And up came
William Bee
With Georgie Sprat, my overseer, and Thomas Slye, my
tabourer,
   "Farewell," she laughed, and vanished with a Suffolk
courtesie.

I leapt away to Rockland, and from Rockland on to
Hingham,
   From Hingham on to Norwich, sirs!   I hardly heard
a while
The throngs that followed after, with their shouting and
their laughter,
   For a shadow danced beside me, my companion of a
mile!

At Norwich, by St Giles his gate, I entered, and the Mayor
in state,
   With all the rosy knights and squires for twenty miles
about,
With trumpets and with minstrelsy, was waiting there to
welcome me;
   And, as I skipt into the street, the City raised a shout.

They gave me what I did not seek!   I fed on roasted
swans a week!
   They pledged me in their malmsey, and they lined me
warm with ale!
They sleeked my skin with red-deer pies, and all that runs
and swims and flies;
   But, through the clashing wine-cups, O, I heard her
clanking pail.

And, rising from his crimson chair, the worshipful and
        portly Mayor
    Bequeathed me forty shillings every year that I should
        live,
With five good angels in my hand that I might drink while
        I could stand !
    They gave me golden angels !   What I lacked they
        could not give.

They made Will Kemp, thenceforward, sirs, Freeman of
        Marchaunt Venturers !
    They hoped that I would dance again from Norwich up
        to York ;
Then they asked me, all together, had I met with right
        May weather,
    And they praised my heels of feather, and my heart, my
        heart of cork.

.   .   .   .   .   .

As I came home by Sudbury, by little red-roofed Sudbury,
    I waited for my bare-foot maid, among her satin kine.
I heard a peal of wedding-bells, of treble, bass, and tenor
        bells :
    "Ring well," I cried, "this bridal morn !   You soon
        shall ring for mine !"

I found her foot-prints in the grass, just where she stood
        and saw me pass,
    I stood within her own sweet field and waited for my
        May.
I laughed.   The dance has turned about !   I stand within :
        she'll pass without,
    And—*down the road the wedding came, the road I danced
        that day !*

I saw the wedding-folk go by, with laughter and with
          minstrelsy,
  I gazed across her own sweet hedge, I caught her happy
          smile,
I saw the tall young butcher pass to little red-roofed Sudbury,
  His bride upon his arm, my lost companion of a mile.

Down from his table leapt the motley Fool.
His bladder bounced from head to ducking head,
His crackling laugh rang high,—"Sir John, I danced
In February, and the song says May!
A fig for all your poets, liars all!
Away to Fenchurch Street, lasses and lads,
They hold high revel there this May-day morn.
Away!" The mad-cap throng echoed the cry.
He drove them with his bauble through the door;
Then, as the last gay kerchief fluttered out,
He gave one little sharp sad lingering cry
As of a lute-string breaking.   He turned back
And threw himself along a low dark bench;
His jingling cap was crumpled in his fist,
And, as he lay there, all along Cheapside
The happy voices of his comrades rang:—

          Out of the woods we'll dance and sing
          Under the morning-star of Spring,
          Into the town with our fresh boughs
          And knock at every sleeping house,
                    Not sighing,
                    Or crying,
          Though Love knows no denying!
          Then, round your summer queen and king,
          Come, young lovers, dance and sing,
                    Dance and sing!

His motley shoulders heaved.   I touched his arm,
"What ails you, sir?"   He raised his thin white face,
Wet with the May-dew still.   A few stray petals

Clung in his tangled hair.   He leapt to his feet,
"'Twas February, but I danced, boy, danced
In May!   Can you do this?"   Forward he bent
Over his feet, and shuffled it, heel and toe,
Out of the Mermaid, singing his old song—
> A-maying,
> A-playing,
> For Love knows no gain-saying!
> Wisdom trips not?   Even so,—
> Come, young lovers, trip and go,
> Trip and go.

Five minutes later, over the roaring Strand,
Chorus, I heard him crow, and half the town
Reeled into music under his crimson comb.

VI.—BIG BEN.

Gods, what a hubbub shook our cobwebs out
The day that Chapman, Marston, and our Ben
Waited in Newgate for the hangman's hands.
Chapman and Marston had been flung there first
For some imagined insult to the Scots
In *Eastward Hoe*, the play they wrote with Ben.
But Ben was famous now, and our brave law
Would fain have winked and passed the big man by.
The lesser men had straightway been condemned
To have their ears cut off, their noses slit
With other tortures.

             Ben had risen at that.
He gripped his cudgel, called for a quart of ale,
Then, like Helvellyn with his rocky face
And mountain-belly, he surged along Cheapside,
Snorting with wrath, and rolled into the gaol,
To share their punishment.

                "There is my mark!
'Tis not the first time you have branded me,"
Said our big Ben, and thrust his broad left thumb,
Branded with T for Tyburn, into the face
Of every protest.   "That's the mark you gave me
Because I killed my man in Spitalfields,
A duel honest as any your courtiers fight.
But I was no Fitzdotterel, claimed no gules
And azure, only red blood and the blue sky,
I never robbed one silk-worm for my hose.
I was Ben Jonson, out of Annandale,
Brick-layer in common to the good Lord God.

You branded me.   I am Ben Jonson still.
You cannot rub it out."
                          The Mermaid Inn
Buzzed like a hornet's nest upon the day
Fixed for their mutilation.   And the stings
Were ready, too.   For rapiers flashed and clashed
Among the tankards.   Dekker was there, and Lodge.
Brome (Jonson's body-servant whom he taught
His art of verse, and, more than that, to love him)
With half a dozen more.   They planned to meet
The prisoners going to Tyburn and attempt
A desperate rescue.

                          All at once, we heard
A great gay song come marching down the street,
A single voice and twenty marching men,
Then the full chorus, twenty voices strong :—

    The prentice whistles at break of day
      All under fair roofs and towers,
  When the old Cheape openeth every way
      Her little sweet inns like flowers :
  And he sings like a lark, both early and late
      To think, if his house take fire,
  At the good *Green Dragon* in Bishopsgate
      He may drink to his heart's desire.

Chorus : Or sit at his ease in the old *Cross Keys*
        And drink to his heart's desire.

  But I, as I walk by *Red Rose Lane*,
      Tho' it warmeth my heart to see
  The Swan, The Golden Hind, and *The Crane*
      With the door set wide for me,
  Tho' Signs like daffodils paint the Strand
      When the thirsty bees begin,
  Of all the good taverns in England
      My choice is—*The Mermaid Inn.*

Chorus : There is much to be said for the *Saracen's Head,*
        But—my choice is the *Mermaid Inn.*

Into the tavern they tumbled, those roaring boys.
"Now broach your ripest and your best," they cried,
"All's well! They are all released! They are on the
    way!
Old Camden and young Selden worked the trick.
Where is Dame Dimpling? Where's our jolly hostess?
Tell her the Mermaid Tavern will have guests:
We are sent to warn her. She must raid Cook's Row,
And make their ovens bellow. Nobody dines
This day with old Duke Humphrey. Red-deer pies,
Castles of almond crust, three roasted peacocks,
And one immortal barrel of red wine;
One gorgeous, rolling, hooped and cob-webbed tun
Of Venus' blood, mighty enough to drown
All the white roses out of Araby
In crimson, drench the great grey beard of Jove
And turn it to a sunset! Big enough
To frighten Bacchus and make Gargantua drunk!
The gods will pay for it! Ben is on the way!"
Then all the rafters rang with song again:—

    There was a Prince—long since, long since!—
        To Eastcheape did resort,
    For that he loved *The Blue Boar's Head*
        Far better than Crown or Court:
    But old King Harry in Westminster
        Hung up, for all to see,
    Three bells of power, in St Stephen's Tower,
        Yea, bells of a thousand and three!

Chorus: Three bells of power, in a timber tower,
            Thirty thousand and three.

    For Harry the Fourth was a godly king,
        And loved great godly bells!
    He bade them ring, and he bade them swing
        Till a man might hear nought else.

In every tavern it soured the sack
   With discord and with din,
But they drowned it all in a madrigal
   Like this, at *The Mermaid Inn.*

Chorus : They drowned it all in a madrigal
          Like this, at *The Mermaid Inn.*

"But how did Camden work it ?"—nobody knows.
They will be here anon.   Better ask Selden.
He's the magician.   "Ah, here comes Dame Dimpling !"—
And into the rollicking tumult our good Dame,
A Dame of only two and thirty springs,
All lavender and roses and white kerchief,
Bustled, to lay the tables.
                      Fletcher flung
His arm around her waist and kissed her cheek ;
But all she said was " *One—two—three—four—five—*
Six, at a pinch, in yonder window-seat ! "
"A health to our Dame Dimpling !" Beaumont cried,
And Dekker, leaping on the old black settle,
Led all their chaos into a song again :—

What is the Mermaid's merriest toast ?
   Our hostess—good Dame Dimpling !
Who is it rules the Mermaid roast ?
Who is it bangs the Mermaid host,
Tho' her hands be soft as her heart almost ?
       Dame Dimpling !

She stands at the board in her fresh blue gown
   With the sleeves tucked up—Dame Dimpling !
She rolls the white dough up and down,
And her pies are crisp, and her eyes are brown,
So—she is the Queen of all this town,—
       Dame Dimpling !

Her sheets are white as black-thorn bloom,
  White as her neck, Dame Dimpling !
Her lavender sprigs in the London gloom
Make every little bridal-room
A country nook of fresh perfume, —
      Dame Dimpling !

She wears white lace on her dark brown hair ;
  And a rose on her breast, Dame Dimpling !
And who can show you a foot as fair
Or an ankle as neat when she climbs the stair,
Taper in hand, and head in the air,
And a rose in her cheek ?   O, past compare,
      Dame Dimpling !

"But don't forget those oyster-pies," cried Lyly,
"Nor the roast beef," roared Dekker.   "Prove yourself
The Muse of meat and drink."
                        There was a shout
In Bread Street, and our windows all swung wide,
Six heads at each.
                  Nat Field bestrode our sign
And kissed the painted Mermaid on her lips,
Then waved his tankard.   "Here they come," he cried,
"Camden and Selden, Chapman and Marston, too,
And half Will's company with our big Ben
Riding upon their shoulders."   "Look," cried Dekker,
"But where is Atlas now ?   O, let them have it !
A lusty chorus, lads !   Let the roof crack !"
And all the Mermaid clashed and roared again
In thunderous measure to the marching tune
That rolled down Bread Street, forty voices strong :—

  At *Ypres Inn*, by *Wring-wren Lane*,
    Old John of Gaunt would dine :
  He scarce had opened an oyster or twain
    Or drunk one flagon of wine,

When, all along the Vintry Ward,
    He heard the trumpets blow,
And a voice that roared—"If thou love thy Lord,
    Tell John of Gaunt to go!"

Chorus: A great voice roared—"If thou love thy Lord,
            Tell John of Gaunt to go!"

Then, into the room rushed Haviland
    That fair fat Flemish host:
"They are marching hither with sword and brand!
    Ten thousand men—almost!
It is these oysters or thy sweet life,
    Thy blood or the best of the bin!"
"Proud Pump, avaunt!" quoth John of Gaunt,
    "I will dine at the Mermaid Inn!"

Chorus: "Proud Pump, avaunt!" quoth John of Gaunt,
            "There is Wine at the Mermaid Inn!"

And in came Ben like a great galleon poised
High on the white crest of a shouting wave.
And then the feast began.   The fragrant steam
As from the kitchens of Olympus drew
A throng of ragged urchins to our doors.
Ben ordered them a castellated pie
That rolled a cloud around them where they sat
Munching upon the cobble-stones.   Our casements
Dripped with the golden dews of Helicon
And, under the warm feast, our cellarage
Gurgled and foamed in the delicious cool
With crimson freshets. . . .
                            "But tell us," cried Nat Field,
When pipes began to puff.   "How did you work it?"
Camden chuckled and tugged his long white beard.
"Out of the mouth of babes," he said, and shook
His wrinkled hand at Selden.   "O, young man,
There's a career before you!   Selden did it.
Take my advice, my children.   Make young Selden

Solicitor-general to the Mermaid Inn.
That rosy silken smile of his conceals
A scholar! Yes, that suckling lawyer there
Puts my grey beard to shame. His courteous airs
And silken manners hide the nimblest wit
That ever trimmed a sail to catch the wind
Of courtly favour. Mark my words now, Ben,
That youth will sail right up against the wind
By skilful tacking. But you run it fine,
Selden, you run it fine. Take my advice,
And don't be too ironical, my boy,
Or even the king will see it."

                    He chuckled again.
"But tell them of your treatise."

                             "Here it is,"
Said Selden, twisting a lighted paper-spill,
Then, with his round cherubic face a-glow,
Lit his long silver pipe.

                    "Why, first," he said,
"Camden, being Clarencieux King-at-Arms,
I made him read the King this tract I wrote
Against tobacco."

                    And the Mermaid roared
With laughter. "Well, you went the way to hang
All three of them," cried Lyly, "and, as for Ben,
His Trinidado goes to bed with him."
"Green gosling, quack no more," Selden replied,
Smiling that rosy silken smile anew.
"The King's a *critic!* When have critics known
The poet from his creatures, God from me?
How many cite Polonius to their sons
And call it Shakespeare? Well, I took my text
From sundry creatures of our great big Ben,
And called it 'Jonson.'"

                        Camden read it out
Without the flicker of an eye. His beard
Saved us, I think. The King admired his text.
"*There is a man,*" he read, "*lies at death's door*

Thro' taking of Tobacco.   Yesterday,
He voided a bushel of soot."

                        "God bless my soul,
A bushel of soot!   Think of it!" said the King.
"The man who wrote those great and splendid words,"
Camden replied—I had prepared his case
Carefully—"lies in Newgate prison, sire.
His nose and ears await the hangman's knife."

   "Ah," said the shrewd King, goggling his great eyes
Cannily.   "Did he not defame the Scots?"
"That's true," said Camden, "but—sire—only those
Who flout your Majesty and take tobacco.
He is a Scot, himself, and hath the gift
Of preaching."

               Then we gave him Jonson's lines
Against Virginia.   "Neither do thou lust
After that tawny weed; for who can tell,
Before the gathering and the making up,
What alligarta may have spawned thereon."
Or words to that effect.

                     "Magneeficent!"
Spluttered the King, "who knows? who knows, indeed?
That's a grand touch—that alligarta, Camden!"

"The Scot who wrote those great and splendid words,"
Said Camden, "languishes in Newgate, sire,
His ears and nose . . ."

               And there, as we arranged
With Inigo Jones, the ladies of the court
Assailed the King in tears.   Their masque and ball
Would all be ruined.   All their Grecian robes,
Procured at vast expense, were wasted now.
The masque was not half-written, Master Jones
Had lost his poets!   They were all in gaol!
Their noses and their ears . . .

                  "God bless my soul,"
Spluttered the King again, goggling his eyes,
"What d'you make of it, Camden?"

                    "I should say
A Puritan plot, sire; for these justices—
Who love tobacco—use their law, it seems,
To flout your Majesty at every turn.
If this continue, sire, there'll not be left
A loyal ear or nose in all your realm!"
At that, our noble monarch well-nigh swooned.
He hunched his body, padded as it was
Against the assassin's knife, six inches deep
With great green quilts, wagged his enormous head,
Then, in a dozen words, he wooed destruction:
"It is presumption, and a high contempt
In subjects to dispute what kings can do,"
He whimpered, "Even as it is blasphemy
To thwart the will of God."

                  He waved his hand,
And rose. "These men must be released," he said.
Then—as I think—to seek a safer place,
He waddled from the room, his rickety legs
Doubling beneath that great green feather-bed
He calls his "person."—"I shall dream to-night
Of spiders, Camden!"—But in half an hour
Inigo Jones was armed with Right Divine
To save such ears and noses as the ball
Required for its perfection. Think of that!
And let this earthly ball remember, too,
That Chapman, Marston, and our great big Ben
Owe their poor adjuncts to—ten Grecian robes,
And "Jonson" on tobacco! England loves
Her poets, O supremely, when they're dead.

"But Ben has narrowly escaped her love,"
Said Chapman gravely.

                "What d'you mean?" said Lodge.
And, as he spoke, there was a sudden hush.
A tall gaunt woman with great burning eyes,
And white hair blown back softly from a face
Ethereally fierce, as might have looked

Cassandra in old age, stood at the door.
"Where is my Ben?" she said.

                              "Mother!" cried Ben.
He rose and caught her in his mighty arms.
Her labour-reddened, large-boned hands entwined
Behind his neck.

                    "She brought this to the gaol,"
Said Chapman, quietly, tossing a phial across
To Camden, "And he meant to take it, too,
Before the hangman touched him.   Half an hour,
And you'd have been too late to save big Ben.
He has lived too long in ancient Rome to love
A slit nose and the pillory.   He'd have wrapped
His purple round him like an Emperor."
The gaunt old woman heard him.   "Do not think
His mother was a churl!" she cried, and stood
Flaming before us like a Roman sibyl,
"I had another phial for myself!"
Ben drew her back into his arms.   She hid
Her face upon his breast.   He led her aside.
"There's Roman blood in both of them," said Dekker,
"Don't look.   She is weeping now."

                              And, while Ben held
That gaunt old body sobbing against his heart,
Dekker, to make her think they paid no heed,
Began to sing ; and, very softly now,
Full forty voices echoed the refrain :—

          The Cardinal's Hat is a very good inn,
              And so is the *Puritan's Head* ;
          But I know a sign of a Wine, a Wine
              That is better when all is said.
          It is whiter than Venus, redder than Mars,
              It was old when the world begun ;
          For all good inns are moons or stars,
              But *The Mermaid* is their Sun.

     Chorus : They are all alight like moons in the night,
              But *The Mermaid* is their Sun.

Therefore, when priest or parson cries
    That inns like flowers increase,
I say that mine inn is a church likewise,
    And I say to them "Be at peace!"
An host may gather in dark St Paul's
    To salve their souls from sin;
But the Light may be where "two or three"
    Drink Wine in *The Mermaid Inn*.

Chorus: The Light may be where "two or three"
    Drink Wine in *The Mermaid Inn*.

VII.—THE BURIAL OF A QUEEN.

'Twas on an All Souls' Eve that our good Inn
—Whereof, for ten years now, myself was host—
Heard and took part in its most eerie tale.
    It was a bitter night; and master Ben,
—His hair now flecked with grey, though youth still fired
His deep and ageless eyes,—in the old oak-chair,
Over the roaring hearth, puffed at his pipe;
A little sad, as often I found him now
Remembering vanished faces.   Yet the years
Brought others round him.   Wreaths of Heliochrise
Gleamed still in that great tribe of Benjamin,
Burned still across the malmsey and muscadel.
The son o' the goldsmith, Herrick,—a name like thyme
Crushed into sweetness by a bare-foot maid
Milking, at dewy dawn, in Elfin-land,—
Was often with us now.   But on this night
He had forsaken us for the *Devil's Tavern*
Where Donne and Marmion supped.

                              This left with Ben,
John Ford, wrapped in his cloak, brooding aloof,
Drayton and Lodge and Drummond of Hawthornden.
    Suddenly, in the porch, I heard a sound
Of iron that grated on the flags.   A spade
And pick came edging through the door.

                              "O, room!
Room for the master-craftsman," muttered Ford,
And grey old sexton Scarlet hobbled in.
    He shuffled off the snow that clogged his boots,

—On my clean rushes!—brushed it from his cloak
Of Northern Russet, wiped his rheumatic knees,
Blew out his lanthorn, hung it on a nail,
Leaned his rude pick and spade against the wall,
Flung back his rough frieze hood, flapped his gaunt arms,
And called for ale.

             "Come to the fire," said Lodge.
"Room for the wisest counsellor of kings,
The kindly sage that puts us all to bed,
And tucks us up beneath the grass-green quilt."
"Plenty of work, eh Timothy?" said Ben.
"Work? Where's my liquor? O, ay, there's work to spare,"
Old Scarlet croaked, then quaffed his creaming stoup,
While Ben said softly—"Pity you could not spare,
You and your Scythe-man, some of the golden lads
That I have seen here in the Mermaid Inn!"
Then, with a quiet smile he shook his head
And turned to master Drummond of Hawthornden.
Well—songs are good, but flesh and blood are better.
The grey old tomb of Horace glows for me
Across the centuries, with one little fire
Lit by a girl's light hand.   Then, under breath
Yet with some passion, he murmured this brief rhyme :—

I.

Dulce ridentem, laughing through the ages,
  Dulce loquentem, O, fairer far to me,
Rarer than the wisdom of all his golden pages
  Floats the happy laughter of his vanished Lalage.

II.

Dulce loquentem,—we hear it and we know it!
  Dulce ridentem,—so musical and low!
"Mightier than marble is my song!"   Ah, did the poet
  Know why little Lalage was mightier even so?

III.

Dulce ridentem—thro' all the years that sever,
   Clear as o'er yon hawthorn-hedge we heard her passing
      by—
Lalagen amabo—a song may live for ever!—
   Dulce loquentem, but Lalage must die.

"I'd like to learn that rhyme," the sexton said.
"I've a fine memory, sir!   If you should start me,
I shouldn't wonder but I'd call to mind
Hundreds of ancient ballads.   Long 'uns, too."
And then—a strange thing happened.

                                    I saw John Ford
"With folded arms and melancholy hat"
(As in our Mermaid jest he still would sit)
Watching old Scarlet like a man in trance.
The sexton gulped his ale and smacked his lips.
"Work, you were saying?" he croaked, "Ah, and to spare,
We fills 'em faster than the spades can dig."
And, all at once, the lights burned low and blue.
Ford leaned right forward, with his grim black eyes
Widening.

            "Why, that's a marvellous ring!" he said,
And pointed to the sexton's gnarled old hand
Spread on that black oak-table like the claw
Of some great bird of prey.   "A ruby worth
The ransom of a queen!"   The fire leapt up!
The sexton stared at him;
Then stretched his hand out, with its blue-black nails,
Full in the light, a grim earth-coloured hand,
But bare as it was born.

                        "There was a ring!
I could have sworn it!   Red as blood!" cried Ford.
And Ben and Lodge and Drummond of Hawthornden
All stared at him.   For such a silent soul
Was master Ford that, when he suddenly spake,
It struck the rest as dumb as if the Sphinx

Had opened its cold stone lips.   He would sit mute
Brooding, aloof, for hours, his cloak around him,
A staff between his knees, as if prepared
For a long journey, a lonely pilgrimage
To some dark tomb; a strange and sorrowful soul,
Yet not—as many thought him—harsh or hard,
But of a most kind patience.   Though he wrote
In blood, they say, the blood came from his heart;
And all the sufferings of this world he took
To his own soul, and bade them pasture there;
Till out of his compassion, he became
A monument of bitterness.   He rebelled;
And so fell short of that celestial height
Whereto the greatest only climb, who stand
By Shakespeare, and accept the Eternal Law.
These find, in law, firm footing for the soul,
The strength that binds the stars, and reins the sea,
The base of being, the pillars of the world,
The pledge of honour, the pure cord of love,
The form of truth, the golden floors of heaven.
These men discern a height beyond all heights,
A depth below all depths, and never an end
Without a pang beyond it, and a hope;
Without a heaven beyond it, and a hell.
For these, despair is like a bubble pricked,
An old romance to make young lovers weep.
For these, the law becomes a fiery road,
A Jacob's ladder through that vast abyss,
Lacking no rung from realm to loftier realm,
Nor wanting one degree from dust to wings.
These, at the last, radiant with victory,
Lay their strong hands upon the wingèd steeds
And fiery chariots, and exult to hold,
Themselves, the throbbing reins, whereby they steer
The stormy splendours.
                              He, being less, rebelled,
Cried out for unreined steeds, and unruled stars,
An unprohibited ocean and a truth

Untrue; and the equal thunder of the law
Hurled him to night and chaos, who was born
To shine upon the forehead of the day.
And yet—the voice of darkness and despair
May speak for heaven where heaven would not be heard,
May fight for heaven where heaven would not prevail,
And the consummate splendour of that strife,
Swallowing up all discords, all defeat,
In one huge victory, harmonising all,
Make Lucifer, at last, at one with God.

    There,—on that All Souls' Eve, you might have thought
A dead man spoke, to see how Drayton stared,
And Drummond started.
                "You saw no ruby ring,"
The old sexton muttered sullenly. "If you did,
The worse for me, by all accounts. The lights
Burned low. You caught the firelight on my fist.
What was it like, this ring?"
                "A band of gold,
And a great ruby, heart-shaped, fit to burn
Between the breasts of Laïs. Am I awake
Or dreaming?"
             "Well,—that makes the second time!
There's many have said they saw it, out of jest,
To scare me. For the astrologer did say
The third time I should die. Now, did you see it?
Most likely some one's told you that old tale!
You hadn't heard it, now?"
              Ford shook his head.
"What tale?" said Ben.
             "O, you could make a book
About my life. I've talked with quick and dead,
And neither ghost nor flesh can fright me now!
I wish it was a ring, so 's I could catch him,
And sell him; but I've never seen him yet.
A white witch told me, if I did, I'd go
Clink, just like that, to heaven or t'other place,

Whirled in a fiery chariot with ten steeds
The way Elijah went.   For I have seen
So many mighty things that I must die
Mightily.

        Well,—I came, sirs, to my craft
The day mine uncle Robert dug the grave
For good Queen Katharine, she whose heart was broke
By old King Harry, a very great while ago.
Maybe you've heard about my uncle, sirs?
He was far-famed for his grave-digging.
In depth, in speed, in neatness, he'd no match!
They've put a fine slab to his memory
In Peterborough Cathedral—*Robert Scarlet,*
Sexton for half a century, it says,
In Peterborough Cathedral, where he built
The last sad habitation for two queens,
And many hundreds of the common sort.
And now himself, who for so many built
Eternal habitations, others have buried.
Obiit anno ætatis, ninety-eight,
July the second, fifteen ninety-four.
  "We should do well, sir, with a slab like that,
Shouldn't we?"   And the sexton leered at Lodge.
"Not many boasts a finer slab than that.
There's many a king done worse.   Ah, well, you see,
He'd a fine record.   Living to ninety-eight,
He buried generations of the poor,
A countless host, and thought no more of it
Than digging potatoes.   He'd a lofty mind
That found no satisfaction in small deeds.
But from his burying of two queens he drew
A lively pleasure.   Could he have buried a third,
It would indeed have crowned his old white hairs.
But he was famous, and he thought, perchance,
A third was mere vain-glory.   So he died.
I helped him with the second."

                The old man leered
To see the shaft go home.

                              Ben filled the stoup
With ale. "So that," quoth he, "began the tale
About this ruby ring?"   "But who," said Lodge,
"Who was the second queen?"

                              "A famous queen,
And a great lover! When you hear her name,
Your hearts will leap. Her beauty passed the bounds
Of modesty, men say, yet—she died young!
We buried her at midnight. There were few
That knew it; for the high State Funeral
Was held upon the morrow, Lammas morn.
Anon you shall hear why. A strange thing that,—
To see the mourners weeping round a hearse
That held a dummy coffin. Stranger still
To see us lowering the true coffin down
By torchlight, with some few of her true friends,
In Peterborough Cathedral, all alone."

   "Old as the world," said Ford. "It is the way
Of princes. Their true tears and smiles are seen
At dead of night, like ghosts raised from the grave!
And all the luxury of their brief, bright noon,
Cloaks but a dummy throne, a mask of life;
And, at the last, drapes a false catafalque,
Holding a vacant urn, a mask of death.
But tell, tell on!"
                     The sexton took a draught
Of ale and smacked his lips.

                           "My uncle lived
A mile or more from Peterborough then.
And, past his cottage, in the dead of night,
Her royal coach came creeping through the lanes,
With scutcheons round it and no crowd to see,
And heralds carrying torches in their hands,
And none to admire, but him and me, and one,
A pedlar-poet, who lodged with us that week
And paid his lodging with a bunch of rhymes.
By these, he said, my uncle Robert's fame

Should live, as in a picture, till the crack
Of doom.   My uncle thought that he should pay
Four pence beside ; but, when the man declared
The thought unworthy of these august events,
My uncle was abashed.

                  And, truth to tell,
The rhymes were mellow, though here and there he
    swerved
From truth to make them so.   Nor would he change
' June' to ' July' for all that we could say.
' I never said the month was June,' he cried,
' And if I did, Shakespeare hath jumped an age !
Gods, will you hedge me round with thirty nights ?
" June " rhymes with " moon " ! '   With that, he flung
    them down
And strode away like Lucifer, and was gone,
Before old Scarlet could approach again
The matter of that four-pence.

                      Yet his rhymes
Have caught the very colours of that night !
I can see through them,
Ay, just as through our cottage window-panes,
Can see the great black coach,
Carrying the dead queen past our garden-gate.
The roses bobbing and fluttering to and fro,
Hide, and yet show the more by hiding, half.
And, like smoked glass through which you see the
    sun,
The song shows truest when it blurs the truth.
This is the way it goes."

                He rose to his feet,
Picked up his spade, and struck an attitude,
Leaning upon it.   " I've got to feel my spade,
Or I'll forget it.   This is the way I speak it,
Always."   And, with a schoolboy's rigid face.
And eyes fixed on the rafters, he began,
Sing-song, the pedlar-poet's bunch of rhymes :—

As I went by the cattle-shed
   The grey dew dimmed the grass,
And, under a twisted apple-tree,
Old Robin Scarlet stood by me.
" Keep watch !   Keep watch to-night," he said,
   " There's things 'ull come to pass.

" Keep watch until the moon has cleared
   The thatch of yonder rick ;
Then I'll come out of my cottage-door
To wait for the coach of a queen once more ;
And—you'll say nothing of what you've heard,
   But rise and follow me quick."

" And what 'ull I see if I keep your trust,
   And wait and watch so late ? "
" Pride," he said, " and Pomp," he said,
" Beauty to haunt you till you're dead,
And Glorious Dust that goes to dust,
   Passing the white farm-gate.

" You are young and all for adventure, lad,
   And the great tales to be told :
This night, before the clock strike one,
Your lordliest hour will all be done ;
But you'll remember it and be glad,
   In the days when you are old ! "

All in the middle of the night
   My face was at the pane ;
When, creeping out of his cottage-door,
To wait for the coach of a queen once more,
Old Scarlet, in the moon-light,
   Beckoned to me again.

He stood beneath a lilac-spray,
   Like Father Time for dole,
In Reading Tawny cloak and hood,
With mattock and with spade he stood,
And, far away to southward,
   A bell began to toll.

He stood beneath a lilac-spray,
   And never a word he said;
But, as I stole out of the house,
He pointed over the orchard boughs,
Where, not with dawn or sunset,
   The Northern sky grew red.

I followed him, and half in fear,
   To the old farm-gate again;
And, round the curve of the long white road,
I saw that the dew-dashed hedges glowed
Red with the grandeur drawing near,
   And the torches of her train.

They carried her down with singing,
   With singing sweet and low,
Slowly round the curve they came,
Twenty torches dropping flame,
The heralds that were bringing her
   The way we all must go.

'Twas master William Dethick,
   The Garter King of Arms,
Before her royal coach did ride,
With none to see his Coat of Pride,
For peace was on the country-side,
   And sleep upon the farms;

Peace upon the red farm,
   Peace upon the grey,
Peace on the heavy orchard trees,
And little white-walled cottages,
Peace upon the wayside,
   And sleep upon the way.

So master William Dethick,
   With forty horse and men,
Like any common man and mean
Rode on before the Queen, the Queen,
And—only a wandering pedlar
   Could tell the tale again.

How, like a cloud of darkness,
   Between the torches moved
Four black steeds and a velvet pall
Crowned with the Crown Imperiall
And—on her shield—the lilies,
   The lilies that she loved.

Ah, stained and ever stainless,
   Ah, white as her own hand,
White as the wonder of that brow,
Crowned with colder lilies now,
White on the velvet darkness,
   The lilies of her land!

The witch from over the water,
   The fay from over the foam,
The bride that rode thro' Edinbro' town
With satin shoes and a silken gown,
A queen, and a great king's daughter,—
   Thus they carried her home,

With torches and with scutcheons,
　　Unhonoured and unseen,
With the lilies of France in the wind a-stir,
And the Lion of Scotland over her,
Darkly, in the dead of night,
　　They carried the Queen, the Queen!

The sexton paused and took a draught of ale.
"'Twas there," he said, "I joined 'em at the gate,
My uncle and the pedlar.   What they sang,
The little shadowy throng of men that walked
Behind the scutcheoned coach with bare bent heads
I know not; but 'twas very soft and low.
They walked behind the rest, like shadows flung
Behind the torch-light, from that strange dark hearse.
And, some said, afterwards, they were the ghosts
Of lovers that this queen had brought to death.
A foolish thought it seemed to me, and yet
Like the night-wind they sang.   And there was one
An olive-coloured man,—the pedlar said
Was like a certain foreigner that she loved,
One Chastelard, a wild French poet of hers.
Also the pedlar thought they sang 'farewell'
In words like this, and that the words in French
Were written by the hapless Queen herself,
When as a girl she left the vines of France
For Scotland and the halls of Holyrood:—

I.

Though thy hands have plied their trade
　　Eighty years without a rest,
Robin Scarlet, never thy spade
　　Built a house for such a guest!
Carry her where, in earliest June,
　　All the whitest hawthorns blow.
Carry her under the midnight moon,
　　Singing very soft and low.

Slow between the low green larches, carry the lovely lady
　　sleeping,
　　Past the low white moon-lit farms, along the lilac-
　　　　shadowed way!
Carry her through the summer darkness, weeping, weeping,
　　weeping, weeping!
　　Answering only, to any that ask you, whence ye carry
　　　　her,—*Fotheringhay!*

II.

　　She was gayer than a child!
　　—Let your torches droop for sorrow.—
　　Laughter in her eyes ran wild!
　　—Carry her down to Peterboro'.—
　　Words were kisses in her mouth!
　　—Let no word of blame be spoken.—
　　She was Queen of all the South!
　　—In the North, her heart was broken.—
They should have left her in her vineyards, left her heart to
　　her land's own keeping,
　　Left her white breast room to breathe, and left her light
　　　　foot free to dance.
Out of the cold grey northern mists, we carry her weeping,
　　weeping, weeping,—
　　　　O, ma patrie,
　　　　La plus chérie,
　　Adieu, plaisant pays de France!

III.

　　Many a red heart died to beat
　　—Music swelled in Holyrood!—
　　Once, beneath her fair white feet.
　　—Now the floors may rot with blood—

She was young and her deep hair—
—*Wind and rain were all her fate !*—
Trapped young Love as in a snare.
—*And the wind's a sword in the Canongate !*
                    Edinboro' !
                    Edinboro' !
Music built the towers of Troy, but thy grey walls are built
        of sorrow !
Wind-swept hills, and sorrowful glens, of thrifty sowing and
            iron reaping,
    What if her foot were fair as a sunbeam, how should it
            touch or melt your snows?
                What if her hair were a silken mesh?
                Hands of steel can deal hard blows,
                Iron breast-plates bruise fair flesh !
                Carry her southward, palled in purple,
                Weeping, weeping, weeping, weeping,
    What had their rocks to do with roses?   Body and soul
        she was all one rose?

Thus, through the summer night, slowly they went,
We three behind,—the pedlar-poet and I,
And Robin Scarlet.   The moving flare that ringed
The escutcheoned hearse, lit every leaf distinct
Along the hedges and woke the sleeping birds,
But drew no watchers from the drowsier farms.
Thus, through a world of innocence and sleep,
We brought her to the doors of her last home,
In Peterborough Cathedral.   Round her tomb
They stood, in the huge gloom of those old aisles,
The heralds with their torches, but their light
Struggled in vain with that tremendous dark.
Their ring of smoky red could only show
A few sad faces round the purple pall,
The wings of a stone angel overhead,
The base of three great pillars, and, fitfully,
Faint as the phosphorus glowing in some old vault,
One little slab of marble, far away.

Yet, or the darkness, or the pedlar's words
Had made me fanciful, I thought I saw
Bowed shadows praying in those unplumbed aisles,
Nay, dimly heard them weeping, in a grief
That still was built of silence, like the drip
Of water from a frozen fountain-head.

We laid her in her grave. We closed the tomb.
With echoing footsteps all the funeral went;
And I went last to close and lock the doors;
Last, and half frightened of the enormous gloom
That rolled along behind me as one by one
The torches vanished. O, I was glad to see
The moonlight on the kind turf-mounds again.

But, as I turned the key, a quivering hand
Was laid upon my arm. I turned and saw
That foreigner with the olive-coloured face.

From head to foot he shivered, as with cold.
He drew me into the shadow of the porch.
'Come back with me,' he whispered, and slid his hand
—Like ice it was!—along my wrist, and slipped
A ring upon my finger, muttering quick,
As in a burning fever, 'All the wealth
Of Eldorado for one hour! Come back!
I must go back and see her face again!
I was not there, not there, the day she—died.
You'll help me with the coffin. Not a soul
Will know. Come back! One moment, only one!'

I thought the man was mad, and plucked my hand
Away from him. He caught me by the sleeve,
And sank upon his knees, lifting his face
Most piteously to mine. 'One moment! See!
I loved her!'
I saw the moonlight glisten on his tears,
Great, long, slow tears they were; and then—my God—
As his face lifted and his head sank back
Beseeching me—I saw a crimson thread
Circling his throat, as though the headsman's axe
Had cloven it with one blow, so shrewd, so keen,

The head had slipped not from the trunk.
                                                    I gasped ;
And, as he pleaded, stretching his head back,
The wound, O like a second awful mouth,
The wound began to gape.
                                        I tore my cloak
Out of his clutch.   My keys fell with a clash.
I left them where they lay, and with a shout
I dashed into the broad white empty road.
There was no soul in sight.   Sweating with fear
I hastened home, not daring to look back ;
But as I turned the corner, I heard the clang
Of those great doors, and knew he had entered in.

Not till I saw before me in the lane
The pedlar and my uncle did I halt
And look at that which clasped my finger still
As with a band of ice.
                                My hand was bare !
I stared at it and rubbed it.   Then I thought
I had been dreaming.   There had been no ring !
The poor man I had left there in the porch,
Being a Frenchman, talked a little wild,
But only wished to look upon her grave.
And I—I was the madman !   So I said
Nothing.   But all the same, for all my thoughts,
I'd not go back that night to find the keys,
No, not for all the rubies in the crown
Of Prester John.
                        The high State Funeral
Was held on Lammas Day.   A wondrous sight
For Peterborough !   For myself, I found
Small satisfaction in a catafalque
That carried a dummy coffin.   None the less,
The pedlar thought that as a Solemn Masque,
Or Piece of Purple Pomp, the thing was good,
And worthy of a picture in his rhymes ;
The more because he said it shadowed forth

The ironic face of Death.

                        The Masque, indeed,
Began before we buried her.   For a host
Of Mourners—Lords and Ladies—on Lammas eve,
Panting with eagerness of pride and place,
Arrived in readiness for the morrow's pomp,
And at the Bishop's Palace they found prepared
A mighty supper for them, where they sat
All at one table.   In a Chamber hung
With scutcheons and black cloth, they drank red wine
And feasted, while the torches and the queen
Crept through the darkness of Northampton lanes.

At seven o'clock on Lammas Morn they woke,
After the Queen was buried ; and at eight
The Masque set forth, thus pictured in the rhymes
With tolling bells, which on the pedlar's lips
Had more than paid his lodging.   Thus he spake it,
Slowly, sounding the rhymes like solemn bells,
And tolling, in between, with lingering tongue :—

Toll !—From the Palace the Releevants creep,—
    A hundred poor old women, nigh their end,
Wearing their black cloth gowns, and on each head
An ell of snow-white holland which, some said,
        Afterwards they might keep,
—*Ah, Toll !*—with nine new shillings each to spend,
    For all the trouble that they had, and all
    The sorrow of walking to this funeral.

Toll !—And the Mourning Cloaks in purple streamed
    Following, a long procession, two by two,
Her Household first.   With these, Monsieur du Preau,
Her French Confessor, unafraid to show
        The golden Cross that gleamed
About his neck, warned what the crowd might do
    Said *I will wear it, though I die for it !*
    So subtle in malice was that Jesuit.

Toll!—Sir George Savile in his Mourner's Gown
    Carried the solemn Cross upon a Field
Azure, and under it by a streamer borne
    Upon a field of Gules, an Unicorn
        Argent and, lower down,
A scrolled device upon a blazoned shield,
    Which seemed to say—I AM SILENT TILL THE END!—
    Toll! Toll!—IN MY DEFENCE, GOD ME DEFEND!

Toll! and a hundred poor old men went by,
    Followed by two great Bishops.—*Toll, ah toll!*—
Then, with White Staves and Gowns, four noble lords;
Then sixteen Scots and Frenchmen with drawn swords;
        Then, with a Bannerol,
Sir Andrew Noel, lifting to the sky
    The Great Red Lion.   Then the Crown and Crest
    Borne by a Herald on his glittering breast.

And now—ah now, indeed, the deep bell tolls!—
    That empty Coffin, with its velvet pall,
Borne by six Gentlemen, under a canopy
Of purple, lifted by four knights, goes by.
        The Crown Imperiall
Burns on the Coffin-head.   Four Bannerols
    On either side, uplifted by four squires,
    Roll on the wind their rich heraldic fires.

Toll! The Chief Mourner—the fair Russell!—*toll!*—
    Countess of Bedford—*toll!*—they bring her now,
Weeping under a purple Cloth of State,
Till, halting there before the Minster Gate,
        Having in her control
The fair White Staves of office, with a bow
    She gives them to her two great Earls again,
    Then sweeps them onward in her mournful train.

Toll! At the high Cathedral door the Quires
    Meet them and lead them, singing all the while
A mighty *Miserere* for her soul!
Then, as the rolling organ—*toll, ah toll!*—
        Floods every glimmering aisle
With ocean-thunders, all those knights and squires
    Bring the false Coffin to the central nave
    And set it in the Catafalque o'er her grave.

The Catafalque was made in Field-bed wise
    Valanced with midnight purple, fringed with gold:
All the Chief Mourners on dark thrones were set
Within it, as jewels in some huge carcanet:
        Above was this device
IN MY DEFENCE, GOD ME DEFEND, inscrolled
    Round the rich Arms of Scotland, as to say
    ' Man judged me. I abide the Judgment Day.' "

The sexton paused anew. All looked at him,
And at his wrinkled, grim, earth-coloured hand,
As if, in that dim light, beclouded now
With blue tobacco-smoke, they thought to see
The smouldering ruby again.
            " Ye know," he said,
" How master William Wickham preached that day?"
Ford nodded. " I have heard of it. He showed
Subtly, O very subtly, after his kind,
That the white Body of Beauty such as hers
Was in itself Papistical, a feast,
A fast, an incense, a burnt-offering,
And an Abomination in the sight
Of all true Protestants. Why, her very name
Was Mary!"
          " Ay, that's true, that's very true!"
The sexton mused. " Now that's a strange deep thought!
The Bishop missed a text in missing that.
Her name, indeed, was Mary!"
                " Did you find

Your keys again?"   "Ay, sir, I found them!"   "Where?"
"Strange you should ask me that!   After the throng
Departed, and the Nobles were at feast,
All in the Bishop's Palace—a great feast
And worthy of their sorrow—I came back
Carrying my uncle's second bunch of keys
To lock the doors and search, too, for mine own.
'Twas growing dusk already, and as I thrust
The key into the lock, the great grey porch
Grew cold upon me, like a tomb.

        I pushed
Hard at the key—then stopped—with all my flesh
Freezing, and half in mind to fly; for, sirs,
The door was locked already, and—*from within!*

I drew the key forth quietly and stepped back
Into the Churchyard, where the graves were warm
With sunset still, and the blunt carven stones
Lengthened their homely shadows, out and out,
To Everlasting.   Then I plucked up heart,
Seeing the foot-prints of the mighty Masque
Along the pebbled path.   A queer thought came
Into my head that all the world without
Was but a Masque, and I was creeping back,
Back from the Mourner's Feast to Truth again.
Yet—I grew bold, and tried the southern door.
 'Twas locked, but held no key on the inner side
To foil my own, and softly, softly, click,
I turned it, and with heart, sirs, in my mouth,
Pushed back the studded door and entered in . . .
 Stepped straight out of the world, I might have said,
Out of the dusk into a night so deep,
So dark, I trembled like a child. . . .

          And then
I was aware, sirs, of a great sweet wave
Of incense.   All the gloom was heavy with it,
As if her Papist Household had returned
To pray for her poor soul; and, my fear went.

                     L

But either that strange incense weighed me down,
Or else from being sorely over-tasked,
A languor came upon me, and sitting there
To breathe a moment, in a velvet stall,
I closed mine eyes.

               A moment, and no more,
For then I heard a rustling in the nave,
And opened them ; and, very far away,
As if across the world, in Rome herself,
I saw twelve tapers in the solemn East,
And saw, or thought I saw, cowled figures kneel
Before them, in an incense-cloud.

                      And then,
Maybe the sunset deepened in the world
Of masques without—clear proof that I had closed
Mine eyes but for a moment, sirs, I saw
As if across a world-without-end tomb,
A tiny jewelled glow of crimson panes
Darkening and brightening with the West.

                        And then,
Then I saw something more—Queen Mary's vault,
And—it was open ! . . .

                Then, I heard a voice,
A strange deep broken voice, whispering love
In soft French words, that clasped and clung like hands;
And then—two shadows passed against the West,
Two blurs of black against that crimson stain,
Slowly, O very slowly, with bowed heads,
Leaning together, and vanished into the dark
Beyond the Catafalque.

                 Then—I heard him pray,—
And knew him for the man that prayed to me,—
Pray as a man prays for his love's last breath !
And then, O sirs, it caught me by the throat,
And I, too, dropped upon my knees and prayed ;
For, as in answer to his prayer, there came
A moan of music, a mighty shuddering sound
From the great organ, a sound that rose and fell

Like seas in anger, very far away;
And then a peal of thunder, and then it seemed,
As if the graves were giving up their dead,
A great cowled host of shadows rose and sang :—

> ' Dies iræ, dies illâ,
> Solvet sæclum in favilla,
> Teste David cum Sibylla.'

I heard her sad, sad, little, broken voice,
Out in the darkness. 'Ay, and David, too,
His blood is on the floors of Holyrood,
To speak for me.' Then that great ocean-sound
Swelled to a thunder again, and heaven and earth
Shrivelled away; and in that huge slow hymn
Chariots were driven forth in flaming rows,
And terrible trumpets blown from deep to deep.

And then, ah then, the heart of heaven was hushed,
And—in the hush—it seemed an angel wept,
Another Mary wept, and gathering up
All our poor wounded, weary, way-worn world,
Even as a mother gathers up her babe,
Soothed it against her breast, and rained her tears
On the pierced feet of God, and melted Him
To pity, and over His feet poured her deep hair.

The music died away. The shadows knelt.
And then—I heard a rustling nigh the tomb,
And heard—and heard—or dreamed I heard—farewells,
Farewells for everlasting, deep farewells;
Bitter as blood, darker than any death.
And, at the last, as in a kiss, one word,
One whispering edge of sweetness, like a sword
For sharpness, drawn along a soft white throat ;
And, for its terrible longing, like a sigh
Across great waters, very far away,—
Sweetheart!

And then, like doors, like world-without-end doors
That shut for Everlasting, came a clang,
And ringing, echoing, through the echo of it,
One terrible cry that plucked my heart-strings out,
Mary!   And on the closed and silent tomb,
Where there were two, one shuddering shadow lay,
And then—I, too,—reeled, swooned and knew no more.

Sirs, when I woke, there was a broad bright shaft
Of moonlight, slanting through an Eastern pane
Full on her tomb and that black Catafalque.
And on the tomb there lay—my bunch of keys!
I struggled to my feet,
Ashamed of my wild fancies, like a man
Awaking from a drunken dream.   And yet,
When I picked up the keys, although that storm
Of terror had all blown by and left me calm,
I lifted up mine eyes to see the scroll
Round the rich crest of that dark canopy,
IN MY DEFENCE, GOD ME DEFEND.   The moon
Struck full upon it; and, as I turned and went,
God help me, sirs, though I were loyal enough
To good Queen Bess, I could not help but say,
Amen!
And yet, methought it was not I that spake,
But some deep soul that used me for a mask,
A soul that rose up in this hollow shell
Like dark sea-tides flooding an empty cave.
I could not help but say with my poor lips,
Amen!   Amen!
                              Sirs, 'tis a terrible thing
To move in great events.   Since that strange night
I have not been as other men.   The tides
Would rise in this dark cave "—he tapped his skull—
" Deep tides, I know not whence; and when they rose
My friends looked strangely upon me and stood aloof.
And once, my uncle said to me—indeed,
It troubled me strangely,—' Timothy,' he said,

'Thou art translated!   I could well believe
Thou art two men, whereof the one's a fool,
The other a prophet.   Or else, beneath thy skin
There lurks a changeling!   What hath come to thee?'
And then, sirs, then—well I remember it!
'Twas on a summer eve, and we walked home
Between high ghostly hedges white with may—
And uncle Robin, in his holy-day suit
Of Reading Tawny, felt his old heart swell
With pride in his great memories.   He began
Chanting the pedlar's tune, keeping the time
Thus, jingle, jingle, slowly, with his keys:—

I.

Douglas in the moonless night
   —*Muffled oars on blue Loch Leven*—
Took her hand, a flake of white
   —*Beauty slides the bolts of Heaven!*—
Little white hand, like a flake of snow,
   When they saw it, his Highland crew
Swung together, and murmured low,
   Douglas, wilt *thou* die, then, too?
And the pine-trees whispered, weeping,
   Douglas, Douglas, tender and true!

'Little white hand like a tender moon-beam, soon shall you
      set the broadswords leaping!
   It is the Queen! the Queen!' they whispered, watching
      her soar to the saddle anew:
'There will be trumpets blown in the mountains, a mist of
      blood on the heather, and weeping,
   Weeping, weeping, and thou, too, dead for her, Douglas,
      Douglas, tender and true?'

II.

Carry the queenly lass along !
— *Cold she lies, cold and dead,—*
   She whose laughter was a song,
      —*Lapped around with sheets of lead !—*
   She whose blood was wine of the South,
      —*Light her down to a couch of clay—*
And a royal rose her mouth,
      And her body made of may !
   —*Lift your torches weeping, weeping,*
      Light her down to a couch of clay.

They should have left her in her vineyards, left her heart to
      her land's own keeping,
   Left her white breast room to breathe, and left her light
      foot free to dance !
Hush ! Between the solemn pinewoods, carry the lovely
      lady sleeping,
   Out of the cold grey Northern mists, with banner and
      scutcheon, plume and lance,
Carry her southward, palled in purple, weeping, weeping,
      weeping, weeping,—

            O, ma patrie,
            La plus chérie,
      Adieu, plaisant pays de France.

Well, sirs, that dark tide rose within my brain !
I snatched his keys and flung them over the hedge,
Then flung myself down on a bank of ferns
And wept and wept and wept.
                              It puzzled him.
Perchance he feared my mind was going and yet,
O, sirs, if you consider it rightly now,
With all those ages knocking at his doors,
With all that custom clamouring for his care,
Is it so strange a grave-digger should weep ?

Well—he was kind enough and heaped my plate
That night at supper.
But I could never dig my graves at ease
In Peterborough Churchyard.   So I came
To London—to St Mary Magdalen's.
And thus, I chanced to drink my ale one night
Here in the Mermaid Inn.   'Twas All Souls' Eve,
And, on that bench, where master Ford now sits
Was master Shakespeare.   Well, the lights burned low,
And just like master Ford to-night he leaned
Suddenly forward.   'Timothy,' he said,
'That's a most marvellous ruby!'
                                            My blood froze!
I stretched my hand out bare as it was born;
And he said nothing, only looked at me.
Then, seeing my pipe was empty, he bade me fill
And lit it for me.
                          Peach, the astrologer,
Was living then; and that same night I went
And told him all my trouble about this ring.
He took my hand in his, and held it—thus—
Then looked into my face and said this rhyme :—

> *The ruby ring, that only three*
> *While Time and Tide go by, shall see,*
> *Weds your hand to history.*
>
> *Honour and pride the first shall lend;*
> *The second shall give you gold to spend;*
> *The third—shall warn you of your end.*

Peach was a rogue, some say, and yet he spake
Most truly about the first," the sexton mused,
"For master Shakespeare, though they say, in youth,
Outside the theatres, he would hold your horse
For pence, prospered at last, bought a fine house
In Stratford, lived there like a squire, they say.
And here, here he would sit, for all the world
As he were but a poet!   God bless us all,

And then—to think!—he rose to be a squire!
A deep one, masters!   Well, he lit my pipe!"

"Why did they bury such a queen by night?"
Said Ford.   "Kings might have wept for her.   Did Death
Play epicure and glutton that so few
Were bidden to such a feast?   Once on a time
I could have wept, myself, to hear a tale
Of beauty buried in the dark.   And hers
Was loveliness, far, far beyond the common!
Such beauty should be marble to the touch
Of time, and clad in purple to amaze
The moth.   But she was kind and soft and fair,
A woman, and so she died.   But, why the dark?"

"Sir, they gave out the coffin was too heavy
For gentlemen to bear!"—"For kings to bear?"
Ford flashed at him.   The sexton shook his head,—
"Nay!   Gentlemen to bear!   But—the true cause—
Ah, sir, 'tis unbelievable, even to me,
A sexton, for a queen so fair of face!
And all her beds, even as the pedlar said,
Breathing Arabia, sirs, her walls all hung
With woven purple wonders and great tales
Of amorous gods, and mighty mirrors, too,
Imaging her own softness, night and dawn,
When through her sumptuous hair she drew the combs;
And like one great white rose-leaf half her breast
Shone through it, firm as ivory."

                                        "Ay," said Lodge,
Murmuring his own rich music under breath,
"*About her neck did all the graces throng,
And lay such baits as did entangle death.*"

"Well, sir, the weather being hot, they feared
She would not hold the burying!" . . .

                                        "In some sort,"

Ford answered slowly, "if your tale be true,
She did not hold it.   Many a knightly crest
Will bend yet over the ghost of that small hand."

There was a hush, broken by Ben at last,
Who turned to Ford—"How now, my golden lad?
The astrologer's dead hand is on thy purse!"

Ford laughed, grimly, and flung an angel down.
"Well, cause or consequence, rhyme or no rhyme,
There is thy gold.   I will not break the spell,
Or thou mayst live to bury us one and all!"
    "And, if I live so long," the old man replied,
Lighting his lanthorn, "you may trust me, sirs,
Mine Inn is quiet, and I can find you beds
Where Queens might sleep all night and never move.
Good-night, sirs, and God bless you, one and all."

    He shouldered pick and spade.   I opened the door.
The snow blew in, and, as he shuffled out,
There, in the strait dark passage, I could swear
I saw a spark of red upon his hand,
Like a great smouldering ruby.
                              I gasped.   He stopped.
He peered at me.
                    "Twice in a night," he said.
"Nothing," I answered, "only the lanthorn-light."
He shook his head.   "I'll tell you something more!
There's nothing, nothing now in life or death
That frightens me.   Ah, things used to frighten me!
But never now!   I thought I had ten years;
But if the warning comes and says 'Thou fool,
This night!'   Why, then, I'm ready!"
                              I watched him go,
With glimmering lanthorn up the narrow street,
Like one that walked upon the clouds, through snow
That seemed to mix the City with the skies.

On Christmas Eve we heard that he was dead.

VIII.—*FLOS MERCATORUM.*

FLOS MERCATORUM! On that night of nights,
We drew from out our Mermaid cellarage
All the old glory of London in one cask
Of magic vintage. Never a city on earth—
Rome, Paris, Florence, Bagdad—held for Ben
The colours of old London ; and, that night,
We staved them like a wine, and drank, drank deep !

'Twas Master Heywood, whom the Mermaid Inn
Had dubbed our London laureate, hauled the cask
Out of its ancient harbourage. "Ben," he cried,
Bustling into the room with Dekker and Brome,
"The prentices are up !" Ben raised his head
Out of the chimney-corner where he drowsed,
And listened, reaching slowly for his pipe.

"*Clerk of the Bow Bell,*" all along the Cheape
There came a shout that swelled into a roar.
    "What ! Will they storm the Mermaid ?" Heywood
        laughed,
"They are turning into Bread Street !"
                                    Down they came !
We heard them hooting round the poor old Clerk—
"Clubs ! Clubs ! The rogue would have us work all
        night !
He rang ten minutes late ! Fifteen, by Paul's !"
And over the hubbub rose, like a thin bell,
The Clerk's entreaty—"Now, good boys, good boys,

Children of Cheape, be still, I do beseech you!
I took some forty winks, but then . . ."   A roar
Of wrathful laughter drowned him—" Forty winks!
Remember Black May-day!   We'll make you wink!"
There was a scuffle, and into the tavern rushed
Gregory Clopton, Clerk of the Bow Bell,—
A tall thin man, with yellow hair a-stream,
And blazing eyes.

         " Hide me," he clamoured, "quick!
These picaroons will murder me!"

              I closed
The thick oak doors against the coloured storm
Of prentices in red and green and ray,
Saffron and Reading Tawny.   Twenty clubs
Drubbed on the panels as I barred them out;
And even our walls and shutters could not drown
Their song that, like a mocking peal of bells,
Under our windows, made all Bread Street ring :—

       "Clerk of the Bow Bell,
          With the yellow locks,
        For thy late ringing
          Thy head shall have knocks!"

Then Heywood, seeing the Clerk was all a-quake,
Went to an upper casement that o'er-looked
The whole of Bread Street.   Heywood knew their ways,
And parleyed with them till their anger turned
To shouts of merriment.   Then, like one deep bell
His voice rang out, in answer to their peal :—

       "Children of Cheape,
         Hold you all still!
        You shall have Bow Bell
         Rung at your will!"

Loudly they cheered him.   Courteously he bowed,
Then firmly shut the window; and, ere I filled
His cup with sack again, the crowd had gone.

"My clochard, sirs, is warm," quavered the Clerk.
"I do confess I took some forty winks!
They are good lads, our prentices of Cheape,
But hasty!"

        "Wine!" said Ben.   He filled a cup
And thrust it into Gregory's trembling hands.
"Yours is a task," said Dekker, "a great task!
You sit among the gods, a lord of time,
Measuring out the pulse of London's heart."

  "Ay, sir, above the hours and days and years,
I sometimes think. 'Tis a great Bell—the Bow!
And hath been, since the days of Whittington."

  "The good old days," growled Ben. "Both good and
      bad
Were measured by my Bell," the Clerk replied.
And, while he spoke, warmed by the wine, his voice
Mellowed and floated up and down the scale,
As if the music of the London bells
Lingered upon his tongue. "I know them all,
And love them, all the voices of the bells.
FLOS MERCATORUM! That's the Bell of Bow
Remembering Richard Whittington. You should hear
The bells of London when they tell his tale.
Once, after hearing them, I wrote it down.
I know the tale by heart now, every turn."

  "Then ring it out," said Heywood.

                     Gregory smiled
And cleared his throat.

                "You must imagine, sirs,
The Clerk, sitting on high, among the clouds,
With London spread beneath him like a map.
Under his tower, a flock of prentices
Calling like bells, of little size or weight,
But bells no less, ask that the Bell of Bow
Shall tell the tale of Richard Whittington,
As thus."

           Then Gregory Clopton, mellowing all
The chiming vowels, and dwelling on every tone

In rhythm or rhyme that helped to swell the peal
Or make it sound like ringing, tossed the tenor
And trolled this legend of the London bells :—

I.

Clerk of the Bow Bell, four-and-twenty prentices,
   All upon a Hallowe'en, we prithee, for our joy,
Ring a little turn again for sweet Dick Whittington,
   Flos Mercatorum, and a barefoot boy !—

"Children of Cheape," did that old Clerk answer,
   "You will have a peal, then, for well may you know,
All the bells of London remember Richard Whittington
   When they hear the voice of the big Bell of Bow ! "—

Clerk with the yellow locks, mellow be thy malmsey !
   He was once a prentice, and carolled in the Strand !
Ay, and we are all, too, Marchaunt Adventurers,
   Prentices of London, and lords of Engeland.

Children of Cheape, did that old Clerk answer,
   "Hold you, ah hold you, ah hold you all still !
Souling if you come to the glory of a Prentice,
   You shall have the Bow Bell rung at your will !"

"Whittington ! Whittington ! O, turn again, Whittington,
   Lord Mayor of London," the big bell began :
"Where was he born ? O, at Pauntley in Gloucestershire,
   Hard by Cold Ashton, Cold Ashton," it ran.

"*Flos Mercatorum,*" mourned the bell of All Hallowes,
   "There was he an orphan, O, a little lad alone !"
"Then we all sang," echoed happy St Saviour's,
   "Called him, and lured him, and made him our own.

Told him a tale as he lay upon the hillside,
  Looking on his home in the meadow-lands below!"
"Told him a tale," clanged the bell of Cold Abbey;
  "Told him the truth," boomed the big Bell of Bow!

Sang of a City that was like a blazoned missal-book
  Black with open gables, carven and inscrolled;
Every street a coloured page, and every sign a hieroglyph,
  Dusky with enchantments, a City paved with gold.

"Younger son, younger son, up with stick and bundle!"—
  Even so we rung for him—"But—kneel before you go;
Watch, by your painted shield, in little Pauntley Chancel,
  Look upon the coloured panes that hold your Arms
    a-glow,—

Coat of Gules and Azure; but the proud will not
    remember it!
  And the Crest a Lion's Head, until the new be won!
Far away, remember it!   And O, remember this, too,—
  Every barefoot boy on earth is but a younger son."

Proudly he answered us, beneath the painted window,—
  "Though I be a younger son, the glory falls to me:
While my brother bideth by a little land in Gloucestershire,
  All the open Earth is mine, and all the Ocean-sea.

Yet will I remember, yet will I remember,
  By the chivalry of God, until my day be done,
When I meet a gentle heart, lonely and unshielded,
  Every barefoot boy on earth is but a younger son!"

Then he looked to Northward for the tall ships of Bristol;
  Far away, and cold as death, he saw the Severn shine:
Then he looked to Eastward, and he saw a string of colours
  Trickling through the grey hills, like elfin drops of wine;

Down along the Mendip dale the chapmen and their horses,
    Far away, and carrying each its little coloured load,
Winding like a fairy-tale, with pack and corded bundle,
    Filed like a crimson thread along the silver road.

Quick he ran to meet them, stick and bundle on his
        shoulder !
    Over by Cold Ashton, he met them trampling down,—
White shaggy horses with their packs of purple spicery,
    Crimson kegs of malmsey, and the silks of London town.

When the chapmen asked of him the bridle-path to Dorset,
    Blithely he showed them, and he led them on their way,
Led them through the fern with their bales of breathing
        Araby,
    Led them to a bridle-path that saved them half a day.

Merrily shook the silver bells that hung the broidered
        bridle-rein,
    Chiming to his hand, as he led them through the fern,
Down to deep Dorset, and the wooded Isle of Purbeck,
    Then—by little Kimmeridge—they led him turn for turn.

Down by little Kimmeridge, and up by Hampshire forest-
        roads,
    Round by Sussex violets, and apple-bloom of Kent,
Singing songs of London, telling tales of London,
    All the way to London, with packs of wool they went.

"London was London, then ! A clean, clear moat
Girdled her walls that measured, round about,
Three miles or less. She is big and dirty now,"
Said Dekker.
            "Call it a silver moat," growled Ben,
"That's the new poetry ! Call it crystal, lad !
But, till you kiss the Beast, you'll never find
Your Fairy Prince. Why, all those crowded streets,

Flung all their filth, their refuse, rags and bones,
Dead cats and dogs, into your clean clear moat,
And made it sluggish as old Acheron.
Fevers and plagues, death in a thousand shapes
Crawled out of it.   London was dirty, then;
And till you kiss that fact, you'll never see
The glory of this old Jerusalem!"

   " Ay, 'tis the fogs that make the sunset red,"
Answered Tom Heywood.   "London is earthy, coarse,
Grimy and grand.   You must make dirt the ground,
Or lose the colours of friend Clopton's tale.
Ring on!"   And, nothing loth, the Clerk resumed:—

II.

Bravely swelled his heart to see the moat of London
      glittering
   Round her mighty wall—they told him—two miles long!
Then—he gasped as, echoing in by grim black Aldgate,
   Suddenly their shaggy nags were nodding through a
      throng!

Prentices in red and ray, marchaunts in their saffron,
   Aldermen in violet, and minstrels in white,
Clerks in homely hoods of budge, and wives with crimson
      wimples,
   Thronging as to welcome him that happy summer night.

"Back," they cried, and "Clear the way," and caught the
      ringing bridle-reins:
   "Wait! the Watch is going by, this vigil of St John!"
Gruffly laughed the chapmen then, reining their great
      white horses back,
   "When the pageant passes, lad, we'll up and follow on!"

There, as thick the crowd surged, beneath the blossomed
    ale-poles,
  Lifting up to Whittington a fair face afraid,
Swept against his horse by a billow of mad-cap prentices,
  Hard against the stirrup breathed a green-gowned maid.

Swift he drew her up and up, and throned her there before
    him,
  High above the throng with her laughing April eyes,
Like a Queen of Faërie on the great pack-saddle.
  "Hey!" laughed the chapmen, "the prentice wins the
    prize!"

"Whittington! Whittington! the world is all before
    you!"
  Blithely rang the bells and the steeples rocked and
    reeled!
Then—he saw her eyes grow wide, and, all along by
    Leaden Hall,
  Drums rolled, earth shook, and shattering trumpets
    pealed.

Like a marching sunset, there, from Leaden Hall to
    Aldgate,
  Flared the crimson cressets—O, her brows were haloed
    then!—
Then the stirring steeds went by with all their mounted
    trumpeters,
  Then, in ringing harness, came a thousand marching men.

Marching—marching—his heart and all the halberdiers,
  And his pulses throbbing with the throbbing of the
    drums;
Marching—marching—his blood and all the burganets!
  "Look," she cried, "O, look," she cried, "and now the
    morrice comes!"

Dancing—dancing—her eyes and all the Lincoln Green,
    Robin Hood and Friar Tuck, dancing through the town!
"Where is Marian?"   Laughingly she turned to Richard
        Whittington,
    "Here," he said, and pointed to her own green gown.

Dancing—dancing—her heart and all the morrice bells!
    Then there burst a mighty shout from thrice a thousand
        throats!
Then, with all their bows bent, and sheaves of peacock
    arrows,
    Marched the tall archers in their white silk coats,

White silk coats, with the crest of London City
    Crimson on the shoulder, a sign for all to read,—
Marching—marching—and then the sworded henchmen,
    Then, William Walworth, on his great stirring steed.

Flos Mercatorum, ay, the fish-monger, Walworth,—
    He whose nets of silk drew the silver from the tide,
He who saved the king when the king was but a prentice,—
    Lord Mayor of London, with his sword at his side!

All the book of London, the pages of adventure,
    Passed before the prentice on that vigil of St John:
Then the chapmen shook their reins,—"We'll ride behind
        the revelry,
    Round again to Cornhill!   Up, and follow on!"

Riding on his pack-horse, above the shouting multitude,
    There she turned and smiled at him, and thanked him
        for his grace:
"Let me down by *Red Rose Lane*," and, like a wave of
        twilight
    While she spoke, her shadowy hair—touched his tingling
    face,

When they came to *Red Rose Lane*, beneath the blossomed
    ale-poles,
  Light along his arm she lay, a moment, leaping down :
Then she waved "farewell" to him, and down the Lane
    he watched her
  Flitting through the darkness in her gay green gown.

All along the Cheape, as he rode among the chapmen,
  Round by *Black Friars*, to the *Two-Necked Swan*,
Coloured like the sunset, prentices and maidens
  Danced for red roses on the vigil of St John.

Over them were jewelled lamps in great black galleries,
  Garlanded with beauty, and burning all the night ;
All the doors were shadowy with orpin and St John's wort,
  Long fennel, green birch, and lilies of delight.

"He should have slept here at the Mermaid Inn,"
Said Heywood as the chanter paused for breath.
"What ? Has our Mermaid sung so long ? " cried Ben.
"Her beams are black enough. There was an Inn,"
Said Tom, "that bore the name ; and through its heart
There flowed the right old purple. I like to think
It was the same, where Lydgate took his ease
After his hood was stolen ; and Gower, perchance ;
And, though he loved the *Tabard* for a-while,
I like to think the Father of us all,
The old Adam of English minstrelsy caroused
Here in the Mermaid Tavern. Ay, who knows ?
Perhaps Dan Chaucer, with his kind shrewd face
Fresh as an apple o'er his fur-fringed gown,
One plump hand sporting with his golden chain,
Looked out from that old casement o'er the sign,
And saw the pageant, and the shaggy nags,
With Whittington, and his green-gowned maid, go by.
  "O, very like," said Clopton, "for the bells
Left not a head indoors that night." He drank
A draught of malmsey—and thus renewed his tale :—

III.

"*Flos Mercatorum*," mourned the bell of All Hallowes,
　"There was he an orphan, O, a little lad alone,
Rubbing down the great white horses for a supper!"
　"Ay," boomed the Bow Bell, "his hands were his own!"

Where did he sleep?　On a plump white wool-pack
　Open to the moon on that vigil of St John,
Sheltered from the dew, where the black-timbered gallery
　Frowned above the yard of the *Two-Necked Swan.*

Early in the morning, clanged the bell of St Martin's,
　Early in the morning, with a groat in his hand,
Mournfully he parted with the jolly-hearted chapmen,
　Shouldered his bundle and walked into the *Strand;*

Walked into the *Strand*, and back again to *West Cheape*,
　Staring at the wizardry of every painted sign,
Dazed with the steeples and the rich heraldic cornices
　Drinking in the colours of the Cheape like wine.

All about the booths now, the parti-coloured prentices
　Fluted like a flock of birds along a summer lane,
Green linnets, red caps, and gay gold-finches,—
　　*What d'ye lack, and what d'ye lack, and what d'ye lack
　　　again?*

"Buy my dainty doublets, cut on double taffetas,
　Buy my Paris thread," they cried, and caught him by
　　the hand.
"Laces for your Heart's-Delight, and lawns to make her
　　love you,
　Cambric for her wimple, O, the finest in the land."

Ah, but he was hungry, foot-sore, weary,
  Knocking at the doors of the armourers that day !
What d'ye lack ? they asked of him ; but no man lacked
    a prentice :
  When he told them what he lacked, they frowned and
      turned away.

Hard was his bed that night, beneath a cruel archway,
  Down among the hulks, with his heart growing cold !
London is a rare town, but O, the streets of London,
  Red though their flints be, they are not red with gold.

Pale in the dawn, ere he marched on his adventure,
  Starving for a crust, did he kneel a-while again,
Then, upon the fourth night, he cried, O, like a wounded
      bird,
  Let me die, if die I must, in *Red Rose Lane.*

Like a little wounded bird he trailed through the darkness,
  Laid him on a door-step, and then—O, like a breath
Pitifully blowing out his life's little rush-light,
  Came a gush of blackness, a swoon, deep as death.

Then he heard a rough voice ! Then he saw a lanthorn !
  Then he saw a bearded face, and blindly wondered
      whose :
Then—a marchaunt's portly legs, with great Rose-
      Windows,
  Bigger than St Paul's, he thought, embroidered on his
      shoes.

"Alice !" roared the voice, and then, O like a lilied angel,
  Leaning from the lighted door a fair face afraid,
Leaning over *Red Rose Lane*, O, leaning out of Paradise,
  Drooped the sudden glory of his green-gowned maid !

    "O, mellow be thy malmsey," grunted Ben,
    Filling the Clerk another cup.

"The peal,"
Quoth Clopton, "is not ended, but the pause
In ringing, chimes to a deep inward ear
And tells its own deep tale.   Silence and sound,
Darkness and light, mourning and mirth,—no tale,
No painting, and no music, nay, no world,
If God should cut their fruitful marriage-knot.
A shallow sort to-day would fain deny
A hell, sirs, to this boundless universe.
To such I say 'no hell, no Paradise!'
Others would fain deny the topless towers
Of heaven, and make this earth a hell indeed.
To such I say, 'the unplumbed gulfs of grief
Are only theirs for whom the blissful chimes
Ring from those unseen heights.'   This earth, mid-way,
Hangs like a belfry where the ringers grasp
Their ropes in darkness, each in his own place,
Each knowing, by the tune in his own heart,
Never by sight, when he must toss through heaven
The tone of his own bell.   Those bounded souls
Have never heard our chimes!   Why, sirs, myself
Simply by running up and down the scale
Descend to hell or soar to heaven.   My bells
Height above height, deep below deep, respond!
Their scale is infinite.   Dare I, for one breath,
Dream that one note hath crowned and ended all,
Sudden I hear, far, far above those clouds,
Like laughing angels, peal on golden peal,
Innumerable as drops of April rain,
Yet every note distinct, round as a pearl,
And perfect in its place, a chime of law,
Whose pure and boundless mere arithmetic
Climbs with my soul to God."

                              Ben looked at him,
Gently.   "Resume, old moralist," he said.
"On to thy marriage-bells!"

                              "The fairy-tales
Are wiser than they know, sirs.   All our woes

Lead on to those celestial marriage-bells.
The world's a-wooing; and the pure City of God
Peals for the wedding of our joy and pain !
This was well seen of Richard Whittington;
For only he that finds the London streets
Paved with red flints, at last shall find them paved
Like to the perfect City, with pure gold.
Ye know the world ! what was a London waif
To Hugh Fitzwarren's daughter ?   He was fed
And harboured; and the cook declared she lacked
A scullion.   So, in Hugh Fitzwarren's house,
He turned the jack, and scoured the dripping-pan.
How could he hope for more?

       This Marchaunt's house
Was builded like a great high-gabled inn,
Square, with a galleried courtyard, such as now
The players use.   Its rooms were rich and dim
With deep-set coloured panes and massy beams.
Its ancient eaves jutted o'er Red Rose Lane
Dark as the eyebrows of a mage asleep.
Its oaken stair coiled upward through a dusk
Heavy with fume of scented woods that burned
To keep the plague away,—a gloom to embalm
A Pharaoh, but to dull the cheek and eye
Of country lads like Whittington.

         His throat
Grew dry, thinking of things that he scarce knew
Had struck root in his heart,—sun-dappled ferns
By Little Pauntley, where the larches drooped
Their long green fingers, and that wood of firs
Where the wild pigeons built such careless nests
—Ten dry twigs, crossed, to bear their pretty twins.—
Yet when her eyes met his, as young eyes meet
In April, one ache wrestled with another,
Until his boyish longing forged the dream
That he might see her stand knee-deep, some day,
In his own ferns, embraced by clinging fronds,
Ferns that were fringe to all his fairy-lands,

Ferns that had shaken the richness of his heart
And pulled it all to pieces like loose loam,
Ready for rarer seeds.
                              At night he crept
Wearily into a low dark vaulted den,
A cobwebbed cellar, where the cook had strewn
His bed of straw.   And there all beauty died.
There, in the musty gloom, with trembling hands
He kept his rush-light burning.   Often he started
Bolt upright, while an evil-smelling scurry
Rustled his yellow bed, and beady eyes
Peered at him from the crannies of the wall.
Or, if he slept, he saw a human face
Gnawed by grey shadows, like that pigeon's head
The rats had eaten, in his cote, at home.
He fought with hideous nightmares, fought and fled
Down endless tunnels, . . .
Hunted by horrible human souls that took
The shape of monstrous rats, great chattering snouts,
That talked together and vanished, . . .
Shapes of demoniac cunning and grey greed,
That gnaw through beams and undermine tall towns,
To carry the smouldering blue-fires of the plague
Under the Marchaunt's house and the King's hall.
Nightly the prentice waged his lonely war
With all the powers of darkness.
                                        'If the light
Do break upon me, by the grace of God,'
So did he vow, 'O, then will I remember,
Then, then, will I remember, ay, and help
To build that lovelier City which is paved
For rich and poor alike, with purest gold.'
Ah, sirs, he kept his vow.   Ye will not smile
If, at the first, the best that he could do
Was with his first poor penny-piece to buy
A cat, and bring her home, under his coat
By stealth (or else that termagant, the cook,
Had drowned it in the water-butt, nor deemed

The water worse to drink).   So did he quell
First his own plague, but bettered others, too.

Now, in those days, Marchaunt Adventurers
Shared with their prentices the happy chance
Of each new venture.   Each might have his stake,
Little or great, upon the glowing tides
Of high romance that washed the wharfs of Thames ;
And every lad in London had his groat
Or splendid shilling on some fair ship at sea.

So, on an April eve, Fitzwarren called
His prentices together ; for, ere long,
The *Unicorn*, his tall new ship, must sail
Beyond the world to gather gorgeous webs
From Eastern looms, great miracles of silk
Dipt in the dawn by wizard hands of Ind ;
Or, if they chanced upon that fabled coast
Where Sydon, river of jewels, like a snake
Slides down the gorge its coils of crimson fire,
Perchance a richer cargo,—rubies, pearls,
Or gold bars from the Gates of Paradise.
And many a moon, at least, a faërie foam
Would lap Blackfriars wharf, where London lads
Gazed in the sunset down that misty reach
For old black battered hulks and tattered sails
Bringing their dreams home from the uncharted sea.
And one flung down a groat—he had no more.
One staked a shilling, one a good French crown ;
And one an angel, O, light-winged enough
To reach Cathay ; and not a lad but bought
His pennyworth of wonder.
                              So they thought,
Till all at once Fitzwarren's daughter cried
' Father, you have forgot poor Whittington ! '
' 'Snails,' laughed the rosy marchaunt, ' but that's true !
Call Whittington !   The lad must stake his groat !
'Twill bring us luck ! '

                              'Whittington! Whittington!'
Down the dark stair, like a gold-headed bird,
Fluttered sweet Alice.   'Whittington! Richard! Quick!
Quick with your groat now for the *Unicorn!*'

  'A groat!' cried Whittington, standing there aghast,
With brown bare arms, still coloured by the sun,
Among his pots and pans.   'Where should I find
A groat?   I staked my last groat in a cat!'
—'What! have you nothing?   Nothing but a cat?
Then stake the cat,' she said; and the quick fire
That in a woman's mind out-runs the thought
Of man, lit her grey eyes.
                              Whittington laughed
And opened the cellar-door.   Out sailed his wealth,
Waving its tail, purring, and rubbing its head
Now on his boots, now on the dainty shoe
Of Alice, who straightway, deaf to his laughing prayers,
Caught up the cat, whispered it, hugged it close,
Against its grey fur leaned her glowing cheek,
And carried it off in triumph.
                              Red Rose Lane
Echoed with laughter as with amber eyes
Blinking, the grey cat in a seaman's arms
Went to the wharf.   'Ay, but we need a cat,'
The captain said.   So, when the painted ship
Sailed through a golden sunrise down the Thames
A grey tail waved upon the misty poop,
And Whittington had his venture on the seas.

It was a nine days' jest, and soon forgot.
But, all that year,—ah, sirs, ye know the world
For all the foolish boasting of the proud
Looks not beneath the coat of Taunton serge
For Gules and Azure.   A prince that comes in rags
To clean your shoes and, out of his own pride,
Waits for the world to paint his shield again
Must wait for ever and a day.

                                             The world
Is a great hypocrite, hypocrite most of all
When thus it boasts its purple pride of race,
Then with eyes blind to all but pride of place
Tramples the scullion's heraldry underfoot,
Nay, never sees it, never dreams of it,
Content to know that, here and now, his coat
Is greasy . . .

                         So did Whittington find at last
Such nearness was most distant; that to see her,
Talk with her, serve her thus, was but to lose
True sight, true hearing.   He must save his life
By losing it; forsake, to win, his love ;
Go out into the world to bring her home.
It was but labour lost to clean the shoes,
And turn the jack, and scour the dripping-pan.
For every scolding blown about her ears
The cook's great ladle fell upon the head
Of Whittington ; who, beneath her rule, became
The scullery's general scapegoat.   It was he
That burned the pie-crust, drank the hippocras,
Dinted the silver beaker. . . .

                                   Many a month
He chafed, till his resolve took sudden shape
And, out of the dark house at the peep of day,
Shouldering bundle and stick again, he stole
To seek his freedom, and to shake the dust
Of London from his shoes. . . .

                                 You know the stone
On Highgate, where he sate awhile to rest,
With aching heart, and thought 'I shall not see
Her face again.'   There, as the coloured dawn
Over the sleeping City slowly bloomed,
A small black battered ship with tattered sails
Blurring the burnished glamour of the Thames
Crept, side-long, to a wharf.

                             Then, all at once,
The London bells rang out a welcome home ;

And, over them all, tossing the tenor on high,
    The Bell of Bow, a sun among the stars,
Flooded the morning air with this refrain :—

'Turn again, Whittington !   Turn again, Whittington !
    Flos Mercatorum, thy ship hath come home !
Trailing from her cross-trees the crimson of the sunrise,
Dragging all the glory of the sunset thro' the foam.
                Turn again, Whittington !
                Turn again, Whittington,
                    Lord Mayor of London !

Turn again, Whittington !   When thy hope was darkest,
    Far beyond the sky-line a ship sailed for thee ;
Flos Mercatorum, O, when thy faith was blindest,
    Even then thy sails were set beyond the Ocean-sea.'

So he heard and heeded us, and turned again to London,
    Stick and bundle on his back, he turned to *Red Rose
        Lane*,
Hardly hearing as he went the chatter of the prentices,—
    *What d'ye lack, and what d'ye lack, and what d'ye lack
        again ?*

Back into the scullery, before the cook had missed him,
    Early in the morning his labours he began :
Once again to clean the shoes and clatter with the water-pail,
    Once again to scrub the jack and scour the dripping-pan.

All the bells of London were pealing as he laboured ;
    Wildly beat his heart, and his blood began to race ;
Then—there came a light step and there, O there, beside
    him
    Stood his lady Alice, with a light upon her face.

'Quick,' she said, 'O, quick,' she said, 'they want you,
    Richard Whittington!'
  'Quick,' she said, and, while she spoke, her lighted eyes
    betrayed
All that she had hidden long, and all she still would hide
    from him.
  So—he turned and followed her, his green-gowned maid.

•   .   .   .   .

  There, in a broad dark oaken-panelled room
  Rich with black carvings and great gleaming cups
  Of silver, sirs, and massy halpace built
  Half over *Red Rose Lane*, Fitzwarren sat;
  And, at his side, O, like an old romance
  That suddenly comes true and fills the world
  With April colours, two bronzed seamen stood,
  Tattered and scarred, and stained with sun and brine.
  '*Flos Mercatorum*,' Hugh Fitzwarren cried,
  Holding both hands out to the pale-faced boy,
  'The prentice wins the prize!   Why, Whittington,
  Thy cat hath caught the biggest mouse of all!'
  And, on to the table, tilting a heavy sack,
  One of the seamen poured a glittering stream
  Of rubies, emeralds, opals, amethysts,
  That turned the room to an Aladdin's cave,
  Or magic goblet brimmed with dusky wine
  Where clustering rainbow-coloured bubbles clung
  And sparkled, in the halls of Prester John.

  'And that,' said Hugh Fitzwarren, 'is the price
  Paid for your cat in Barbary, by a king
  Whose house was rich in gems, but sorely plagued
  With rats and mice.   Gather it up, my lad,
  And praise your master for his honesty;
  For, though my cargo prospered, yours out-shines
  The best of it.   Take it, my lad, and go;
  You're a rich man; and, if you use it well,

Riches will make you richer, and the world
Will prosper in your own prosperity.
The miser, like the cold and barren moon,
Shines with a fruitless light.   The spendthrift fool
Flits like a Jack-o-Lent over quags and fens;
But he that's wisely rich gathers his gold
Into a fruitful and unwasting sun
That spends its glory on a thousand fields
And blesses all the world.   Take it and go.'

Blankly, as in a dream, Whittington stared.
'How should I take it, sir?   The ship was yours,
And . . .'
                'Ay, the ship was mine; but in that ship
Your stake was richer than we knew.   'Tis yours.'
'Then,' answered Whittington, 'if this wealth be mine,
Who but an hour ago was all so poor,
I know one way to make me richer still.'
He gathered up the glittering sack of gems,
Turned to the halpace, where his green-gowned maid
Stood in the glory of the coloured panes.
He thrust the splendid load into her arms,
Muttering—'Take it, lady!   Let me be poor!
But rich, at least, in that you not despise
The waif you saved.'
                —'Despise you, Whittington?'—
'O, no, not in the sight of God!   But I
Grow tired of waiting for the Judgment Day:
I am but a man.   I am a scullion now;
But I would like, only for half an hour,
To stand upright and say "I am a king!"
Take it!'
                And, as they stood, a little apart,
Their eyes were married in one swift level look,
Silent, but all that souls could say was said.

.   .   .   .

And
'I know a way,' said the Bell of St Martin's.
 'Tell it, and be quick,' laughed the prentices below!
'Whittington shall marry her, marry her, marry her!
 Peal for a wedding,' said the big Bell of Bow.

Kingly he shall take his wealth, and cast it on the sea again.
 He shall have his caravels to traffic for him now;
He shall see his royal sails rolling up from Araby,
 And the crest—a honey-bee—golden at the prow.

Whittington! Whittington! The world is all a fairy tale!—
 Even so we sang for him.—But O, the tale is true!
Whittington he married her, and on his April marriage-day,
 O, we sang, we sang for him, like lavrocks in the blue.

Far away from London, these happy prentice lovers
 Wandered through the summer to his western home
  again,
Down by deep Dorset to the wooded isle of Purbeck,
 Round to little Kimmeridge, by many a lover's lane.

There did they abide as in a dove-cote hidden
 Deep in happy woods until the bells of duty rang;
Then they rode the way he went, a barefoot boy to London,
 Round by Hampshire forest-roads, but as he rode he
  sang :—

Kimmeridge in Dorset is the happiest of places!
 All the little homesteads are thatched with beauty there!
All the old ploughmen, there, have happy smiling faces,
 Christmas roses in their cheeks, and crowns of silver hair.

Blue as are the eggs in the nest of the hedge-sparrow,
  Gleam the little rooms in the homestead that I know :
Death, I think, has lost the way to Kimmeridge in Dorset ;
  Sorrow never knew it, or forgot it long ago !

Kimmeridge in Dorset, Kimmeridge in Dorset,
  Though I may not see you more thro' all the years to be,
Yet will I remember the little happy homestead
  Hidden in that Paradise where God was good to me.

.   .   .   .

So they turned to London, and with mind and soul he
    laboured,
  Flos Mercatorum, for the mighty years to be,
Fashioning, for profit—to the years that should forget
    him !—
  This, our sacred City that must shine upon the sea.

London was a City when her hearts were great and simple !
  Rosaries of prayer were hung in Paternoster Row,
Gutter Lane was Guthrun's, then ; and, bright with painted
    missal-books,
  Ave Mary Corner, sirs, was fairer than ye know.

London was mighty when her marchaunts loved their
    merchandise,
  Bales of Eastern magic that empurpled wharf and quay :
London was mighty when her booths were a dream-market
  Loaded with the colours of the sunset and the sea.

There, in all their glory, with the Virgin on their bannerols,
  Glory out of Genoa, the Mercers might be seen,
Walking to their Company of Marchaunt Adventurers ;—
  Gallantly they jetted it in scarlet and in green.

There, in all the glory of the lordly Linen Armourers,
 Walked the Marchaunt Taylors with the Pilgrim of their
   trade,
Fresh from adventuring in Italy and Flanders,
 Flos Mercatorum, for a green-gowned maid.

Flos Mercatorum! Can a good thing come of Nazareth?
 High above the darkness, where our duller senses drown,
Lifts the splendid Vision of a City, built on merchandize,
 Fairer than that City of Light that wore the violet crown,

Lifts the sacred vision of a far-resplendent City
 Flashing, like the heart of heaven, its messages afar,
Trafficking, as God Himself, through all His interchanging
   worlds,
 Holding up the scales of law, weighing star by star,

Stern as Justice, in one hand the sword of Truth and
   Righteousness;
 Blind as Justice, in one hand the everlasting scales,
Lifts the sacred Vision of that City from the darkness,
 Whence the thoughts of men break out, like blossoms,
   or like sails!

Ordered and harmonious, a City built to music,
 Lifting, out of chaos, the shining towers of law,—
Ay, a sacred City, and a City built of merchandize,
 Flos Mercatorum, was the City that he saw."

" And by that light," quoth Clopton, " did he keep
His promise. He was rich; but in his will
He wrote those words which should be blazed with gold
In London's *Liber Albus:*—

The desire
And busy intention of a man, devout
And wise, should be to fore-cast and secure
The state and end of this short life with deeds
Of mercy and pity, especially to provide
For those whom poverty insulteth ; those
To whom the power of labouring for the needs
Of life, is interdicted.

He became
The Father of the City.   Felons died
Of fever in old Newgate.   He rebuilt
The prison.   London sickened from the lack
Of water, and he made fresh fountains flow.
He heard the cry of suffering and disease,
And built the stately hospital that still
Shines like an angel's lanthorn through the night,
The stately halls of St Bartholomew.
He saw men wrapt in ignorance, and he raised
Schools, colleges, and libraries.   He heard
The cry of the old and weary, and he built
Houses of refuge.
                    Even so he kept
His prentice vows of Duty, Industry,
Obedience, words contemned of every fool
Who shrinks from law ; yet were those ancient vows
The adamantine pillars of the State.
Let all who play their Samson be well warned
That Samsons perish, too !
                    His monument
Is London !"
                    " True," quoth Dekker, "and he deserves
Well of the Mermaid Inn for one good law
Rightly enforced.   He pilloried that rogue
Will Horold, who in Whittington's third year
Of office, as Lord Mayor, placed certain gums
And spices in great casks, and filled them up
With feeble Spanish wine, to have the taste

And smell of Romeney,—Malmsey ! "
        " Honest wine,
Indeed," replied the Clerk, " concerns the State,
That solemn structure touched with light from heaven,
Which he, our merchant, helped to build on earth.
And, while he laboured for it, all things else
Were added unto him, until the bells
More than fulfilled their prophecy.
         One great eve,
Dame Alice, leaning from her casement, saw
Another Watch, and mightier than the first,
Billowing past the newly painted doors
Of Whittington Palace—so men called his house
In Hart Street, fifteen yards from old Mark Lane,—
A thousand burganets and halberdiers,
A thousand archers in their white silk coats,
A thousand mounted men in ringing mail,
A thousand sworded henchmen ; then, his Guild,
Advancing, on their splendid bannerols
The Virgin, glorious in gold ; and then,
Flos Mercatorum, on his great stirring steed
Whittington !   On that night he made a feast
For London and the King.   His feasting hall
Gleamed like the magic cave that Prester John
Wrought out of one huge opal.   East and West
Lavished their wealth on that great Citizen
Who, when the King from Agincourt returned
Victorious, but with empty coffers, lent
Three times the ransom of an Emperor
To fill them—on the royal bond, and said
When the King questioned him of how and whence,
' I am the steward of your City, sire !
There is a sea, and who shall drain it dry ? '
  Over the roasted swans and peacock pies,
The minstrels in the great black gallery tuned
All hearts to mirth, until it seemed their cups
Were brimmed with dawn and sunset, and they drank
The wine of gods.   Lord of a hundred ships,

Under the feet of England, Whittington flung
The purple of the seas.   And when the Queen,
Catharine, wondered at the costly woods
That burned upon his hearth, the Marchaunt rose,
He drew the great sealed parchments from his breast,
The bonds the King had given him on his loans,
Loans that might drain the Mediterranean dry.
'They call us hucksters, madam, we that love
Our City,' and, into the red-hot heart of the fire,
He tossed the bonds of sixty thousand pounds.
'The fire burns low,' said Richard Whittington.
Then, overhead, the minstrels plucked their strings;
And, over the clash of wine-cups, rose a song
That made the old timbers of their feasting-hall
Shake, as a galleon shakes in a gale of wind,
When she rolls glorying through the Ocean-sea :—

Marchaunt Adventurers, O what shall it profit you
    Thus to seek your kingdom in the dream-destroying sun?
Ask us why the hawthorn brightens on the sky-line :
    Even so our sails break out when spring is well begun!
Flos Mercatorum!   Blossom wide, ye sails of England,
    Hasten ye the kingdom, now the bitter days are done!
Ay, for we be members, one of another,
    Each for all, and all for each, quoth Richard Whit-
        tington !

Chorus: Marchaunt Adventurers,
                Marchaunt Adventurers,
    Marchaunt Adventurers, the Spring is well begun!
Break, break out on every sea, O, fair white sails of
        England !
    'Each for all, and all for each,' quoth Richard Whit-
        tington.

Marchaunt Adventurers, O what 'ull ye bring home again?
    Woonders and works and the thunder of the sea !
Whom will ye traffic with?   The King of the sunset !—
    What shall be your pilot, then?—A wind from Galilee !

—Nay, but ye be marchaunts, will ye come back empty-
      handed?—
  Ay, we be marchaunts, though our gain we ne'er shall
      see!
Cast we now our bread upon the waste wild waters;
  After many days it shall return with usury.

Chorus: Marchaunt Adventurers,
                 Marchaunt Adventurers,
  What shall be your profit in the mighty days to be?
Englande! Englande! Englande! Englande!
  Glory everlasting and the lordship of the sea.

  What need to tell you, sirs, how Whittington
Remembered? Night and morning, as he knelt
In those old days, O, like two children still,
Whittington and his Alice bowed their heads
Together, praying.
               From such simple hearts,
O never doubt it, though the whole world doubt
The God that made it, came the steadfast strength
Of England, all that once was her strong soul,
The soul that laughed and shook away defeat
As her strong cliffs hurl back the streaming seas.
Sirs, in his old age, Whittington returned
And stood with Alice, by the silent tomb
In little Pauntley church.
                There, to his Arms,
The Gules and Azure, and the Lion's Head
So proudly blazoned on the painted panes,
(O, sirs, the simple wistfulness of it
Might move hard hearts to laughter, but I think
Tears tremble through it, for the Mermaid Inn)
He added his new crest, the hard-won sign
And lowly prize of his own industry,
The Honey-bee. And, far away, the bells
Peal softly from the pure white City of God.

Ut fragrans nardus
Fama fuit iste Ricardus.

With folded hands he waits the Judgment now.
Slowly our dark bells toll across the world
For him who waits the reckoning, his accompt
Secure, his conscience clear, his ledger spread
A *Liber Albus*, flooded with pure light.

Flos Mercatorum,
Fundator presbyterorum, . . .

Slowly the dark bells toll for him who asks
No more of men, but that they may sometimes
Pray for the souls of Richard Whittington,
Alice, his wife, and (as themselves of old
Had prayed) the father and mother of each of them.
Slowly the great notes fall and float away :—

Omnibus exemplum
Barathrum vincendo morosum
Condidit hoc templum . . .
Pauperibus pater . . .
Finiit ipse dies
Sis sibi Christe quies.   Amen."

IX.—RALEIGH.

BEN was our only guest that day. His tribe
Had flown to their new shrine—the Apollo Room,
To which, though they enscrolled his golden verse
Above their doors like some great-fruited vine,
Ben still preferred our *Mermaid*, and to smoke
Alone in his old nook ; perhaps to hear
The voices of the dead,
The voices of his old companions,
Hovering near him,—Will and Kit and Rob.

" Our Ocean-shepherd from the main-deep sea,
Raleigh," he muttered, as I brimmed his cup,
" Last of the men that broke the fleets of Spain,
'Twas not enough to cage him, sixteen years,
Rotting his heart out in the Bloody Tower,
But they must fling him forth in his old age
To hunt for El Dorado. Then, mine host,
Because his poor old ship *The Destiny*
Smashes the Spaniard, but comes tottering home
Without the Spanish gold, our gracious king,
To please a catamite,
Sends the old lion back to the Tower again.
The friends of Spain will send him to the block
This time. That male Salome, Buckingham,
Is dancing for his head. Raleigh is doomed."

A shadow stood in the doorway. We looked up ;
And there, but O, how changed, how worn and grey,

Sir Walter Raleigh, like a hunted thing
Stared at us.

            "Ben," he said, and glanced behind him.
Ben took a step towards him.

                    "Tell me quickly,"
Whispered the old man in a husky voice,
Half timorous and half cunning, so unlike
His old heroic self that one might weep
To hear it, "Ben, I have given them all the slip!
I may be followed!   Can you hide me here
Till it grows dark?"
Ben drew him quickly in, and motioned me
To lock the door.   "Till it grows dark," he cried,
"My God, that you should ask it!"

                      "Do not think,
Do not believe that I am quite disgraced,"
The old man faltered, "for they'll say it, Ben;
And when my boy grows up, they'll tell him, too,
His father was a coward.   I do cling
To life, for many reasons, not from fear
Of death.   No, Ben, I can disdain that still;
But—there's my boy!"

                 Then all his face went blind.
He dropped upon Ben's shoulder and sobbed outright,
"They are trying to break my pride, to break my pride!"
The window darkened, and I saw a face
Blurring the panes.   Ben gripped the old man's arm
And led him gently to a room within,
Out of the way of guests.

                "Your pride," he said,
"That is the pride of England!"

                   At that name
England!—
As at a signal-gun, heard in the night
Far out at sea, the weather-and-world-worn man,
That once was Raleigh, lifted up his head.
Old age and weakness, weariness and fear,
Fell from him like a cloak.   He stood erect.

His eager eyes, full of wide sea-washed dawns,
Burned for a moment with immortal youth,
While tears blurred mine to see him.

                             "You do think,
That England will remember?   You do think it?"
He asked with a great light upon his face.
Ben bowed his head in silence.

.   .   .   .   .   .

                       "I have wronged
My cause by this," said Raleigh.   "Well they know it
Who left this way for me.   I have flung myself
Like a blind moth into this deadly light
Of freedom.   Now, at the eleventh hour,
Is it too late?   I might return and . . ."
                                    "No!
Not now!" Ben interrupted.   "I'd have said
Laugh at the headsmen, sixteen years ago,
When England was awake.   She will awake
Again.   But now, while our most gracious king,
Who hates tobacco, dedicates his prayers
To Buckingham, that male Salome . . . no!
This is no land for men that, under God,
Shattered the fleet invincible."
                        A knock
Startled us, at the outer door.   "My friend
Stukeley," said Raleigh, "if I know his hand.
He has a ketch will carry me to France,
Waiting at Tilbury."
                    I let him in,—
A lean and stealthy fellow, Sir Lewis Stukeley,—
I liked him little.   He thought much of his health,
More of his money-bags, and most of all
On how to run with all men all at once
For his own profit.   At the *Mermaid Inn*
Men disagreed in friendship and in truth;
But he agreed with all men, and his life
Was one soft quag of falsehood.   Fugitives
Must use false keys, I thought; and there was hope

For Raleigh if such a man would walk one mile
To serve him now.   Yet my throat moved to see him
Usurping, with one hand on Raleigh's arm,
A kind of ownership.   *Lend me ten pounds,*
Were the first words he breathed in the old man's ear,
And Raleigh slipped his purse into his hand.

.   .   .   .

Just over Bread Street hung the bruised white moon
When they crept out.

                    Sir Lewis Stukeley's watch-dog,
A derelict bo'sun with a mulberry face,
Met them outside.   "The coast quite clear, eh, Hart?"
Said Stukeley.   "Ah, that's good.   Lead on, then, quick."
And there, framed in the cruddle of moonlit clouds
That ended the steep street, dark on its light,
And standing on those glistening cobble-stones
Just where they turned to silver, Raleigh looked back
Before he turned the corner.   He stood there,
A figure like foot-feathered Mercury,
Tall, straight and splendid, waving his plumed hat
To Ben, and taking his last look, I felt,
Upon our Mermaid Tavern.   As he paused,
His long fantastic shadow swayed and swept
Against our feet.   Then, like a shadow, he passed.

"It is not right," said Ben, "it is not right.
Why did they give the old man so much grace?
Witness and evidence are what they lack.
Would you trust Stukeley—not to draw him out?
Raleigh was always rash.   A phrase or two
Will turn their murderous axe into a sword
Of righteousness. . . .

                    Why, come to think of it,
Blackfriar's wharf, last night I landed there,
And—no, by God!—Raleigh is not himself,
The tide will never serve beyond Gravesend.
It is a trap!   Come on!   We'll follow them!

Quick!   To the river-side! . . ."
                                     We reached the wharf
Only to see their wherry, a small black cloud
Dwindling far down that running silver road.
Ben touched my arm.
" Look there," he said, pointing up stream.
                                               The moon
Glanced on a cluster of pikes, like silver thorns,
Three hundred yards away, a little troop
Of weaponed men, embarking hurriedly.
Their great black wherry clumsily swung about,
Then, with twelve oars for legs, came striding down,
An armoured beetle on the glittering trail
Of some small victim.
                             Just below our wharf
A little dinghy waddled.
Ben cut the painter, and without one word
Drew her up crackling thro' the lapping water,
Motioned me to the tiller, thrust her off,
And, pulling with one oar, backing with the other,
Swirled her round and down, hard on the track
Of Raleigh.
Ben was an old man now, but tough,
O tough as a buccaneer.   We distanced them.
His oar-blades drove the silver boiling back.
By Broken Wharf the beetle was a speck.
It dwindled by Queen Hythe and the Three Cranes.
By Bellyn's Gate we had left it out of sight.
By Custom House and Galley Keye we shot
Thro' silver all the way, without one glimpse
Of Raleigh.   Then a dreadful shadow fell,
And over us the Tower of London rose
Like ebony; and on the glittering reach
Beyond it, I could see the small black cloud
That carried the great old seaman slowly down
Between the dark shores whence in happier years
The throng had cheered his golden galleons out,
And watched his proud sails filling for Cathay.

There, as through lead, we dragged by Traitor's Gate
There, in the darkness, under the Bloody Tower,
There, on the very verge of victory,
Ben gasped and dropped his oars.
"Take one and row," he said, "my arms are numbed.
We'll overtake him yet!"   I clambered past him,
And took the bow oar.

               Once, as the pace flagged,
Over his shoulder he turned his great scarred face
And snarled, with a trickle of blood on his coarse lips,
"Hard!" . . .
And blood and fire ran through my veins again,
For half a minute more.

               Yet we fell back.
Our course was crooked now.   And suddenly
A grim black speck began to grow behind us,
Grow like the threat of death upon old age.
Then, thickening, blackening, sharpening, foaming, swept
Up the bright line of bubbles in our wake,
That armoured wherry, with its long twelve oars,
All well together now.

            "Too late," gasped Ben.
His ash-grey face uplifted to the moon,
One quivering hand upon the thwart behind him,
A moment.   Then he bowed over his knees
Coughing.   "But we'll delay them.   We'll be drunk,
And hold the catch-polls up."

               We drifted down
Before them, broadside on.   They sheered aside.
Then, feigning a clumsy stroke, Ben drove our craft
As they drew level, right in among their blades.
There was a shout, an oath.   They thrust us off,
And then we swung our nose against their bows
And pulled them round with every well-meant stroke,
A full half-minute, ere they won quite free,
Cursing us for a pair of drunken fools.

We drifted down behind them.

"There's no doubt,"
Said Ben, "the headsman waits behind all this
For Raleigh.   This is a play to cheat the soul
Of England, teach the people to applaud
The red fifth act."
Without another word we drifted down,
For centuries it seemed, until we came
To Greenwich.
Then up the long white burnished reach there crept,
Like little sooty clouds, the two black boats
To meet us.
"He is in the trap," said Ben,
"And does not know it yet.   See where he sits
By Stukeley as by a friend."
Long after this,
We heard how Raleigh, simply as a child,
Seeing the tide would never serve him now,
And they must turn, had taken from his neck
Some trinkets that he wore.   "Keep them," he said
To Stukeley, "in remembrance of this night."
He had no doubts of Stukeley when he saw
The wherry close beside them.   He but wrapped
His cloak a little closer round his face.

Our boat rocked in their wash when Stukeley dropped
The mask.   We saw him give the sign, and heard
His high-pitched quavering voice—*In the King's name!*

Raleigh rose to his feet.   "I am under arrest?"
He said, like a dazed man.
And Stukeley laughed.
Then as he bore himself to the grim end,
All doubt being over, the old sea-king stood
Among those glittering points, a king indeed.
The black boats rocked.   We heard his level voice,
Sir Lewis, these actions never will turn out
To your good credit.   Across the moonlit Thames
It rang contemptuously, cold as cold steel,

And passionless as the judgment that ends all.

.   .   .   .

Some three months later, Raleigh's widow came
To lodge a se'nnight at the Mermaid Inn.
His house in Bread Street was no more her own,
But in the hands of Stukeley, who had reaped
A pretty harvest . . .
She kept close to her room, and that same night,
Being ill and with some fever, sent her maid
To fetch the apothecary from Friday Street,
Old Galen, as the Mermaid christened him.
At that same moment, as the maid went out,
Stukeley came in.   He met her at the door ;
And, chucking her under the chin, gave her a letter,
" Take this up to your mistress.   It concerns
Her property," he said ; " say that I wait,
And would be glad to speak with her."
                                        The wench
Looked pertly into his face and tripped upstairs.
I scarce could trust my hands.
                                " Sir Lewis," I said,
" This is no time to trouble her.   She is ill."
" Let her decide," he answered, with a sneer.
Before I found another word to say
The maid tripped down again.   I scarce believed
My senses when she beckoned him up the stair.
Shaking from head to foot, I blocked the way.
" Property !"   Could the crux of mine and thine
Bring widow and murderer into one small room ?
" Sir Lewis," I said, " she is ill.   It is not right !
She never would consent."
                                He sneered again,
" You are her doctor ?   Out of the way, old fool !
She has decided !"
                        " Go," I said to the maid,
" Fetch the apothecary.   Let it rest
With him."
                        She tossed her head.   Her quick eyes glanced,

Showing the white, like the eyes of a vicious mare.
She laughed at Stukeley, loitered, then—obeyed.

And so we waited, till the wench returned,
With Galen at her heels.   His wholesome face,
Russet and wrinkled like an apple, peered
Shrewdly at Stukeley, twinkled once at me
And passed in silence, leaving a whiff of herbs
Behind him on the stair.

                          Five minutes later
To my amazement, that same wholesome face
Leaned from the lighted door above, and called
"Sir Lewis Stukeley!"

                          Sir Judas hastened up.
The apothecary followed him within.
The door shut, I was left there in the dark
Bewildered; for my heart was hot with thoughts
Of those last months.   Our Summer's Nightingale,
Our Ocean-Shepherd from the Main-deep Sea,
The Founder of our Mermaid Fellowship,
Was this his guerdon—at the Mermaid Inn?
Was this that maid-of-honour whose romance
With Raleigh, once, had been a kingdom's talk?
Could Bess Throckmorton slight his memory thus?
"It is not right," I said, "it is not right.
She wrongs him deeply."

                          I leaned against the porch
Staring into the night.   A ghostly ray
Above me, from her window, bridged the street
And rested on the goldsmith's painted sign
Opposite.

                          I could hear the muffled voice
Of Stukeley overhead, persuasive, bland;
And then, her own, cooing, soft as a dove
Calling its mate from Eden cedar-boughs,
Flowed on and on; and then—all my flesh crept
At something worse than either, a long space
Of silence that stretched threatening and cold,

Cold as a dagger-point pricking the skin
Over my heart.
                          Then came a stifled cry,
A crashing door, a footstep on the stair,
Blundering like a drunkard's heavily down;
And with his gasping face one tragic mask
Of horror,—may God help me to forget,
Some day the frozen awful eyes of one
Who, fearing neither hell nor heaven, has met
That ultimate weapon of the gods, the face
And serpent tresses that turn flesh to stone—
Stukeley stumbled, groping his way out,
Blindly, past me, into the sheltering night.

.   .   .   .

It was the last night of another year
Before I understood what punishment
Had overtaken Stukeley.
                          Ben and Brome—
Ben's ancient servant, but turned poet now—
Sat by the fire with the old apothecary
To see the New Year in.
                          The starry night
Had drawn me to the door.   Could it be true
That our poor earth no longer was the hub
Of those white wheeling orbs?   I scarce believed
The strange new dreams; but I had seen the veils
Rent from vast oceans and huge continents,
Till what was once our comfortable fire,
Our cosy tavern, and our earthly home
With heaven beyond the next turn in the road,
All that resplendent fabric of our world
Shrank to a glow-worm, lighting up one leaf
In one small forest, in one little land,
Among those wild infinitudes of God.
A tattered wastrel wandered down the street,
Clad in a seaman's jersey, staring hard
At every sign.   Beneath our own, the light
Fell on his red carbuncled face, I knew him,—

The bo'sun, Hart.
                    He pointed to our sign
And leered at me.   "That's her," he said, "no doubt,
The sea-witch with the shiny mackerel tail
Swishing in wine.   That's what Sir Lewis meant.
He called it blood.   Blood is his craze, you see.
This is the Mermaid Tavern, sir, no doubt?"
I nodded.   "Ah, I thought as much," he said.
"Well—happen this is worth a cup of ale."
He thrust his hand under his jersey and lugged
A greasy letter out.   It was inscribed
The apothecary at the Mermaid Tavern.
   I led him in.   "I knew it, sir," he said,
While Galen broke the seal.   "Soon as I saw
That sweet young naked wench curling her tail
In those red waves.—The old man called it blood—
Blood is his craze, you see.—But you can tell
'Tis wine, sir, by the foam.   Malmsey, no doubt.
And that sweet wench to make you smack your lips
Like oysters, with her slippery tail and all!
Why, sir, no doubt, this was the Mermaid Inn."

"But this," said Galen, lifting his grave face
To Ben, "this letter is from all that's left
Of Stukeley.   The good host, there, thinks I wronged
Your Ocean-shepherd's memory.   From this letter,
I think I helped to avenge him.   Do not wrong
His widow, even in thought.   She loved him dearly.
You know she keeps his poor grey severed head
Embalmed ; and so will keep it till she dies ;
Weeps over it alone.   I have heard such things
In wild Italian tales.   But *this* was true.
Had I refused to let her speak with Stukeley
I feared she would go mad.   This letter proves
That I—and she perhaps—were instruments,
Of some more terrible chirurgery
Than either knew.
                    "Ah, when I saw your sign,"

The bo'sun interjected, " I'd no doubt
That letter was well worth a cup of ale."

  "Go—paint your bows with hell-fire somewhere else,
Not at this inn," said Ben, tossing the rogue
A good French crown. "Pickle yourself in hell."
And Hart lurched out into the night again,
Muttering, "Thank you, sirs. 'Twas worth all that.
No doubt at all."

              "There are some men," said Galen,
Spreading the letter out on his plump knees,
"Will heap up wrong on wrong; and, at the last,
Wonder because the world will not forget
Just when it suits them, cancel all they owe,
And, like a mother, hold its arms out wide
At their first cry. And, sirs, I do believe
That Stukeley, on that night, had some such wish
To reconcile himself. What else had passed
Between the widow and himself I know not;
But she had lured him on until he thought
That words and smiles, perhaps a tear or two,
Might make the widow take the murderer's hand
In friendship, since it might advantage both.
Indeed, he came prepared for even more.
Villains are always fools. A wicked act,
What is it but a false move in the game,
A blind man's blunder, a deaf man's reply,
The wrong drug taken in the dead of night?
I always pity villains.

                I mistook
The avenger for the victim. There she lay
Panting, that night, her eyes like summer stars.
Her pale gold hair upon the pillows tossed
Dishevelled, while the fever in her face
Brought back the lost wild roses of her youth
For half an hour. Against a breast as pure
And smooth as any maid's her soft arms pressed
A bundle wrapped in a white embroidered cloth.
She crooned over it as a mother croons

Over her suckling child.   I stood beside her.
—That was her wish, and mine, while Stukeley stayed.—
And, over against me, on the other side,
Stood Stukeley, gnawing his nether lip to find
She could not, or she would not, speak one word
In answer to his letter.
                              "Lady Raleigh,
You wrong me, and you wrong yourself," he cried,
"To play like a green girl when great affairs
Are laid before you.   Let me speak with you,
Alone."
            "But I am all alone," she said,
"Far more alone than I have ever been
In all my life before.   This is my doctor.
He must not leave me."
                              Then she lured him on,
Played on his brain as a musician plays
Upon the lute.
                    "Forgive me, dear Sir Lewis,
If I am grown too gay for widowhood.
But I have pondered for a long, long time
On all these matters.   I know the world was right,
The King was right, and Buckingham was right ;
And Spain was right, Sir Lewis.   Yes, and you,
You, too, were right ; and my poor husband wrong.
You see I knew his mind so very well.
I knew his every gesture, every smile.
I lived with him.   I think I died with him.

It is a strange thing, marriage.   For my soul
(As if myself were present in this flesh)
Beside him, slept in his grey prison-cell
On that last dreadful dawn.   I heard the throng
Murmuring round the scaffold, far away ;
And, with the smell of sawdust in my nostrils,
I woke bewildered as himself, to see
That tall, black-cassocked figure by his bed.
I heard the words that made him understand :

The Body of our Lord . . . *take and eat this!*
I rolled the small sour flakes beneath my tongue
With him.   I caught, with him, the gleam of tears,
Far off, on some strange face of sickly dread.
The Blood . . . and the cold cup was in my hand,
Cold as an axe-heft washed with waterish red.
I heard his last poor cry to wife and child.—
Could any that heard forget it?—*My true God
Hold you both in His arms, both in His arms!*
And then—that last poor wish, a thing to raise
A smile in some.   I have smiled at it myself
A thousand times.
                    Give me my pipe, he said,
*My old Winchester clay, with the long stem,
And half an hour alone.   The crowd can wait.
They have not waited half so long as I.*
And then, O then, I know what soft blue clouds,
What wavering rings, fragrant ascending wreaths
Melted his prison-walls to a summer haze,
Through which I think he saw the little port
Of Budleigh Salterton, like a sea-bird's nest
Among the Devon cliffs . . . the tarry quay
Where in his boyhood he had flung a line
For bass or whiting-pollock.   I remembered
(Had he not told me, on some summer night
His arm about my neck, kissing my hair)
He used to sit there, gazing out to sea;
Fish, and for what?   Not all for what he caught
And handled; but for rainbow-coloured things,
The water-drops that jewelled his thin line,
Flotsam and jetsam of the sunset clouds,
While the green water gurgling through the piles,
Heaving and sinking, helped him to believe
The fast-bound quay a galleon plunging out
Superbly for Cathay.   There would he sit
Listening, a radiant boy, child of the sea,
Listening to some old seaman's glowing tales,
His grey eyes rich with pictures. . . .

                        Then he saw,
And I with him, that gathering in the West,
To break the Fleet Invincible. O, I heard
The trumpets and the neighings and the drums,
The sound of guns at sea, like a long soft fall
Of white chalk cliffs, crumbling slowly away.
I watched the beacons on a hundred hills.
I drank that wine of battle from *his* cup,
And gloried in it, lying against his heart.
I sailed with him and saw the unknown worlds.
The slender ivory towers of old Cathay
Rose for us over lilac-coloured seas
That crumpled a sky-blue foam on long shores
Of shining sand, shores of so clear a glass
They drew the sunset-clouds into their bosom
And hung that City of Vision in mid air
Girdling it round, as with a moat of sky,
Hopelessly beautiful, O, yet I heard—
Heard from his blazoned poops the trumpeters
Blowing proud calls, while overhead the flag
Of England floated from white towers of sail . .
And yet, and yet I knew that he was wrong.
And soon he knew it, too.
                    I saw the cloud
Of doubt assail him, in the Bloody Tower,
When, being withheld from sailing the high seas
For sixteen years, he spread a prouder sail,
Took up his pen and, walled about with stone,
Began to write—his *History of the World*.
And emperors came, like Lazarus from the grave,
To wear his purple. And the night disgorged
Its empires, till, O, like the swirl of dust
Around their marching legions, that dim cloud
Of doubt closed round him. Was there any man
So sure of heart and brain as to record
The simple truth of things himself had seen?
Then who could plumb that night? The work broke off!
He knew that he was wrong. I knew it, too!

Once more that stately structure of his dreams
Melted like mist.   His eagles perished like clouds.
Death wound a thin horn through the centuries.
The grave resumed his forlorn emperors.
His empires crumbled back to a little ash
Knocked from his pipe . . .
He dropped his pen in homage to the truth.
The truth?   *O, eloquent, just, and mighty Death !*

Then, when he forged, out of one golden thought,
A key to open his prison ; when the King
Released him for a tale of faërie gold
Under the tropic palms ; when those grey walls
Melted before his passion ; do you think
The gold that lured the King was quite the same
As that which Raleigh saw ?   You know the song :

    'Say to the King,' quoth Raleigh,
       'I have a tale to tell him :
          Wealth beyond derision,
             Veils to lift from the sky,
    Seas to sail for England,
        And a little dream to sell him,
          Gold, the gold of a vision
            That angels cannot buy.'

Ah, no !   For all the beauty and the pride,
Raleigh was wrong ; but not so wrong, I think,
As those for whom his kingdoms oversea
Meant only glittering dust.   The fight he waged
Was not with them.   They never worsted him.
It was the *Destiny* that brought him home
Without the Spanish gold. . . . O, he was wrong,
But such a wrong in Gloriana's day,
Was more than right, was immortality.
He had just half an hour to put all this
Into his pipe and smoke it . . .
                The red fire,

The red heroic fire that filled his veins
When the proud flag of England floated out
Its challenge to the world—all gone to ash?
What? Was the great red wine that Drake had quaffed
Vinegar? He must fawn, haul down his flag,
And count all nations nobler than his own;
Tear out the lions from the painted shields
That hung his poop, for fear that he offend
The pride of Spain? Treason to sack the ships
Of Spain? The wounds of slaughtered Englishmen
Cried out—*there is no law beyond the line !*
Treason to sweep the seas with Francis Drake?
Treason to fight for England?

                 If it were so,
The times had changed and quickly. He had been
A school-boy in the morning of the world,
Playing with wooden swords and winning crowns
Of tinsel; but his comrades had outgrown
Their morning-game, and gathered round to mock
His battles in the sunset. Yet he knew
That all his life had passed in that brief day;
And he was old, too old to understand
The smile upon the face of Buckingham,
The smile on Cobham's face at that great word
England !

       He knew the solid earth was changed
To something less than dust among the stars . . .
And O, be sure he knew that he was wrong,
That gleams would come—
Gleams of a happier world for younger men,
That Commonwealth, far off. This was a time
Of sadder things, destruction of the old
Before the new was born. At least he knew
It was his own way that had brought the world
Thus far, England thus far ! How could he change,
He who loved England as a man might love
His mistress, change from year to fickle year?
For the new years would change, even as the old.

No—he was wedded to that old first love,
Crude flesh and blood, and coarse as meat and drink,
The woman—England; no fine angel-isle,
Ruled by that male Salome—Buckingham!
Better the axe than to live on and wage
These new and silent and more deadly wars
That play at friendship with our enemies.
Such times are evil.   Not of their own desire
They lead to good, blind agents of that Hand
Which now had hewed him down, down to his knees,
But in a prouder battle than men knew.

His pipe was out.   The guard was at the door.
Raleigh was not a god.   But when he climbed
The scaffold, I believe he looked a man.
And when the axe fell, I believe that God
Set on his shoulders that immortal head
Which he desired on earth.
                                          O, he was wrong!
But when that axe fell, not one shout was raised.
That mighty throng around that crimson block
Stood silent—like the hushed black cloud that holds
The thunder.   You might hear the headsman's breath.
Stillness like that is dangerous, being charged
Sometimes with thought, Sir Lewis!   England sleeps!
What if, one day, the Stewart should be called
To know that England wakes?   What if a shout
Should thunder-strike Whitehall, and the dogs lift
Their heads along the fringes of the crowd
To catch a certain savour that I know,
The smell of blood and sawdust? . . .
                                          Ah, Sir Lewis,
'Tis hard to find one little seed of right
Among so many wrongs.   Raleigh was wrong,
And yet—it was because he loved his country,
Next to himself, Sir Lewis, by your leave,
His country butchered him.   You did not know
That I was only third in his affections?

The night I told him—we were parting then—
I had begged the last disposal of his body,
Did he not say, with O, so gentle a smile,
Thou hadst not always the disposal of it
In life, dear Bess. 'Tis well it should be thine
In death !"—

        "The jest was bitter at such an hour,
And somewhat coarse in grain," Stukeley replied.
"Indeed I thought him kinder."

                 "Kinder," she said,
Laughing bitterly.

        Stukeley looked at her.
She whispered something, and his lewd old eyes
Fastened upon her own.   He knelt by her.
"Perhaps," he said, "your woman's wit has found
A better way to solve this bitter business."
Her head moved on the pillow with little tossings.
He touched her hand.   It leapt quickly away.
She hugged that strange white bundle to her breast,
And writhed back, smiling at him, across the bed.
"Ah, Bess," he whispered huskily, pressing his lips
To that warm hollow where her head had lain,
"There is one way to close the long dispute,
Keep the estates unbroken in your hands
And stop all slanderous tongues, one happy way.
We have some years to live ; and why alone?"

  "Alone?" she sighed.   "My husband thought of that.
He wrote a letter to me, long ago,
When he was first condemned.   He said—he said—
Now let me think—what was it that he said?—
I had it all by heart.—*Beseech you, Bess,*
Hide not yourself for many days, he said."

  "True wisdom that," quoth Stukeley, "for the love
That seeks to chain the living to the dead
Is but self-love at best !"

             "And yet," she said,
"See how his poor heart's torn between two cares,
Love of himself and care of me, as thus :

Love God! Begin to repose yourself on Him!
Therein you shall find true and lasting riches;
But all the rest is nothing. When you have tired
Your thoughts on earthly things, when you have travelled
Through all the glittering pomps of this proud world,
You shall sit down by Sorrow in the end.
Begin betimes, and teach your little son
To serve and fear God also.
Then God will be a husband unto you,
And unto him a father; nor can Death
Bereave you any more. When I am gone,
No doubt you shall be sought unto by many,
For the world thinks that I was very rich.
No greater misery can befall you, Bess,
Than to become a prey and, afterwards,
To be despised."

          " Human enough," said Stukeley,
" And yet—self-love, self-love ! "

                " Ah, no," quoth she,
" You have not heard the end : *God knows, I speak it*
Not to dissuade you—not to dissuade you, mark—
From marriage. That will be the best for you,
Both in respect of God and of the world.
Was *that* self-love, Sir Lewis? Ah, not all.
And thus he ended : *For his father's sake*
That chose and loved you in his happiest times,
Remember your poor child! The Everlasting,
Infinite, Powerful, and Inscrutable God,
Keep you and yours, have mercy upon me,
And teach me to forgive my false accusers. . . .
Wrong, even in death, you see. Then—*My true wife,*
Farewell!
Bless my poor boy! Pray for me! My true God
Hold you both in His arms, both in His arms!

I know that he was wrong. You did not know,
Sir Lewis, that he had left me a little child.

Come closer, you shall see its orphaned face.
The sad, sad relict of a man that loved
His country . . . all that's left to me. Come, look!"
She beckoned Stukeley nearer. He bent down
Curiously. Her feverish fingers drew
The white wrap from the bundle in her arms,
And, with a smile that would make angels weep,
She showed him, pressed against her naked breast,
Terrible as Medusa, the grey flesh
And shrivelled face, embalmed, the thing that dropped
Into the headsman's basket, months agone,—
The head of Raleigh.

               Half her body lay
Bare, while she held that grey babe to her heart;
But Judas hid his face.
"Living," she said, "he was not always mine;
But—dead—I shall not wean him. . . ."

                         Then I, too,
Covered my face . . . I cannot tell you more.
There was a dreadful silence in that room,
Silence that, as I know, shattered the brain
Of Stukeley. . . . When I dared to raise my head
Beneath that silent thunder of our God,
The man had gone. . . .

                 This is his letter, sirs,
Written from Lundy Island: *For God's love,*
Tell them it is a cruel thing to say
That I drink blood. I have no secret sin.
A thousand pound is not so great a sum;
And that was all they paid me, every penny.
Salt water, that is all the drink I taste
On this rough island. Somebody has taught
The sea-gulls how to wail around my hut
All night, like lost souls. And there is a face,
A dead man's face that laughs in every storm,
And sleeps in every pool along the coast.
I thought it was my own, once. But I know

These actions never, never, on God's earth,
Will turn out to their credit who believe
That I drink blood.
                              He crumpled up the letter
And tossed it into the fire.
                              "Galen," said Ben,
"I think you are right—that one should pity villains."
.   .   .   .

The clock struck twelve.   The bells began to peal.
We drank a cup of sack to the New Year.
"New songs for *you*, lad, all as fresh as may,"
Said Ben to Brome, "but I shall never live
To hear them."
                              All was not so well, indeed,
With Ben, as hitherto.   Age had come upon him.
He dragged one foot as in paralysis.
The critics bayed against the old lion, now,
And called him arrogant.   "My brain," he said,
"Is yet unhurt, although, set round with pain,
It cannot long hold out."   He never stooped,
Never once pandered to that vitiate hour.
His coat was thread-bare.   Weeks had passed of late
Without his voice resounding in our inn.
"The statues are defiled, the gods dethroned,
The Ionian movement reigns, not the free soul.
And, as for me," he said, "I have lived too long.
Well—I can weave the old threnodies anew."
Then, filling his cup, he murmured, soft and low,
A new song, breaking on an ancient shore :—

                              I.

Marlowe is dead, and Greene is in his grave,
    And sweet Will Shakespeare long ago is gone !
Our Ocean-shepherd sleeps beneath the wave ;
Robin is dead, and Marlowe in his grave.

Why should I stay to chant an idle stave,
    And in my Mermaid Tavern drink alone?
For Kit is dead, and Greene is in his grave,
    And sweet Will Shakespeare long ago is gone.

II.

Where is the singer of the Faërie Queen?
    Where are the lyric lips of Astrophel?
Long, long ago, their quiet graves were green;
Ay, and the grave, too, of their Faërie Queen!
And yet their faces, hovering here unseen,
    Call me to taste their new-found œnomel;
To sup with him who sang the Faërie Queen;
    To drink with him whose name was Astrophel.

III.

I drink to that great Inn beyond the grave!
—If there be none, the gods have done us wrong,—
Ere long I hope to chant a better stave
In some great Mermaid Inn beyond the grave;
And quaff the best of earth that heaven can save,
    Red wine like blood, deep love of friends, and song.
I drink to that great Inn beyond the grave,
    And hope to greet my golden lads ere long.

He raised his cup and drank in silence.   Brome
Drank with him, too.   The bells had ceased to peal.
Galen shook hands, and bade us all good-night.
Then Brome, a little wistfully, I thought,
Looked at his old-time master and prepared
To follow.   "Good-night—Ben," he said, a pause
Before he spoke the name. "Good-night! Good-night!
My dear old Brome," said Ben.
                                And, at the door,
Brome whispered to me, " He is lonely now.

There are not many left of his old friends,
We all go out—like this—into the night.
But what a fleet of stars," he said, and shook
My hand, and smiled, and pointed to the sky.

And, when I looked into the room again,
The lights were very dim, and I believed
That Ben had fallen asleep.   His great grey head
Was bowed across the table, on his arms,
Then, all at once, I knew that he was weeping,
And like a shadow I crept back again,
And stole into the night.
                          There as I stood
Under the painted sign, I could have vowed
That I, too, heard the voices of the dead,
The voices of his old companions,
Gathering round him in that lonely room ;
Till all the timbers of the Mermaid Inn
Trembled above me with their ghostly song—

    " Say to the King," quoth Raleigh,
      " I have a tale to tell him,
        Wealth beyond derision,
          Veils to lift from the sky ;
    Seas to sail for England
      And a little dream to sell him,
        Gold, the gold of a vision,
          That angels cannot buy."

    Fair thro' the walls of his dungeon,
      —What were the stones but a shadow ?—
        Streamed the light of the rapture,
          The lure that he followed of old,
    The dream of his old companions,
      The vision of El Dorado,
        The fleet that they never could capture,
          The city of sunset gold.

Yet did they sail the seas
  And, dazed with exceeding wonder,
    Straight thro' the sunset-glory
      Plunge into the dawn:
Leaving their home behind them,
  By a road of splendour and thunder,
    They came to their home in amazement
      Simply by sailing on.

THE WINE-PRESS.

A TALE OF WAR.

DEDICATION.

(To those who believe that Peace is the corrupter of nations.)

I.

PEACE? When have we prayed for peace?
  Over us burns a star
Bright, beautiful, red for strife!
Yours are only the drum and the fife
And the golden braid and the surface of life.
  Ours is the white-hot war.

II.

Peace? When have we prayed for peace?
  Ours are the weapons of men.
Time changes the face of the world.
Your swords are rust! Your flags are furled
And ours are the unseen legions hurled
  Up to the heights again.

III.

Peace?   When have we prayed for peace?
  Is there no wrong to right?
Wrong crying to God on high
Here where the weak and the helpless die,
And the homeless hordes of the City go by,
  The ranks are rallied to-night.

IV.

Peace?   When have we prayed for peace?
  Are ye so dazed with words?
Earth, heaven, shall pass away
Ere for your passionless peace we pray.
Are ye deaf to the trumpets that call us to-day,
  Blind to the blazing swords?

PRELUDE.

I.

SANDALPHON, whose white wings to heaven up-bear
    The weight of human prayer,
Stood silent in the still eternal light
    Of God, one dreadful night.
His wings were clogged with blood, and foul with mire,
    His body seared with fire,
"Hast thou no word for Me?" the Master said.
    The angel sank his head.

II.

"Word from the nations of the East and West,"
    He moaned, "that blood is best:
The patriot prayers of either half of earth.
    Hear Thou, and judge their worth.
Out of the obscene seas of slaughter, hear
    First, the first nation's prayer:
*O God, deliver Thy people. Let Thy sword
    Destroy our enemies, Lord.*

III.

Pure as the first, as passionate in trust
    That their own cause is just,
Puppets as fond in those dark hands of greed,
    As fervent in their creed,

As blindly moved, as utterly betrayed,
    As urgent for thine aid,
Out of the obscene seas of slaughter, hear
    The second nation's prayer:
O God, deliver Thy people.   Let Thy sword
    Destroy our enemies, Lord.

IV.

Over their slaughtered children, one great cry
    From either enemy;
From either host, thigh-deep in filth and shame,
    One prayer, one and the same;
With Thee, with Thee, Lord God of Sabaoth,
    It rests to answer both.
Out of the obscene seas of slaughter, hear,
    From East and West one prayer:
O God, deliver Thy people.   Let Thy sword
    Destroy our enemies, Lord."

V.

Then, on the cross of His creative pain,
    God bowed His head again.
Then East and West, over all seas and lands,
    Out-stretched His piercéd hands.
Then, down in hell, they chuckled, "West and East,
    Each holds one hand, at least. . . ."

"And yet," Sandalphon whispered, "men deny
    The eternal Calvary."

I.

A MURDERED man, ten miles away,
  Will hardly shake your peace,
Like one red stain upon your hand;
And a tortured child in a distant land
Will never check one smile to-day,
  Or bid one fiddle cease.

Not for a little news from hell
  Shall London strive or cry.
Tho' thought would shatter like dynamite
These granite hills that bury the right,
We must not think.   We must not tell
  The truth for which men die.

To watch the mouth of a harlot foam
  For the blood of Baptist John
Is a fine thing while the fiddles play;
For blood and lust are the mode to-day,
And lust and blood were the mode of Rome,
  And we go where Rome has gone.

The plaudits round the circus roll!
  On the old track we swing.
"Unrest," we say, "is in the air;"
And a flea is in the lap-dog's chair.
But the unrest that troubles the soul
  Is a more difficult thing.

Unrest that has no lot or part
  In anything but truth;
Unrest, unrest, whose passions draw
From founts of everlasting law,
Unrest that nerves the out-worn heart,
  And calls, like God, to youth;

The truth that tickles no sweet sense,
  The pillow of stone by night,
Unrest that no man's art can heal,
Unrest that girds the brain with steel,
And, over earth's indifference,
  Like God, calls up the light;

The truth that all might know, but all
  With one consent, refuse;
To call on *that*, to break our pact
Of silence, were to make men *act*.
Good taste forbids that trumpet-call,
  And a censor sends our news.

It comes along a little wire
  Sunk in a deep sea;
It thins in the clubs to a little smoke
Between one joke and another joke;
For a city in flames is less than the fire
  That comforts you and me.

Play up, then, fiddles! Play, bassoon!
  The plains are soaked with red.
Ten thousand slaughtered fools, out there,
Clutch at their wounds and taint the air,
And . . . here is an excellent cartoon
  On what the Kaiser said.

On with the dance!   In England yet
     The meadow-grass is green.
Play up, play up, and play your part!
It is not that we lack the heart
But that fate deftly swings the net
     And blood is best unseen.

God shields our eyes from too much light,
     Clothes the fine brain with clay;
He wraps mankind in swaddling bands
Till the trumpet ring across all lands—
"The time is come to stand upright
     And flood the world with day."

Not yet, O God, not yet the gleam
     When all the world shall wake!
Grey and immense comes up the dawn
And yet the blinds are not withdrawn,
And, in the dusk, one hideous dream
     Forbids the day to break!

          .   .   .   .   .   .

Around a shining table sat
     Five men in black tail-coats;
And, what their sin was, none could say;
For each was honest, after his way,
(Tho' there are sheep, and armament firms,
     With all that this "connotes.")

One was the friend of a merchant prince,
     One was the foe of a priest,
One had a brother whose heart was set
On a gold star and an epaulette,
And—where the rotten carcass lies,
     The vultures flock to feast.

But—each was honest after his way,
  Lukewarm in faith and old;
And blood, to them, was only a word,
And the point of a phrase their only sword,
And the cost of war, they reckoned it
  In little disks of gold.

They were cleanly groomed.   They were not
    to be bought.
  And their cigars were good.
But they had pulled so many strings
In the tinselled puppet-show of kings
That, when they talked of war, they thought
  Of sawdust, not of blood;

Not of the crimson tempest
  Where the shattered city falls:
They thought, behind their varnished doors,
Of diplomats, ambassadors,
Budgets, and loans and boundary-lines,
  Coercions and re-calls;

Forces and Balances of Power;
  Shadows and dreams and dust;
And how to set their bond aside
And prove they lied not when they lied,
And which was weak, and which was strong,
  But—never which was just.

Yet they were honest, honest men.
  Justice could take no wrong.
The blind arbitrament of steel,
The mailed hand, the armoured heel,
Could only prove that Justice reigned
  And that her hands were strong.

For *they* were strong.   So might is right,
 And reason wins the day.
And, if at a touch on a silver bell
They plunged three nations into hell,
The blood of peasants is not red
 A hundred miles away.

But, if one touch on a silver bell
 Should loose, beyond control,
A blind immeasurable flood
Of lust and hate and tears and blood,
Unknown immeasurable powers
 That swept to an unseen goal,

Beyond their guidance for one hour,
 Beyond their utmost ken,
No huddled madman, crowned with straw,
Could so transgress his own last law . . .
So a secretary struck the bell
 For these five honest men.

II.

WITH brown arms folded, by his hut, Johann,
  The young wood-cutter, waited.   A bell tolled,
The sunset fires along the mountain ran,

The bucket at the well dripped a thin gold,
  He saw the peaks like clouds of lilac bloom
Above him, then the pine-woods, fold on fold,

Around him, slowly filled with deep blue gloom.
  Sleep, Dodi, sleep, he heard his young wife say,
Hushing their child behind him in the room.

Then, like a cottage casement, far away,
  A star thrilled in a pale green space of sky;
And then, like stars, with tiny ray on ray,

He saw the homely village-lights reply:
  And earth and sky were mingled in one night,
And all that vast dissolving pageantry

Drew to those quintessential points of light,
  Still as the windless candles in a shrine,
Significant in the depth as in the height.

O, little blue pigeon, sleep.   Sleep, Dodi, mine,
  She murmured, Sleep, little rose in your rosy bed.
The moon is rocking, rocking to rest in the pine.

Sleep, little blue pigeon,
  Sleep on my breast,
Sleep, while the stars shine,
Sleep, while the big pine
Rocks with the white moon,
  Over your nest.

A great grey cloud sailed slowly overhead.
  She stood behind Johann.   Around his eyes
Her soft hands closed.   "Dodi's asleep," she said.

He drew her hands away.   Then, as the skies
  Darkened, he muttered, "Sonia, you must know.
I've kept the news from you all day."
                                        Surprise

Parted her lips.
                  "To-morrow I must go." ——
"Go?   Where?" —— Clear as a silver bell, one star
Thrilled thro' the clouds.   Her face looked white as snow.

——"To-morrow morning, Sonia.   No, not far!
To join the regiment.   We are called, you see."——
"But why?   What does it mean?"——

                              "Mean, Sonia?   War!

III.

The troop-train couplings clanged like Fate
   Above the bugles' din.
Sweating beneath their haversacks,
With rifles bristling on their backs,
Like heavy-footed oxen
   The dusty men trooped in.

It seemed that some gigantic hand
   Behind the veils of sky
Was driving, herding all these men
Like cattle into a cattle-pen,
So few of them could understand,
   So many of them must die.

Johann was crammed into his truck.
   Far off, he heard a shout.
The corporal cracked a bottle of wine,
And passed the drink along the line.
The iron couplings clanged again,
   And the troop-train rumbled out.

"I left my wife a month's pay,"
   A voice droned at his side.
"This war, they say, will last a year.
God knows what will become of her,
With three to feed."—"Ah, that's the way
   In war," Johann replied.

"They say that war's a noble thing!
  They say it's good to die,
For causes none can understand!
They say it's for the Fatherland!
They say it's for the Flag, the King,
  And none must question why!"

The train shrieked into a tunnel.
  " Duty ?—Yes, that is good.
But when the thing has grown so vast
That no man knows, from first to last,
The reason why he finds himself
  Up to his neck in blood;

When you are trapped and carried along
  By a Power that runs on rails;
Why, open that door, my friends, and see
The way you are fixed.   You think you are free,
But the iron wheels are singing a song
  That stuns our fairy-tales;

When you are lifted up like this
  Between a finger and thumb,
And dropt you don't know where or why,
And told to shoot and butcher and die,
And not to question, not to reply,
But go like a sheep to the shearers,
  A lamb to the slaughter, dumb;

What?   Are the engines, then, our God?
  Does one amongst you know
The *reason* of this bitter work?"—
"Reason?   The devilry of the Turk!
Lock, stock, and barrel, the Sick Man
  And all his tribe must go."

" England, they say, is on our side,"
   Another voice began.
" The paper says it."—" But, I thought . . .
Does no one know why England fought
The great Crimean war, my friends,
   Where blood so freely ran?"—

" O, ay!   They say that England backed
   The wrong horse, a sheer blunder!
She poured out blood *to guarantee*,
For all time, the integrity
Of European Islam."—" Ah!"—
   The train rolled on like thunder.

Michael, the poet, a half Greek,
   Listened to what they said.
Twice his lips parted as to speak,
   And twice he sank his head,
Then a great fire burned in his eyes,
   His sallow cheek flushed red.

" Comrades, comrades, you know not
   The banners that you bear!
There is a sword upon our side,
A sword that is a song," he cried;
Then, through the song, as he whispered it,
   His heart poured like a prayer:

I.

Whose face, whose on high,
   Lifts thro' the sky
      That aureole?
Who, over earth and sea,
   Cries *Victory?*
      Europe, thy soul
      Comes home to thee.

II.

Is it a dream, a cloud
That thus hath rent the shroud
To speak, sublime and proud,
    Thy faith aloud;
Whose eyes make young and fair
All things in earth and air;
The shadow of whose white wing
    Makes violets spring?

III.

Is it the angel of day,
    Whom the blind pray
    Still that their faith
Soundly sleep by night?
    Blood-red, yet white,
    Re-risen, she saith
    Let there be Light!

IV.

Whose are the conquering eyes
That burn thro' those dark skies?
Whose is the voice that cries
    Awake, arise?
For, if she speak one word
To sheathe or draw the sword,
Her nations, on that day,
    Answer her, *Yea!*

V.

It is the angel of God,
    Sun-crowned, fire-shod,
    Bidding hate cease.
Her proud voice on high
    Bids darkness die.
    Her name is Greece,
    Or Liberty.

" *Comrades*," he cried, "*you know not*
   The splendour of your blades !
This war is not as other wars :
The night shrinks with all her stars,
And Freedom rides before you
   On the last of the Crusades.

She rides a snow-white charger
   Tho' her flanks drip with red,
Before her blade's white levin
The Crescent pales in heaven,
Nor shall she shrink from battle
   Till the sun reign overhead ;

Till the dead Cross break in blossom ;
   Till the God we sacrificed,
With that same love He gave us
Stretch out His arms to save us,
Yea, till God save the People,
   And heal the wounds of Christ."

IV.

THEY crept across the valley
    Where the wheat was turning brown.
There was no cloud in the blue sky,
No sight, no sound of an enemy,
When the sharp command rang over them,
    Cover, and *lie down!*

Johann, with four beside him,
    In a cottage garden lay.
Peering over a little wall,
They heard a bird in the eaves call:
And, through the door, a clock ticked
    A thousand miles away.

A thousand miles, a thousand years,
    And all so still and fair,
Then, like some huge invisible train,
Splitting the blue heavens in twain,
Out of the quiet distance rushed
    A thunder of shrieking air.

The earth shook below them,
    And lightnings lashed the sky,
The trees danced in the fires of hell,
The walls burst like a bursting shell;
And a bloody mouth gnawed at the stones
    Like a rat, with a thin cry.

Then, all across the valley,
    Deep silence reigned anew :
There was no cloud in the blue sky,
No sight, no sound of an enemy,
But the red, wet shape beside Johann,
    And that lay silent, too.

A bugle like a scourge of brass
    Whipped thro' nerve and brain ;
Up from their iron-furrowed beds
The long lines with bowed heads
Plunged to meet the hidden Death
    Across the naked plain.

They leapt across the lewd flesh
    That twisted at their feet ;
They leapt across wild shapes that lay
Stark, besmeared with blood and clay
Like the great dead birds, with the glazed eyes,
    That the farmer hangs in the wheat.

Johann plunged onward, counting them,
    Scarecrows that once were men.
He counted them by twos, by fours,
Then, all at once, by tens, by scores !
Cover ! Thro' flesh and nerve and bone
    The bugles rang again.

They lay upon the naked earth,
    Each in his place.
There was no cloud in the blue sky,
No sight, no sound of an enemy.
A brown bee murmured near Johann,
    And the sweat streamed down his face ;

The quiet hills that they must storm
　　Slept softly overhead,
When, in among their sun-lit trees
A sound as of gigantic bees
Whirred, and all the plains were ripped
　　With leaping streaks of lead.

The lightnings leapt among the lines
　　Like a mountain-stream in flood.
Scattering the red clay they ran
A river of fire around Johann,
And, thrice, a spatter of human flesh
　　Blinded him with blood.

Then all the hills grew quiet
　　And the sun slept on the field,
There was no cloud in the blue sky,
No sight, no sound of an enemy ;
But, over them, like a scourge of brass
　　The scornful bugles pealed.

Forward !   At the double,
　　Not questioning what it means !
The long rows of young men
Carried their quivering flesh again
Over those wide inhuman zones
　　Against the cold machines.

Flesh against things fleshless,
　　Never the soul's desire,
Never the flash of steel on steel,
But the brain that is mangled under the wheel,
The nerves that shrivel, the limbs that reel
　　Against a sheet of fire.

They reeled against the thunder,
    Their captain at their head:
They reeled, they clutched at the air, they fell!
Halt!   Rapid fire!   The bugles' yell
Rang along the swaying ranks,
    And they crouched behind their dead.

The levelled rifles cracked like whips
    Against the dark hill brow:
And, for a peasant as for a king,
A dead man makes good covering;
Or, if the man be breathing yet,
    There is none to save him now.

Across a heap of flesh, Johann
    Fired at the unseen mark.
He had not fired a dozen rounds
When the shuddering lump of tattered wounds
Lifted up a mangled head
    And whined, like a child, in the dark.

Its eyes were out.   The raw strings
    Along its face lay red;
It caught the barrel in its hands
    And set it to its head.

Its jaw dropped dumbly, but Johann
    Saw and understood:
The rifle flashed, and the dead man
    Lay quiet in his blood.

Then all along the reeking hills
    And up the dark ravines,
The long rows of young men
Leapt in the glory of life again
To carry their warm and breathing breasts
    Against the cold machines;

Against the Death that mowed them down
With a cold indifferent hand;
And every gap at once was fed
With more life from the fountain-head,
Filled up from endless ranks behind
In the name of the Fatherland,

Mown down! Mown down! Mown down!
Mown down!
They staggered in sheets of fire,
They reeled like ships in a sudden blast,
And shreds of flesh went spattering past,
And the hoarse bugles laughed on high,
Like fiends from hell—*Retire!*

The tall young men, the tall young men,
That were so fain to die,
It was not theirs to question,
It was not theirs to reply.

They had broken their hearts on the cold machines;
And—they had not seen their foe;
And the reason of this butcher's work
It was not theirs to know;
For these tall young men were children
Five short years ago.

Headlong, headlong, down the hill,
They leapt across their dead.
Like madmen, wrapt in sheets of flame,
Yelling out of their hell they came,
And, in among their plunging hordes,
The shrapnel burst and spread.

The shrapnel severed the leaping limbs
  And shrieked above their flight.
They rolled and plunged and writhed like snakes
In the red hill-brooks and the blackthorn brakes.
Their mangled bodies tumbled like elves
  In a wild Walpurgis night.

Slaughter! Slaughter! Slaughter!
  The cold machines whirred on.
And strange things crawled amongst the wheat
With entrails dragging round their feet,
And over the foul red shambles
  A fearful sunlight shone.

And a remnant reached the trenches
  Where the black-mouthed guns lay still.
There was no cloud in the blue sky,
No sight, no sound of an enemy.
The sunlight slept on the valley,
  And the dead slept on the hill.

.   .   .   .   .

But now, beyond the hill, there rose
  A dull and sullen roar,
A sound as of distant breakers
  That burst on a granite shore.

Nearer it boomed and nearer,
  A muffled doomsday din,
A thunder as of assaulting seas
  When the tides are rolling in.

A corporal leapt along the trench
  And shook his blade;
"God sends the Greeks up from the South
  In good time to our aid!

The Turkish dogs are in the trap
    Between us!   God is good!
They are driving them over the ridge of the hill
For our guns, our guns to work their will.
Children of Marko, you shall lap
    Your bellyful of blood."

Down, the dark clouds of Islam poured
    Over the ragged height:
Down, into the valley of wheat,
And the warm dead that lay at their feet,
The men they had slaughtered, slaughtered,
      slaughtered,
    Grinned up at their flight.

Behind, the conquering thunders rolled
    Along the abandoned hill.
Onward the scattering squadrons came
Like madmen, wrapt in a sheet of flame,
Straight for the lurking trenches,
    Where the black-mouthed guns lay still.

And through the masked artillery ran
    A whimper of straining hounds.
"Not yet," the order passed, "lie still,
    Lie still, and lick your wounds."

Johann lay quivering, in a line
    That whined like a leashed wolf-pack,
Leashed by a whisper, sharp as a sword,
At the white of their eyes, I give the word,
Then let the moon be turned to blood,
    And the sun grow black.

Up, up, like plunging bullocks
  The dark-faced Moslems came.
Johann could see their wild eyes shine,
An order hissed along the line,
The black earth yawned like a crimson mouth,
And *slaughter, slaughter, slaughter, slaughter,*
  The trenches belched their flame.

The maxims cracked like cattle-whips
  Above the struggling hordes.
They rolled and plunged and writhed like snakes
In the trampled wheat and the blackthorn brakes,
And the lightnings leapt among them
  Like clashing crimson swords.

The rifles flogged their wallowing herds,
  Flogged them down to die.
Down on their slain the slayers lay,
And the shrapnel thrashed them into the clay,
And tossed their limbs like tattered birds
  Thro' a red volcanic sky.

Then, hard behind the thunder, swept
  Long ranks of arrowy gleams ;
Out of the trenches, down the hill
The level bayonets charged to kill,
And the massed terror that took the shock
  Screamed as a woman screams.

Before Johann a young face rose
  Like a remembered prayer :
He could not halt or swerve aside
In the onrush of that murderous tide,
He jerked his bayonet out of the body
  And swung his butt in the air.

He yelled like a wolf to drown the cry
    Of his own soul in pain,
To stifle the God in his own breast,
He yelled and cursed and struck with the rest,
And the blood bubbled over his boots
    And greased his hands again.

Faces liked drowned things underfoot
    Slipped as he swung round :
A red mouth crackled beneath his boot
    Like thorns in spongy ground.

Slaughter ?   Slaughter ?   So easy it seemed
    This work that he thought so hard !
His eyes lit with a flicker of hell,
He licked his lips, and it tasted well ;
And—once—he had sickened to watch them slaughter
    An ox in the cattle-yard.

For lust of blood, for lust of blood,
    His greasy bludgeon swung :
His rifle-butt sang in the air,
And the things that crashed beneath it there
Were a cluster of grapes in the wine-press
    A savour of wine on his tongue.

Till now the allies' bloody hands
    Across the work could join ;
And, as Johann stretched out his own,
A man that was cleft to the white breast-bone
Writhed up between his knees and fired
    A bullet into his groin.

He clutched at the wound.   He groaned.   He fell
    On the warm breasts of the slain.
Yet, as he swooned, he dreamed he heard
From the lips of Greece one thunder-word,
Freedom !—dreamed that the sons of the mountain
    Doubled the shout again ;

Dreamed—for surely this was a dream—
    He saw them, red from the fight,
Embraced and sobbing, "God is good,
And the blood that seals our brotherhood
Is the red of the dawn that breaks upon Europe."
    Over him swept the night.

V.

MICHAEL had brought a message home. He came,
  Groping, with blind pits where his eyes had been,
And a face glorious with an inner flame,

Whiter than death, and proud with things unseen.
  He came to Sonia; and she stood there, wan,
Watching him, wondering what such pride might mean.

A long low flame along the mountains ran.
He spoke to the air beyond her.

                    " *Sonia*," he said,
" *It was your birthday when I left Johann*

In the field-hospital.   Since you were wed,
  The first, perhaps, without some fond word spoken,
Some gift.   And so he sent this disk of lead

Which came out of his wound.   Wear it in token
  That lovers cannot meet, nor freemen rest,
Until the chains of tyranny be broken.

Tell her," he said—blood washed the golden west—
  " *My wound is healing fast.*"   With fumbling hand
Michael drew out the bullet from his breast.

She took and kissed it.
                    " Ah, but this war is grand ! "
    The blind man murmured.   " Blessed are they that see
The beautiful angel of our Fatherland,

The glory of the angel of Liberty
    Walking thro' all those teeming tents of pain,
The tattered hospitals of our agony,

Where broken men gaze into her eyes again,
    Like happy children.   Sonia, I am told
That wounds broke open for joy, tears flowed like rain

When word came that the Allies would soon hold
    Byzantium, and the mosque that in old days
Belonged to Christ.
                    There, glimmering like pale gold,

High on the walls, they say, thro' a worn haze
    Of whitewash, His crowned Face till time shall cease
Looks down in pity on all our tangled ways,

And yearns to guide us into the way of peace.
    Would God I might be with them, when they ride,
Those hosts of Christ, the Balkan States and Greece,

Along the Golden Horn ! "
                    The sunset died.
    Yet his blind face grew glorious with light,
And, like a soul in ecstasy, he cried :

The Prophet is fallen !   His kingdom is rent asunder !
The blood-stained steeds move on with a sound of thunder !
    The sword of the Prophet is broken.   His cannon are
        dumb.
    The last Crusade rides into Byzantium !

See—on the walls that enshrined the high faith of our
    fathers—
Rich as the dawn thro' the mist that on Bosphorus gathers,
    Gleam the mosaics, the rich encrustations of old,
    Crimson on emerald, azure and opal on gold.

Faint thro' that mist, lo, the Light of the World, the for-
    saken
Glory of Christ, while with terror the mountains are shaken,
    Silently waits ; and the skies with wild trumpets are torn ;
    Waits, and the rivers run red to the Golden Horn ;

Waits, like the splendour of Truth on the walls of Creation ;
Waits, with the Beauty, the Passion, the high Consecration,
    Hidden away on the walls of the world, in a cloud,
    Till the Veil be rent, and the Judgment proclaim Him
    aloud.

Ah, the deep eyes, San Sofia, that deepen and glisten ;
Ah, the crowned Face o'er thine altars, the King that must
    listen,
    Listen and wait thro' the ages, listen and wait,
    For the tramp of a terrible host, and a shout in the gate !

Conquerors, what is your sign, as ye ride thro' the City ?
Is it the sword of wrath, or the sheath of pity ?
    Nay, but a Sword Reversed, let your hilts on high
    Lift the sign of your Captain against the sky !

Reverse the Sword !   The Crescent is rent asunder !
Lift up the Hilt !   Ride on with a sound of thunder !
    Lift up the Cross !   The cannon, the cannon are dumb.
    The last Crusade rides into Byzantium !

Under the apple-tree a shadow stirred.
    An old grey peasant stood there in the night.
"*Michael,*" he said, "*this is bad news we've heard !*"

" *Bad news ?* "—" *O, ay, we're in a pretty plight !*
    They've quarrelled ! "—" *Who ?* "—" *Your great Crusading
        band,*
Greece, and the Balkan States. They're going to fight ! "

—" *Fight ?   Fight ?   For what ?* "—" *Why, don't you
        understand*
    What war is ?   For a port to export prunes,
For Christ, my boy, and for the Fatherland ! "

VI.

Johann had left the tents of death
   And the moan of shattered men.
By God's own grace he was fit to face
   The cold machines again.

It was not his to understand,
   It was only his to know
His hand was against the comrade's hand
   He clasped, a month ago.

It was not his to question,
   It was not his to reply ;
But, over him, the night grew black ;
And his own troop was falling back,
Falling back before the flag
   He had helped to raise on high.

And the guns, the guns that drove them,
   Had thundered with his own !
The men he must kill for a little pay
Had marched beside him, yesterday !
Brothers in blood ! By what foul lips
   Was this war-trumpet blown ?

Back from the heights they had stormed together,
   The gulfs that had gorged their dead,
Back, by the rotting, shot-ripped plain,
Where the black wings fluttered and perched again,
And the yellow beaks in the darkness
   Ripped and dripped and fed.

And once they stayed for water
   By a deep marble well,
Under the walls of a shattered town
They dropt a guttering pine-torch down,
And caught one glimpse of a wine-press
   Choked with the fruits of hell;

One glimpse of the women and children,
   A tangle of red and white!
The naked fruitage hissed in the glare:
They caught the smell of the singeing hair,
And the torch was out, and the wine-press
   Black as the covering night.

And fear went with them down the roads
   Where they had marched in pride;
And villages in panic rout
Poured their rumbling ox-carts out,
And women dropped beneath their loads
   And sobbed by the way-side.

VII.

ONCE, as with bleeding feet they shambled along,
   They came on a way-side fire, a ring of light,
Where old men, women and children, a motley throng,

And their white oxen, heavy with day-long flight,
   Crouched and couched together, on the cold ground,
In a wild blaze of beauty that gashed the night,

Gashed and tattered the gloom like a blood-red wound.
   Now on a blue or an orange sheep-skin cloak
It splashed, and now on the waggons that shadowed them
     round.

But the great black eyes of the oxen, forgetting the yoke,
   Shone with a sheltering pity, so meek, so mild,
While the women lay resting against them; and the smoke

Rolled with the cloud; and Johann, with a heart running
     wild,
   Saw one pale woman that sat in the midst of them,
With a dark-blue robe wrapped round her, suckling a child.

And he thought of the child and the oxen of Bethlehem.

VIII.

BACK, they fell back before the guns,
  Till on one last dark night
They lay along a mountain-ridge
  Entrenched for their last fight.
A pine-wood rolled below them,
  And the moon was all their light.

Johann looked down, in a wild dream,
  On that remembered place :
O, like a ghost, he saw once more
The path that led to his own door,
A white thread, winding thro' the pines,
  And the tears ran down his face.

A ghost on guard among the dead
  With a heart running wild,
For the light of a little window-pane
And all the sorrow of earth again,
A crust of bread, a head on his breast,
  And the cry of his own child ;

The cup of cold water
  That Love would change to wine . . .
Sonia ! Dodi ! O, to creep back ! . . . .
There was a cry in the woods, the crack
Of a pistol, and a startled shout,
  Halt !   Give the counter-sign !

Then all the black unguarded woods
    Behind them spat red flame.
A thousand rifles shattered the night;
And, after the lightning, up the height,
A thousand steady shafts of light,
    The moonlit bayonets came.

Hurled to the trench by the storm of steel
    Under a heap of the slain,
Like one quick nerve in that welter of death,
Johann quivered, blood choked his breath,
And the charge broke over him like a sea,
    And passed like a hurricane.

He crept out in the ghastly moon
    By a black tarpaulined gun.
He stood alone on the moaning height
While the bayonets flashed behind the flight,
Sonia!   Dodi! . . . He turned.   He broke
    For the path, with a stumbling run.

Down by the little white moon-lit thread,
    He rushed thro' the ghostly wood,
A living man in a world of the dead,
    To the place where his own home stood.

For War had "trained" him, strengthened his heart
    To bear that glory agen:
And he was fitted to play his part
    At last, in a "world of men."

The embers of his hut still burned;
    And, in the deep blue gloom,
His bursting eyeballs yet could see
A white shape under the apple-tree,
A naked body, dabbled with red,
    Like a drift of apple-bloom.

She lay like a broken sacrament
    That the dogs have defiled,
Sonia! Sonia! Speak to me!
    He babbled like a child.

The child, the child that lay on her knees. . . .
    Devil nor man may name
The things that Europe must not print,
But only whisper and chuckle and hint,
Lest the soul of Europe rise in thunder
    And swords melt in the flame.

She bore the stigmata of sins
    That devil nor man may tell ;
For O, good taste, good taste, good taste,
    Constrains and serves us well ;
And the censored truth that dies on earth
    Is the crown of the lords of hell.

The quiet moon sailed slowly out
    From a grey cloud overhead,
When, out of the gnarled old apple-tree
There came a moan and, heavily
A patter of blood fell, gout by gout
    On the white breast of the dead.

There came a moan from the apple-tree,
    And the moon showed him there,—
The blind man with his arms stretched wide,
And a nail thro' his hand on either side,
A nail thro' the naked palms of his feet
    And a crown of thorns in his hair.

Johann knelt down before him,
    " *O brother, O Son of Man,*
It was not ours to doubt or reply
When the People were led out to die,
This, this is the end of our Liberty,
    And the goal for which we ran."

O, Christ of the little children. . . .
   Over his naked blade
Johann bowed, bowed and fell,
Gasping *Sonia, Dodi, tell*
Your God in heaven I grow so weary
   Of all that He has made.

Then, still as frost across the world
   The tender moonlight spread,
And, one by one, from the apple-tree
The drops of blood fell heavily,
And the blind man that was crucified
   Spake softly, to the dead.

" *Conquered, we shall conquer !*
   They have not hurt the soul.
For there is another Captain
   Whose legions round us roll,
Battling across the wastes of Death
   Till all be healed and whole.

Till, members of one Body,
   Our agony shall cease ;
Till, like a song thro' chaos,
   His marching worlds increase ;
Till the souls that sit in darkness
   Behold the Prince of Peace ;

Till the dead Cross break in blossom ;
   Till the God we sacrificed,
With that same love He gave us,
Stretch out His arms to save us,
Yea, till God save the People,
   And heal the wounds of Christ."

EPILOGUE.

THE DAWN OF PEACE.

YES—" on our brows we feel the breath
 Of dawn," though in the night we wait!
An arrow is in the heart of Death,
 A God is at the doors of Fate!
The Spirit that moved upon the Deep
 Is moving through the minds of men:
The nations feel it in their sleep.
 A change has touched their dreams again.

Voices, confused and faint, arise,
 Troubling their hearts from East and West.
A doubtful light is in their skies,
 A gleam that will not let them rest:
The dawn, the dawn is on the wing,
 The stir of change on every side,
Unsignalled as the approach of Spring,
 Invincible as the hawthorn-tide.

Have ye not heard, tho' darkness reigns,
 A People's voice across the gloom,
A distant thunder of rending chains,
 And nations rising from their tomb?
Then—if ye will—uplift your word
 Of cynic wisdom, till night fail,
Tell us He came to bring a sword,
 Spit poison in the Holy Grail.

Say that we dream !   Our dreams have woven
   Truths that out-face the burning sun :
The lightnings, that we dreamed, have cloven
   Time, space, and linked all lands in one !
Dreams !   But their swift celestial fingers
   Have knit the world with threads of steel,
Till no remotest island lingers
   Outside the world's great Commonweal.

Tell us that custom, sloth, and fear
   Are strong, then name them "common sense" !
Tell us that greed rules everywhere,
   Then dub the lie "experience" :
Year after year, age after age,
   Has handed down, thro' fool and child,
For earth's divinest heritage
   The dreams whereon old wisdom smiled.

Dreams are they ?   But ye cannot stay them,
   Or thrust the dawn back for one hour !
Truth, Love, and Justice, if ye slay them,
   Return with more than earthly power :
Strive, if ye will, to seal the fountains
   That send the Spring thro' leaf and spray :
Drive back the sun from the Eastern mountains,
   Then—bid this mightier movement stay.

It is the Dawn ! the Dawn !   The nations
   From East to West have heard a cry,—
"Though all earth's blood-red generations
   By hate and slaughter climbed thus high,
Here—on this height—still to aspire,
   One only path remains untrod,
One path of love and peace climbs higher.
   Make straight that highway for our God."

THE SEARCH-LIGHTS

AND OTHER POEMS.

_____

THE PRAYER FOR PEACE.

(WRITTEN AFTER THE ARBITRATION PROPOSALS OF PRESIDENT TAFT IN 1911.)

I.

DARE we—though our hope deferred
  Left us faithless long ago—
Dare we let our hearts be stirred,
  Lift them to the light and *know*,
Cast aside our cynic shields,
Break the sword that Mockery wields,
Know that Truth indeed prevails,
And that Justice holds the scales?
  Britain, kneel!
Kneel, imperial Commonweal!

II.

Dare we know that this great hour
  Dawning on thy long renown,
Marks the purpose of thy power,
  Crowns thee with a mightier crown,

Know that to this purpose climb
All the blood-red wars of Time?
If indeed thou *hast* a goal
Beaconing to thy warrior soul,
     Britain, kneel!
Kneel, imperial Commonweal!

III.

Dare we know what every age
   Writes with an unerring hand,
Read the midnight's moving page,
   Read the stars and understand,—
Out of Chaos ye shall draw,
Linkéd harmonies of Law,
Till, around the Eternal Sun,
All your peoples move in one?
     Britain, kneel!
Kneel, imperial Commonweal!

IV.

Dare we know that wearied eyes,
   Dimmed with dust of every day,
Can, once more, desire the skies
   And the glorious upward way?
Dare we, if the Truth should still
Vex with doubt our alien will,
Take it to our Maker's throne,
Let Him speak with us alone?
     Britain, kneel!
Kneel, imperial Commonweal!

V.

Dare we cast our pride away?
   Dare we tread where Lincoln trod?
All the Future by this day
   Waits to judge us and our God!

Set the struggling peoples free !
Crown with Law their liberty !
Proud with an immortal pride,
Kneel we at our Sister's side,
        Britain, kneel !
Kneel, imperial Commonweal !

THE SWORD OF ENGLAND.

(1912.)

Not as one muttering in a spell-bound sleep
    Shall England speak the word ;
Not idly bid the embattled lightnings leap,
    Nor lightly draw the sword.

Let despots grope by night in a blind dream :
    The cold clear morning star
Should like a trophy in her helmet gleam
    When England sweeps to war.

Not like a derelict, drunk with surf and spray,
    And drifting down to doom ;
But like the Sun-god calling up the day
    Should England rend that gloom.

Not as in trance, at some hypnotic call,
    Nor with a doubtful cry ;
But a clear faith, like a banner above us all,
    Rolling from sky to sky.

She sheds no blood to that vain god of strife
    Whom tonguesters call "renown" ;
She knows that only they who reverence life
    Can nobly lay it down ;

And these shall ride from life and home and love
    Through death and hell that day
But O, her faith, her flag, must burn above ;
    Her soul must lead the way.

THE HEART OF CANADA.

(July 1912.)

BECAUSE her heart is all too proud
  —*Canada ! Canada ! fair young Canada*—
To breathe the might of her love aloud,
  Be quick, O Motherland !
Because her soul is wholly free
  —*Canada kneels, thy daughter, Canada*—
England, look in her eyes and see,
  Honour and understand.

Because her pride at thy masthead shines,
  —*Canada ! Canada !*—queenly Canada
Bows with all her breathing pines,
  All her fragrant firs.
Because our isle is little and old
  —*Canada ! Canada !*—young-eyed Canada
Gives thee, Mother, her hands to hold,
  And makes thy glory hers.

Because thy Fleet is hers for aye,
  —*Canada ! Canada !*—clear-souled Canada,
Ere the war-cloud roll this way,
  Bids the world beware.
Her heart, her soul, her sword are thine
  —*Thine the guns, the guns of Canada !*—
The ships are foaming into line,
  And Canada will be there.

THE SEARCH-LIGHTS.

(1914.)

SHADOW by shadow, stripped for fight,
  The lean black cruisers search the sea.
Night-long their level shafts of light
  Revolve, and find no enemy.
Only they know each leaping wave
May hide the lightning, and their grave.

And in the land they guard so well
  Is there no silent watch to keep?
An age is dying, and the bell
  Rings midnight on a vaster deep.
But over all its waves, once more,
The search-lights move, from shore to shore.

And captains that we thought were dead,
  And dreamers that we thought were dumb,
And voices that we thought were fled,
  Arise, and call us, and we come;
And "search in thine own soul," they cry;
"For there, too, lurks thine enemy."

Search for the foe in thine own soul,
  The sloth, the intellectual pride;
The trivial jest that veils the goal
  For which our fathers lived and died;
The lawless dreams, the cynic Art,
That rend thy nobler self apart.

Not far, not far into the night,
   These level swords of light can pierce;
Yet for her faith does England fight,
   Her faith in this our universe;
Believing Truth and Justice draw
From founts of everlasting law;

Therefore a Power above the State,
   The unconquerable Power returns.
The fire, the fire that made her great
   Once more upon her altar burns.
Once more, redeemed and healed and whole,
She moves to the Eternal Goal.

THE RETURN OF THE HOME-BORN.

ALL along the white chalk coast
    The mist lifts clear.
Wight is glimmering like a ghost.
    The ship draws near.
Little inch-wide meadows
    Lost so many a day,
The first time I knew you
    Was when I turned away.

Island—little island—
    Lost so many a year,
Mother of all I leave behind
    —*Draw me near!*—
Mother of half the rolling world,
    And O, so little and gray,
The first time I found you
    Was when I turned away.

Over yon green water
    Sussex lies.
But the slow mists gather
    In our eyes.
England, little island
    —God, how dear!—
Fold me in your mighty arms,
    Draw me near.

Little tawny roofs of home,
    Nestling in the gray,
Where the smell of Sussex loam
    Blows across the bay . . .
Fold me, teach me, draw me close,
    Lest in death I say
The first time I loved you
    Was when I turned away.

THE BRINGERS OF GOOD NEWS.

LIKE fallen stars the watch-fires gleamed
   Along our menaced age that night!
Our bivouacked century tossed and dreamed
   Of battle with the approaching light.

Rumours of change, a sea-like roar,
   Shook the firm earth with doubt and dread:
The clouds, in rushing legions bore
   Their tattered eagles overhead.

I saw the muffled sentries rest
   On the dark hills of Time.   I saw
Around them march from East to West
   The stars of the unresting law.

I knew that in their mighty course
   They brought the dawn, they brought the day;
And that the unconquerable force
   Of the new years was on the way.

I heard the feet of that great throng!
   I saw them shine, like hope, afar!
Their shout, their shout was like a song,
   And O, 'twas not a song of war!

Yet, as the whole world with their tramp
   Quivered, a signal-lightning spoke,
A bugle warned our darkling camp,
   And, like a thunder-cloud, it woke.

Our search-lights raked the world's wide ends.
    O'er the dark hills a grey light crept.
Down, through the light, that host of friends
    We took for foemen, triumphing swept.

The old century could not hear their cry.
    How should it hear the song they sang?
We bring good news!   It pierced the sky!
    We bring good news!   The welkin rang.

One shout of triumph and of faith;
    And then—our shattering cannon roared!
But, over the reeking ranks of death,
    The song rose like a single sword.

We bring good news!   Red flared the guns!
    We bring good news!   The sabres flashed!
And the dark age with its own sons
    In blind and furious battle clashed.

A swift, a terrible bugle pealed.
    The sulphurous clouds were rolled away.
Embraced, embraced, on that red field,
    The wounded and the dying lay.

We bring good news!   Blood choked the word,
    —*We knew you not; so dark the night!*—
O father, was I worth your sword?
    O son, O herald of the light!

We bring good news!—The darkness fills
    Mine eyes!—Nay, the night ebbs away.
And over the everlasting hills
    The great new dawn led on the day.

THE TRUMPET-CALL.

I.

Trumpeter, sound the great recall!
    Swift, O swift, for the squadrons break,
The long lines waver, mazed in the gloom
        Hither and thither the blind host blunders!
Stand thou firm for a dead Man's sake,
    Firm where the ranks reel down to their doom,
        Stand thou firm in the midst of the thunders,
Stand where the steeds and the riders fall,
    Set the bronze to thy lips and sound
    A rally to ring the whole world round!
Trumpeter, rally us, rally us, rally us!
        Sound the great recall.

II.

Trumpeter, sound for the ancient heights!
Clouds of the earth-born battle cloak
    The heaven that our fathers held from of old;
        And we—shall we prate to their sons of the gain
In gold or bread?   Through yonder smoke
    The heights that never were won with gold
        Wait, still bright with their old red stain,
        For the thousand chariots of God again,
And the steel that swept thro' a hundred fights
    With the Ironsides, equal to life and death,
        The steel, the steel of their ancient faith!
Trumpeter, rally us, rally us, rally us!
        Sound for the sun-lit heights!

III.

Trumpeter, sound for the faith again !
Blind and deaf with the dust and the blood,
   Clashing together we know not whither
     The tides of the battle would have us advance.
Stand thou firm in the crimson flood,
   Send the lightning of thy great cry
    Through the thunders, athwart the storm,
   Sound till the trumpets of God reply
From the heights we have lost in the steadfast sky,
From the Strength we despised and rejected.   Then,
    Locking the ranks as they form and form,
     Lift us forward, banner and lance,
   Mailed in the faith of Cromwell's men,
     When from their burning hearts they hurled
     The gage of heaven against the world !
Trumpeter, rally us, rally us, rally us,
     Up to the heights again.

IV.

Trumpeter, sound for the last Crusade !
Sound for the fire of the red-cross kings,
   Sound for the passion, the splendour, the pity
    That swept the world for a dead Man's sake,
Sound, till the answering trumpet rings
   Clear from the heights of the holy City,
    Sound till the lions of England awake,
   Sound for the tomb that our lives have betrayed ;
    O'er broken shrine and abandoned wall,
    Trumpeter, sound the great recall,
Trumpeter, rally us, rally us, rally us ;
     Sound for the last Crusade !

v.

Trumpeter, sound for the splendour of God!
Sound the music whose name is law,
　　Whose service is perfect freedom still,
　　　The order august that rules the stars!
Bid the anarchs of night withdraw,
　　Too long the destroyers have worked their will,
　　　Sound for the last, the last of the wars!
Sound for the heights that our fathers trod,
　　　When truth was truth and love was love,
　　　With a hell beneath, but a heaven above,
Trumpeter, rally us, up to the heights of it!
　　　Sound for the City of God.

THE CRY IN THE NIGHT.

It tears at the heart in the night, that moan of the wind,
    That desolate moan,
It is worse than the cry of a child.   I can hardly bear
    To hear it, alone.

It is worse than the sobbing of love, when love is estranged ;
    For this is a cry
Out of the desolate ages.   It never has changed.
    It never can die.

A cry over numberless graves, dark, helpless and blind
    From the measureless past,
To the measureless future, a sobbing before the first
    laughter,
    And after the last !

.   .   .   .

From the height of creation, in passion eternal, the Word
    Rushes forth, the loud cry,
Forsaken ! Forsaken ! It cuts through the night like a
    sword !
    Shall it win no reply ?

Not of earth is that height of all sorrow, past time, out
    of space,
    Therefore here, here and now,
Universal, a Calvary, crowned with Thy passionate face,
    Thy thorn-wounded brow.

Ah, could I shrink if Thy heart for each heart upon earth
     Must break like a sea?
Could I hear, could I bear it at all, if I were not a part
     Of this labour in Thee?

Shall I accuse Thee, then? God, I account it my own
     All the grief I can bear,
On Thy Cross of Creation, to balance earth's bliss and
  atone,
     Atone for life there.

If this be the One Way for ever, which not Thine all-might
     Could change, if it would,
Till the truth be untrue, till the dark be the same as the
  light,
     And till evil be good,

Shall I who took part in thine April, shrink now from my
  part
     In thine anguish to be?
If Thy goal be the One goal of all, shall not even man's
  heart
     Endure this, with Thee;

Die with Thee, balancing life, or help Thee to pay
     For our hope with our pain? . . .
O, the voice of the wind in the night! Is it day, then,
  broad day,
     On the blind earth again?

THRICE-ARMED.

Thus only should it come, if come it must,—
   Not with a riot of flags and a mob-born cry,
   But with a noble faith, a conscience high
That, if we fail, we failed not in our trust.
We fought for peace. We dared the bitter thrust
   Of calumny for peace, and watched her die,
   Her scutcheons rent from sky to outraged sky
By felon hands and trampled into the dust.

We proffered justice, and we saw the law
   Cancelled by stroke on stroke of those deft hands
      Which still retain the imperial forger's pen.
They must have blood—Then, at this last, we draw
   The sword, not with a riot of flags and bands,
      But silence, and a mustering of men.

They challenge Truth.   An Empire makes reply,
   East, West, North, South, one honour and one might,
   From sea to sea, from height to war-worn height,
The old word rings out—to conquer or to die.
And we shall conquer!   Though their eagles fly
   Through heaven, around this ancient isle unite
   Powers that were never vanquished in the fight,
The unconquerable Powers that cannot lie.

Though fire destroy her flesh, and many a year
   This land forgot the faith that made her great,
      Now, as her fleets cast off the North Sea foam,
Casting aside all faction and all fear,
   Thrice-armed in all the majesty of her fate,
      Britain remembers, and her sword strikes home.

FORWARD.

"A THOUSAND creeds and battle-cries,
　A thousand warring social schemes,
A thousand new moralities,
　And twenty thousand thousand dreams;

"Each on his own anarchic way,
　From the old order breaking free,
Our ruined world desires," you say,
　"Licence once more, not Liberty."

But ah, beneath the wind-whipt foam
　When storm and change are on the deep,
How quietly the tides come home,
　And how the depths of sea-shine sleep.

And we that march towards a goal,
　Destroying, only to fulfil
The law, the law of that great soul
　Which moves beneath your alien will;

We, that like foemen meet the past
　Because we bring the future, know
We only fight to achieve at last
　A great re-union with our foe;

Re-union in the truths that stand
　When all our wars are rolled away;
Re-union of the heart and hand
　And of the prayers wherewith we pray;

Re-union in the common needs,
  The common strivings of mankind ;
Re-union of our warring creeds
  In the one God that dwells behind.

Then—in that day—we shall not meet
  Wrong with new wrong, but right with right ;
Our faith shall make your faith complete
  When our battalions re-unite.

Forward !—what use in idle words ?—
  Forward, O warriors of the soul !
There will be breaking up of swords
  When that new morning makes us whole.

THE REPEAL.

I DREAMED the Eternal had repealed
  His cosmic code of law last night.
Our prayers had made the Unchanging yield.
  Caprice was king from depth to height.

On Beachy Head a shouting throng
  Had fired a beacon to proclaim
Their licence.   With unmeasured song
  They proved it, dancing in the flame.

They quarrelled.   One desired the sun,
  And one desired the stars to shine.
They closed and wrestled and burned as one,
  And the white chalk grew red as wine.

The furnace licked and purred and rolled,
  A laughing child held up its hands
Like dreadful torches, dropping gold ;
  For pain was dead at their commands.

Painless and wild as clouds they burned,
  Till the restricted Rose of Day
With all its glorious laws returned,
  And the wind blew their ashes away.

THE TRUMPET OF THE LAW.

(PHI BETA KAPPA POEM, READ AT HARVARD
UNIVERSITY, 1915.)

MUSIC is dead. An age, an age is dying!
Shreds of Uranian song, wild symphonies
Tortured by moans of butchered innocents,
Blow past us on the wind. Chaos resumes
His kingdom. All the visions of the world,
The visions that were music, being shaped
By law, moving in measure, treading the road
That suns and systems tread, O who can hear
Their music now? Urania bows her head.

Only the feet that move in order dance,
Only the mind attuned to that dread pulse
Of law, throughout the universe, can sing.
Only the soul that plays its rhythmic part
In that great measure of the tides and suns
Terrestrial and celestial, till it soar
Into the supreme melodies of heaven,
Only that soul, climbing the splendid road
Of law, from height to height, may walk with God,
Shape its own sphere from chaos, conquer death,
Lay hold on life and liberty, and sing.

Yet, since at least, the fleshly heart must beat
In measure, and no new rebellion breaks
That old restriction, murmurs reach it still,
Rumours of that vast music which resolves

Our discords, and to this, to this attuned,
Though blindly, it responds, in notes like these :

There was a song in heaven of old,
    A song the choral seven began,
When God with all His chariots rolled
    The tides of chaos back for man,
When suns revolved and planets wheeled,
    And the great oceans ebbed and flowed,
There is one way of life, it pealed,
    The road of law, the unchanging road.

The Trumpet of the Law resounds
    And we behold, from depth to height,
What glittering sentries walk their rounds,
    What ordered hosts patrol the night,
While wheeling worlds proclaim to us,
    Captained by Thee, thro' nights unknown,—
Glory that would be glorious
    Must keep Thy law to find its own.

Beyond rebellion, past caprice,
    From heavens that comprehend all change,
All space, all time, till time shall cease,
    The Trumpet rings to souls that range,
To souls that in wild dreams annul
    Thy word, confessed by wood and stone,—
Beauty that would be beautiful
    Must keep Thy law to find its own.

He that can shake it, will he thrust
    His careless hands into the fire?
He that would break it, shall we trust
    The sun to rise at his desire?
Constant above our discontent,
    The Trumpet peals in sterner tone,—
Might that would be omnipotent
    Must keep Thy law to find its own.

Ah, though beneath unpitying spheres
   Unreckoned seems our human cry,
In Thy deep law, beyond the years,
   Abides the Eternal memory.
Thy law is light, to eyes grown dull
   Dreaming of worlds like bubbles blown;
And Mercy that is merciful
   Shall keep Thy law and find its own.

Unchanging God, by that one Light
   Through which we grope to Truth and Thee,
Confound not yet our day with night,
   Break not the measures of Thy sea.
Hear not, though grief for chaos cry
   Or rail at Thine unanswering throne
Thy law, Thy law, is Liberty
   And, in Thy law we find our own.

So, to Uranian music, rose our world.
The boughs put forth, the young leaves groped for light.
The wild flower spread its petals as in prayer.
Then, for terrestrial ears, vast discords rose,—
The struggle in the jungle, clashing themes
That strove for mastery; but, above them all,
Ever the mightier measure of the suns
Resolved them into broader harmonies,
That fought again for mastery.   The night
Buried the mastodon.   The warring tribes
Of men were merged in nations.   Wider laws
Embraced them.   Man no longer fought with man,
Though nation warred with nation.   Hatred fell
Before the gaze of love.   For in an hour
When, by the law of might, mankind could rise
No higher, into the deepening music stole,
A loftier theme, a law that gathered all
The laws of earth into its broadening breast
And moved like one full river to the sea,
The law of Love.   The sun stood dark at noon;

Dark as the moon before this mightier power,
And a Voice rang across the blood-stained earth,
I am the Way, the Truth, the Life, the Light.

We heard it, and we did not hear.   In dreams
We caught a thousand fragments of the strain,
But never wholly heard it.   We moved on,
Obeying it a little, till our world
Became so vast, that we could only hear
Stray notes, a golden phrase, a sorrowful cry,
Never the rounded glory of the whole.
So one would sing of death, one of despair,
And one, knowing that God was more than man,
Knowing that the Eternal Power, behind
Our universe, was more than man, would shrink
From crowning Him with human attributes,
And so bereft Him of the highest we knew,
Love, justice, thought, and personality,
And made Him less than man ; made Him a blind
Unweeting force, less than the best in man,
Less than the best that He Himself had made.

Yet though from earth we could no longer hear,
As from a central throne, the harmonies
Of the revolving whole ; yet though from earth
And from earth's Calvary the central scene
Withdrew to dreadful depths beyond our ken—
Withdrew to some deep Calvary at the heart
Of all creation ; yet, O yet, we heard
Hints of that awful music from afar,
Echoes that murmured from eternity,
I am the Way, the Truth, the Life, the Light!

And still the eternal passion undiscerned
Moved like a purple shadow through our world ;
While we, in intellectual chaos, raised
The ancient cry, *Not this man, but Barabbas!*
Then Might grew Right once more, for who could hold

The Right, when the rebellious hearts of men,
Finding the Law too hard in life and thought
And art, proclaimed that right was born of chance,
Born out of nothingness and doomed at last
To nothingness; while all that men have held
Better than dust—love, honour, justice, truth—
Was less than dust, for the blind dust endures;
But love, they said, and the proud soul of man,
Die with the breath, before the flesh decays.
And still, amidst the chaos, Love was born
Suffered and died; and in a myriad forms,
A myriad parables of the Eternal Christ
Unfolded their deep message to mankind.
So, on this last wild winter of His birth,
Though cannon rocked His cradle, heaven might hear,
Once more, the Mother and her infant child.

Will the Five Clock-Towers chime to night?
    —Child, the red earth would shake with scorn.—
But will the Emperors laugh outright
    If Roland rings that Christ is born?—

No belfries pealed for that pure birth.
    There were no high-stalled choirs to sing.
The blood of children smoked on earth;
    For Herod, in those days, was king.—

O, then the Mother and her Son
    Were refugees that Christmas, too?—
Through all the ages, little one,
    That strange old story still comes true.—

Was there no peace in Bethlehem?—
    Yes. There was Love in one poor inn;
And, while His wings were over them,
    They heard those deeper songs begin.—

What songs were they?   What songs were they?
  Did stars of shrapnel shed their light?—
O, little child, I have lost the way,
  I cannot find that inn to-night.—

Is there no peace, then, anywhere?—
  Perhaps, where some poor soldier lies
With all his wounds in front, out there.—
  *You weep?—*He had your innocent eyes.—

Then is it true that Christ's a slave,
  Whom all these wrongs can never rouse?—
They said it.   But His anger drave
  The money-changers from His House.—

Yet He forgave and turned away.—
  Yes, unto seventy times and seven.
But they forget.   He comes one day
  In power, among the clouds of heaven.—

*The Roland rings?—*Yes, little son,
  With iron hammers they dare not scorn.
Roland is breaking them, gun by gun.
  Roland is ringing.   Christ is born.

Born and re-born; for though the Christ we knew
On earth be dead for ever, who shall kill
The Eternal Christ whose law is in our hearts,
Christ, who in this dark hour descends to hell,
And ascends into heaven, and sits beside
The right hand of the Father.   If for men
His law be dead, it lives for childen still,
Children whom men have butchered see His face,
Rest in his arms, and strike our mockery dumb.
So shall the Trumpet of the Law resound
Through all the ages, telling of that child
Whose outstretched arms in Belgium speak for God.

They crucified a Man of old,
  The thorns are shrivelled on His brow.
Prophet or fool or God, behold,
  They crucify Thy children now!
They doubted evil, doubted good,
  And the eternal heavens as well.
Behold, the iron and the blood,
  The visible handiwork of Hell.

Fast to the cross they found it there,
  They found it in the village street,—
A naked child, with sun-kissed hair,
  The nails were through its hands and feet.
For Christ was dead, yes, Christ was dead!
  O Lamb of God, O, little one,
I kneel before your cross instead,
  And the same shadow veils the sun. . . .

And the same shadow veils the sun.

A
BELGIAN CHRISTMAS EVE.

DEDICATION.

THOU whose deep ways are in the sea,
    Whose footsteps are not known,
To-night a world that turned from Thee
    Is waiting—at Thy Throne.

The towering Babels that we raised
    Where scoffing sophists brawl,
The little Antichrists we praised—
    The night is on them all.

The fool hath said . . . The fool hath said . . .
    And we, who deemed him wise,
We, who believed that Thou wast dead,
    How should we seek Thine eyes?

How should we seek to Thee for power,
    Who scorned Thee yesterday?
How should we kneel in this dread hour?
    Lord, teach us how to pray.

Grant us the single heart once more
    That mocks no sacred thing,
The Sword of Truth our fathers wore
    When Thou wast Lord and King.

Let darkness unto darkness tell
    Our deep unspoken prayer;
For, while our souls in darkness dwell,
    We know that Thou art there.

PRELUDE.

UNDER which banner? It was night
   Beyond all nights that ever were.
The Cross was broken. Blood-stained Might
   Moved like a tiger from its lair,
And all that heaven had died to quell
Awoke, and mingled earth with hell.

For Europe, if it held a creed,
   Held it thro' custom, not thro' faith.
Chaos returned in dream and deed,
   Right was a legend—Love, a wraith;
And That from which the world began
Was less than even the best in man.

God in the image of a snake
   Dethroned that dream, too fond, too blind,
The man-shaped God whose heart could break,
   Live, die, and triumph with mankind;
A Super-snake, a Juggernaut,
Dethroned the Highest of human thought.

Choose, England! For the eternal foe
   Within thee, as without, grew strong,
By many a super-subtle blow
   Blurring the lines of right and wrong
In Art and Thought, till nought seemed true
But that soul-slaughtering cry of *New!*

New wreckage of the shrines we made
   Thro' centuries of forgotten tears. . . .
We knew not where their hands had laid
   Our Master.   Twice a thousand years
Had dulled the uncapricious sun.
Manifold worlds obscured the One;

Obscured the reign of Law, our stay,
   Our compass thro' the uncharted sea,
The one sure light, the one sure way,
   The one firm base of Liberty;
The one firm road that men have trod
Thro' Chaos to the Throne of God.

Choose ye!   A hundred legions cried
   Dishonour, or the instant sword!
Ye chose.   Ye met that blood-stained tide.
   A little kingdom kept its word;
And, dying, cried across the night,
Hear us, O earth, We chose the Right.

Whose is the victory?   Though ye stood
   Alone against the unmeasured foe,
By all the tears, by all the blood,
   That flowed, and have not ceased to flow,
By all the legions that ye hurled
Back thro' the thunder-shaken world;

By the old that have not where to rest,
   By lands laid waste and hearths defiled,
By every lacerated breast,
   And every mutilated child,
Whose is the victory?   Answer, ye
Who, dying, smiled at tyranny:—

Under the sky's triumphal arch
*   The glories of the dawn begin.*
Our dead, our shadowy armies, march
*   E'en now, in silence, thro' Berlin—*
Dumb shadows, tattered blood-stained ghosts,
But cast by what swift following hosts!

And answer, England!   At thy side,
*   Thro' seas of blood, thro' mists of tears,*
Thou that for Liberty hast died
*   And livest, to the end of years.*
And answer, earth!   Far off, I hear
The pæans of a happier sphere:—

The trumpet blown at Marathon
*   Exulted over earth and sea:*
But burning angel lips have blown
*   The trumpets of thy Liberty,*
For who, beside thy dead, could deem
The faith, for which they died, a dream?

Earth has not been the same since then,
*   Europe from thee received a soul,*
Whence nations moved in law, like men,
*   As members of a mightier whole,*
Till wars were ended. . . .   In that day,
So shall our children's children say.

A BELGIAN CHRISTMAS EVE.

CHARACTERS.

RADA, wife of the village doctor.
BETTINE, her daughter, aged twelve.
BRANDER ⎫ German soldiers quar-
TARRASCH ⎭ tered in her house during the occupation of the village.

NANKO, an old, half-witted schoolmaster, living in the care of the doctor. He has a delusion that it is always Christmas Eve.
German soldiers.

The action takes place in a Belgian village, during the War of 1914. The scene is a room in the doctor's house. On the right there is a door opening to the street, a window with red curtains, and a desk under the window. On the left there is a large cupboard with a door on either side of it, one leading to a bedroom and the other to the kitchen. At the back an open fire is burning brightly. Over the fireplace there is a reproduction in colours of the Dresden Madonna. The room is lit only by the firelight and two candles in brass candlesticks, on a black oak table, at which the two soldiers are seated, playing cards and drinking beer.

RADA, *a dark handsome woman, sits on a couch to the left of the fire, with her head bowed in her hands, weeping.*

NANKO *sits cross-legged on a rug before the fire, rubbing his hands, snapping his fingers, and chuckling to himself.*

Tarrasch [*throwing down the cards*]. Pish! You have all the luck. [*He turns to* RADA.] Look here, my girl, where is the use of snivelling? We've been killing pigs all day and now we want to unbuckle a bit. You ought to think yourself infernally lucky to be alive at all, and I'm not sure that you will be so fortunate when the other boys come back. Wheedled them out of the house finely, didn't you? On a fine wildgoose chase, too. Hidden money! Refugees don't bury their money and leave the secret behind them. You've been whimpering ever since we two refused to believe you. What's your game, eh? I warn you there'll be hell to pay when they come back.

Rada [*sobbing and burying her face*]. God, be pitiful!

Tarrasch. This is war, this is! And you can't expect war to be all swans and shining armour. No—nor smart uniforms either. Look at the mud my friend and I have already annexed from Belgium. Brander, you know it's a most astonishing fact; but I have remarked it several times. Those women whose eyes glitter at the sight of a spiked helmet are the first to be astonished by the realities of war. They expect the dead to jump up and kiss them and tell them it is all a game, as soon as the battle is ended. No, no, my dear; it's only in war that one sees how small is one's personal happiness in comparison with greater things.

[*He fills a glass and drinks.* BRANDER *lights a cigar.*

Nanko. Exactly. In times of peace we forget those eternal silences. We value life too highly. We become domesticated. Why, I suppose in this magnificent war there have been so many women and children killed that they would fill the great Cloth Hall at Ypres; and, as for the young men, there have been so many slaughtered that their dead bodies would fill St Peter's at Rome. Why, I suppose they would fill the three hundred abbeys of Flanders and all the cathedrals in the world chock-full from floor to belfry, wouldn't they? How Goya would have loved to paint them! Can't you see it?

[*He grows ecstatic over the idea.*

Tournai with its five clock-towers, Ghent, and Bruges,
Louvain and Antwerp, Rheims and Westminster,
Under the round white moon, on Christmas Eve,
With towers of frozen needlework and spires
That point to God; but all their painted panes
Bursting with dreadful arms and gaping faces,

Gargoyles of flesh; and round them, in the snow,
The little cardinals, like gouts of blood,
The little bishops, running like white mice,
Hooded with violet spots, quite, quite dismayed
To find there was no room for them within
Upon that holy night when Christ was born.

But perhaps if Goya were living to-day he would prefer
to pack them into Chicago meat factories, with the intellectuals dancing outside like marionettes, and the uncon-
scious Hand of God pulling the strings. You know one
of their very latest theories is that He is a somnambulist.

Tarrasch [*to* RADA]. You should read Schopenhauer,
my dear, and learn to estimate these emotions at their true
value. You would then be able to laugh at these feelings
which seem to you now so important. It is the mark of
Kultur to be able to laugh at all sentiments.

Nanko. The priests, I suppose, are still balancing themselves on the tight-rope, over the jaws of the crowd. The
poor old Pope did his best for his Master, when the
Emperor asked him for a blessing on his arms. "*I* bless
Peace," said the Pope; but nobody listened. I composed
a little poem about that. I called it St Peter's Christmas.
It went like this :—

And does the Cross of Christ still stand?
    Yes, though His friends may watch from far—
And who is this at His right hand,
    This Rock in the red surf of war?

This, this is he who once denied
    And turned and wept and turned again.
Last night before an Emperor's pride
    He stood and blotted out that stain.

Last night an Emperor bared the sword
    And bade him bless. He stood alone.
Alone in all the world, *his* word
    Confessed—and blessed—a loftier throne.

I hear, still travelling towards the Light,
    In widening waves till Time shall cease,
The Power that breathed from Rome last night
    His infinite whisper—*I bless Peace.*

[TARRASCH *and* BRANDER *applaud ironically.*

Tarrasch. Excellent! Excellent! [*To* RADA.] You should have seen our brave soldiers laughing—do you remember, Brander—at a little village near Termonde. They made the old doctor and his cook dance naked round the dead body of his wife, who had connived at the escape of her daughter from a Prussian officer.

Nanko. Ah, that was reality, wasn't it? None of your provincial respectability about that, none of your shallow conventionality! That's what the age wants—realism!

Tarrasch. It was brutal, I confess; but better than British hypocrisy, eh? There was something great about it, like the neighing of the satyrs in the Venusberg music.

Rada [*sinking on her knees by the couch and sobbing*]. God! God!

Tarrasch. They were beginning to find out the provincialism of their creeds in England. The pessimism of Schopenhauer had taught them much; and if it had not been for this last treachery, this last ridiculous outburst of the middle-class mind on behalf of what they call honour, we should have continued to tolerate (if not to enjoy), in Berlin, those plays by Irishmen which expose so wittily the inferior *Kultur*, the shrinking from reality, of their (for the most part) not intellectual people. I have the honour, madam, to request that you should no longer make this unpleasant sound of weeping. You irritate my nerves. Have you not two men quartered upon you instead of one? And are they not university students? If your husband and the rest of the villagers had not resisted our advance, they might have been alive, too. In any case, your change is for the better.

[*He lights a cigar.*

Nanko. Exactly! Exactly! You remember, Rada, I

used to be a schoolmaster myself in the old days; and if *you* knew what *I* know, you wouldn't cry, my dear. You'd understand that it's entirely a question of the survival of the fittest. A biological necessity, that's what it is. And Haeckel himself has told us that, though we may resign our hopes of immortality, and the grave is the only future for our beloved ones, yet there is infinite consolation to be found in examining a piece of moss or looking at a beetle. That's what the Germans call the male intellect.

Tarrasch. Is this man attempting to be insolent?

[*He rises as if to strike* NANKO.

Brander [*tapping his forehead*]. Take no notice of him. He's only a resident patient. He was not calling you a beetle. He has delusions. He thinks it is always Christmas Eve. That's his little tree in the corner. As Goethe should have said—

> There was a little Christian.
> He had a little tree.
> Up came a Superman
> And cracked him, like a flea.

Tarrasch [*laughing*]. Very good! You should send that to the 'Tageblatt,' Brander.

Well, Rada, or whatever your name is, you'd better find something for us to eat. I'm sick of this whimpering. Wouldn't your Belgian swine have massacred us all, if we'd given them the chance? We've thousands of women and children at home snivelling and saying, "Oh! my God! Oh! my God!" just like you.

Rada [*rising to her feet in sudden anger*]. Then why are you in Belgium, gentlemen?
Is it the husks and chaff that the swine eat,
Or is it simply butchery?

[*They stare at her in silence, overmastered for a moment by her passion. Then, her grief welling up again, she casts herself down on the couch, and buries her face in her hands, sobbing.*

God! God! God!

Brander. Don't you trouble about God. What can *He* do when both sides go down on their marrow-bones? He can't make both sides win, can He?

Nanko. That's how the intellectuals prove He doesn't exist. Either He is not almighty, they say, or else He is unjust enough not to make both sides win. But all those anthropomorphic conceptions are out of date now, even in England, as this gentleman very truly said. You see, it was so degrading, Rada, to think that God had anything in common with mankind (though love was once quite fashionable), and as we didn't know of anything higher than ourselves we were simply compelled to say that He resembled something lower, such as earthquakes, and tigers, and puppet-shows, and ideas of that sort. Reality above all things! You may see God in sunsets; but there was nothing *real* about the *best* qualities of mankind. It's curious. The more intellectual and original you are, the lower you have to go, and the more likely you are to end in the old dance of charlatans and beasts. I suppose that's an argument for tradition and growth. If we call it Evolution, nobody will mind very much.

Rada [*wringing her hands in an agony of grief*]. Oh, God, be pitiful, be pitiful!

Brander [*standing in front of her*]. Look here, we've had enough of this music. I've been watching you, and there's more upon your mind than sorrow for the dead. Why were you so anxious to wheedle us all out of the house? Tarrasch has warned you there'll be hell to pay when the others come back. What was the game, eh? You'd better tell me. You couldn't have thought you were going to escape through our lines to-night.

[*There is a sudden uproar outside, and a woman's scream, followed by the terrified cry of a child.*

Ah! Ah! Father!

Brander. Hear that. The men are mad with brandy and blood and——other things. There's no holding them in, even from the children. You needn't wince. Even from the children, I say. What chance would there be for a fine-looking wench like yourself?

No, you were not going to try that. You've something to hide, here, in the house, eh? Well, now you've got rid of the others, and we've had a drink, we're going to look for it. What is there? [*He points to the bedroom door.*

Rada [*rising to her feet slowly, steadying herself with one hand on the couch and fixing her eyes on his face*]. My bedroom. No. I've nothing here to hide. This is war, isn't it? If I choose to revenge myself on those that have used me badly, people that I hate, by telling you where you can find what everybody wants, money, money—I suppose you want that—isn't that good enough?

Brander. Better come with us, then, and show us this treasure-trove.

Rada [*shrinking back*]. No, no, I dare not. All those dead out there would terrify me, terrify me!

Tarrasch. A pack of lies! What were you up to, eh? Telephoning to the English?

Brander. It has been too much for her nerves. Don't worry her, or she'll go mad. Then there'll be nobody left to get us our supper.

[TARRASCH *wanders round the room, opening drawers and examining letters and other contents at the desk.*

Nanko. That *would* be selfish, Rada. You know it's Christmas Eve. Nobody ought to think of unpleasant things on Christmas Eve. What have you done with the Christmas-tree, Rada?

Brander. And who's to blame? That's what I want to know. You don't blame *us*, do you? We didn't know where we were marching a month ago; and possibly we shall be fighting on your side against somebody else, a year hence.

Nanko. Of course they didn't know! Poor soldiers don't.

Tarrasch [*who has been trying the bedroom door*]. In the meantime, what have you got behind that door? Give me the key.

Rada [*hurriedly, and as if misunderstanding him, opens the cupboard. She speaks excitedly*]. Food! Food! Food for hungry men. Food enough for a wolf pack. Come on, help yourselves!

Tarrasch. Look, Brander! What a larder! Here's a dinner for forty men. Isn't it?

Rada. Better take your pick before the others come.

> [*She thrusts dishes into* BRANDER'S *hands and loads* TARRASCH *with bottles. They lay the table with them,* RADA *seeming to share their eagerness.*

Brander [*looking at his hands*]. Here! Bring me a basin of warm water. There are times when you can't touch food without washing your hands.

> [RADA *hesitates, then goes into the kitchen.*
> BRANDER *holds out a ring to* TARRASCH.

Her husband's ring. I got it off his finger
When he went down. He lay there, doubled up,
With one of those hideous belly wounds. He begged,
Horribly, for a bullet; so, poor devil,
I put him out of his misery. I can't eat
With hands like that. Ugh! Look!

Nanko [*rising and peering at them*]. Ah, but they're red.
Red, aren't they? And there's red on your coat, too.

> [*He fingers it curiously.*

I suppose that's blood, eh? People are such cowards.
Many of them never seem to understand
That man's a fighting animal. They're afraid,
Dreadfully afraid, of the sight of blood.
I think it's a beautiful colour, beautiful!
You know, in the Old Testament, they used
To splash it on the door-posts.

Brander [*pushing him away*]. Go and sit down,
You crazy old devil!

> [RADA *enters with a bowl of water, sets it on a chair, and returns to the couch.* BRANDER *washes his hands.*

Tarrasch.   My hands want washing, too.

My God, you've turned the water into wine.
Get me some fresh.

> [RADA *approaches, stares at the bowl, and moves*
> *back, swaying a little.*

 Brander [*roughly*]. I'll empty it. Give it to me.

> [*He goes out.*

 Nanko. The Old Testament, you know, is full of it.
Who is this, it says, *that cometh from Edom*,
In dyed garments from Bozrah? It was blood
That dyed their garments. And in *Revelations*
Blood came out of the wine-press, till it splashed
The bridles of the horses; and the seas
Were all turned into blood. Doesn't that show
That man's a fighting animal?

 Tarrasch [*again fumbling at the bedroom door*]. Give me
  the key.

 Rada [*thrusting herself between him and the door*]. That
  is my bedroom. You must not go in.

 Tarrasch. Are they so modest, then, in Belgium, madam?
You're fooling us. What is it? Loot? More loot?
The family stocking, eh?

> [BRANDER *enters. He goes to the table and*
> *begins eating.*

 Nanko.   The stocking? No!
The stocking is in the chimney-corner, see.

> [*He shakes an empty stocking that hangs in the*
> *fireplace.*

Bettine and I, we always hang it up
Ready for Santa Claus. It's a good custom.
They do it in Germany. The children there
Believe that Santa Claus comes down the chimney.

 Tarrasch. If I know anything of women's eyes,
It's either money, or a daughter, Rada.
And so—the key! Or else I burst the door.

 Rada [*looks at him for a moment before speaking*]. I
  throw myself upon your mercy, then.
It *is* my little girl. She is twelve years old.
Don't wake her. She has slept all through this night.

I thought I might have hidden her. It's too late.
It's of the other men that I'm afraid,
Not you. But they are drunk. If they come back. . . .
Help me to save her! I'll do anything for you,
Anything! Only help me to get her away!
I'll pray for you every night of my life. I'll pray. . . .

      [*She stretches out her hands pitifully and begins to*
          weep. The men stand staring at her. The
          door opens behind her, and BETTINE, *in her*
          night-dress, steals into the room.

Bettine. Mother—— Oh!

          [*She stops at sight of the strangers.*

Brander. Don't be afraid. I'm Nanko's friend.
What? Don't you know me? I came down the chimney.

Bettine. I don't see any soot upon your face.

          [*She goes nearer.*

Nor on your clothes. That's red paint, isn't it?

Brander. Can't help it. Santa Claus—that is my name.
What's yours?

Bettine.   Bettine.

Brander.   Ah! I've a little girl
At home—about your age, too—called Bettine.

Bettine [*who has been watching him curiously*]. I know.
      You are the British. Mother said
The British would be here before the Boches.
I dreamed that you were coming, and I thought
I heard the marching. Weren't you singing, too?
It made me feel so happy in my sleep.
What were you singing? "It's a long, long way
To——" what d'you call it? *Tipperary?* eh?
What does that mean?

Brander.   A place a long way off.

Bettine. As far as heaven?

Brander.   Almost as far as—home.

Bettine. Well, I suppose it means the Boches must march
A long, long way before they reach it, eh?
There's Canada. They'll have to march through that.
Then India, and that's huge. Why, Nanko says

There are three hundred million people there,
And all their soldiers ride on elephants.
Poor Boches! I'm sorry for them. Nanko says
They're trying to ride across two thousand years
In motor-cars. It's easy enough to ride
Two thousand miles; but not two thousand years.

        [*She runs to the stocking and examines it.*
          TARRASCH *and* BRANDER *return to the table*
          and eat and drink.

There's nothing in the stocking. Never mind,
Nanko, when Christmas really comes, you'll see.

        [*With a sudden note of fear in her voice.*
Mother, where's father?

   Rada [*putting an arm round her*]. He will soon be
     with us.

It's all right, darling.

   Bettine.   Mother, mayn't we try
The new tunes on the gramophone?

   Nanko.   Now, wait!
I've an idea. It's Christmas Eve, you know.
We'll celebrate it. Where's the Christmas-tree?
We'll get that ready first.

        [BETTINE *pulls the little Christmas-tree out from*
          the corner. RADA *glances from the child to the*
          men, as if hoping that her play will win them
          to help her.

   Bettine.   It's nearly a week,
Isn't it, Nanko, since you had your tree?

   Brander. Here, put it on the table.

   Nanko [*clapping his hands*].   Yes, that's best.
I fear that we shall want a new tree, soon.
This one is withered. See how the needles drop.
There's no green left. It's growing old, Bettine.
What shall we hang on it?

   Tarrasch.   What d' you think
Of that now?   [*He hangs his revolver on the tree.*

   Bettine [*laughing merrily*]. Oh! Oh! What a great
     big pistol!

That'll be father's present !   And now what else ?

    Nanko [*eagerly*]. What else ?

    Brander. Well, what do you say to a ring, Bettine ?

How prettily it hangs upon the bough !

Isn't that fine ?   [*He hangs the ring upon the tree.*

    Bettine [*staring at it*]. It's just like father's ring !

    Tarrasch. Now light the little candles.

    Nanko [*clapping his hands and capering*]. Yes, that's

        right !

Light all the little candles on the tree !

Oh, doesn't the pistol shine, doesn't the ring

Glitter !

    Bettine. But, oh, it *is* like father's ring.

He had a little piece of mother's hair

Plaited inside it, just like that.   It *is*

My father's ring !

    Rada.   No ; there are many others,

Bettine, just like it—hundreds, hundreds of others.

    Brander. And now—what's in that package over there ?

    Bettine. Oh, that's the new tunes for the gramophone.

That's father's Christmas present to us all.

    Nanko. Now, what a wonderful man the doctor was !

Nobody else, in these parts, would have thought

Of buying a gramophone.   Let's open it.

    Bettine. Yes !   Yes !   And we'll give father a surprise !

It shall be playing a tune when he comes in !

He won't be angry, will he, mumsy dear ?

        [BRANDER *opens the package.* NANKO *rubs his*

            hands in delight.   They get the gramophone

            ready.

    Nanko. Oh, this will be a merry Christmas Eve.

There now—just see how this kind gentleman

Has opened the package for us.   Now you see

The good of war.   It makes a man efficient,

Sets a man up.   Look at old Peter's legs ;

He's a disgrace to the village, a disgrace !

Nobody shoots him either, so he spoils

Everything ; for you know, you must admit,

Bettine, that war means natural selection—
Survival of the fittest, don't you see?
For instance, *I* survive, and *you* survive:
Don't we?   So Peter shouldn't spoil it all.
They say that all the tall young men in France
Were killed in the Napoleonic wars,
So that most Frenchmen at the present day
Are short and fat.   Isn't that funny, Bettine?

                                        [She laughs.
Which shows us that tall men are not required
To-day   So nobody knows.   Perhaps thin legs
Like Peter's *may* be useful, after all,
In aeroplanes, or something   Every ounce
Makes a great difference there.   Nobody knows.
It's natural selection   See, Bettine?
Ah, now the gramophone's ready   Make it play
A Christmas tune.   That's what the churches do
On Christmas Eve: for all the churches now,
And all the tall cathedrals with their choirs,
What do you think they are, Bettine?   I'll tell you.
I'll whisper it.   *They're great big gramophones!*

                                        [She laughs.
Now for a Christmas tune!

    Tarrasch [adjusting a record]. There's irony
In your idea, my friend, that would delight
The ghost of Nietzsche!   Certainly, it shall play
A Christmas tune.   Here is the very thing.

        *[There is an uproar of drunken shouts in the
            distance.* BRANDER *locks the outer door.*
    Bettine. The inn is full of drunken men to-night,
Mother.   D' you hear them?   Mother, was it an inn
Like that—the one that's in my Christmas piece?

    Brander [to TARRASCH*].* Don't do it, we've had irony
        enough.
Don't start it playing, if you want to keep
This Christmas party to ourselves, my boy.
The men are mad with drink, and—other things.
Look here, Tarrasch, what are we going to do

About this youngster, eh?

Tarrasch.   Better keep quiet
Till morning.   When the men have slept it off
They'll stand a better chance of slipping away.
They're all drunk, officers and men as well.

Brander. That's the most merciful thing that one can
      say.

Nanko. Oh, what a pity! I did think, Bettine,
That we should have some music.   Well—I know!
Tell us the Christmas piece you learned in school.
That's right.   Stand there! No, stand up on this bench.
Your mother tells me that you won the prize
For learning it so beautifully, Bettine.
That's right.   Now, while you say it, I will stand
Here, with a candle.   See, that illustrates
The scene.

> [*He lifts one of the candles to illuminate the picture
> of the Madonna and Child. For a moment he
> speaks with a curious dignity.*

                 You know it is not all delusion
About this Christmas Eve.   The wise men say
That Time is a delusion.   Now then, speak
Your Christmas piece.

Bettine [*with her hands behind her, as if in school, obeying him*]. She laid Him in a manger, because there was no room for them in the inn.

And there were in the same country shepherds abiding in the field, keeping watch over their flock by night,

And lo, the angel of the Lord came upon them, and the glory of the Lord shone round them, and they were sore afraid.

And the angel said unto them, "Fear not: for behold I bring you good tidings of great joy, which shall be to all people.

"For unto you is born this day in the City of David a Saviour, which is Christ the Lord.

"And this shall be a sign unto you; ye shall find the babe wrapped in swaddling clothes, lying in a manger."

And suddenly there was with the angel a multitude of
the heavenly host, praising God, and saying :—
"*Glory to God in the Highest, and on earth peace. . . .*"

> [*There is silence for a moment, then a pistol-shot,
> a scream, and a roar of drunken laughter with-
> out, followed by a furious pounding on the door.*
> BETTINE *runs to her mother.*

Brander. Here, Tarrasch, what the devil are we to do
About this child?   [*He calls through the door.*
                Clear out of this!   The house
Is full.   We want to sleep.

> [*The uproar grows outside, and the pounding is
> resumed.   There is a crash of broken glass at
> the window.*

Bettine.   Mother, I'm frightened!
It is the Boches!   Mother, it is the Boches!
Where are the British, mother?   You said the British
Were sure to be here first!

Brander.   Bundle the child
Into that room, woman, at once!

> [RADA *snatches the revolver from the Christmas-
> tree and hurries* BETTINE *into the bedroom just
> as the other door is burst open and a troop of
> soldiers appear on the threshold, shouting and
> furious with drink.   They sing, with drunken
> gestures, in the doorway:*

"Zum Rhein, zum Rhein, zum deutscher Rhein . . ."

First Soldier.   Come on!
They're in that room.   I saw them!   The only skirts
Left in the village.   Comrades, you've had your fun—
It's time for ours.

Brander.   Clear out of this.   You're drunk.
We want to sleep.

Second Soldier.   Well, hand the women over.

Tarrasch. There are no women here.

First Soldier.   You greedy wolf,
I saw them.

Nanko. Come!   Come!   Come!   It's Christmas Eve!

Second Soldier. Well, if there are no petticoats, where's
    the harm
In letting us poor soldiers take a squint
Through yonder door? By God, we'll do it, too!
Come on, my boys.   [*They make a rush towards the room.*
    Nanko.   Be careful, or you'll smash
The Christmas-tree! You'll smash the gramophone!
            [*A soldier tries the bedroom door. It is opened
                from within, and* RADA *appears on the thres-
                hold with the revolver in her hand.*
First Soldier. Liars! Liars!
    Rada.   There is one woman here,
One woman and a child. . . .
And war, they tell me, is a noble thing.
It is the mother of heroic deeds,
The nurse of honour, manhood.
    Second Soldier.   God, a speech!
    Nanko [*who is hugging his Christmas-tree near the fire
        again*]. Certainly, Rada! You will not deny
That life's a battle.
    Rada.   You hear, drunk as you are,
Up to your necks in blood, you hear this fool,
This poor old fool, piping his dreary cry.
And through his lips, and through his softening brain,
The men that use you, cheat you, drive you out
To slaughter and be slaughtered, teach the world
That this black vampire, sucking at our breasts,
Is good. Men! Men! The stink of your own dead
Is murdering you by legions. All the trains
Of quicklime that your Emperor sends behind you
Can never eat its way through all that flesh—
Three hundred miles of dead! Your dead!
    First Soldier.   Hoch! Hoch!
A speech!
            [*They make a movement towards her, which she
                arrests by raising the revolver.*
    Rada.   I do not hate! I pity you all.
I tell you, you are doing it in a dream.

You are drugged.   You are not awake.
Nanko.   I have sometimes thought
The very same.
Rada.   But you will wake one day.
Listen !   If you have children of your own,
Listen to me . . . the child is twelve years old.
She has never had one hard word spoken to her
In all her life.
Second Soldier. Nor shall she now, by God !
Where is she ?   Bring her out !
First Soldier. Twelve years of age ?
Add two, because her mother loves her so !
That's ripe enough for marriage to a soldier.
          [*They laugh uproariously, and sing again mockingly :*
" Zum Rhein, zum Rhein, zum deutscher Rhein ! "
                              [*They move forward again.*
Rada [*raising the revolver*].   One word.   If you are deaf
to honour, blind
To truth, and if compassion cannot reach you,
Then I appeal to fear !   Yes, you shall fear me.
Listen !   I heard, when I was in that room,
A sound like gun-fire coming from the south :
What if it were the British ?
Soldiers.   Ah !   The swine !
The dogs !
Rada. Bull-dogs ; and slow.   But they are coming,
And, where they hold, they never will let go.
Though they may come too late for me and mine,
You are on your trial now before the world.
You never can escape it.   They are coming,
With justice and the unconquerable law !
I warn you, though their speech is not my own,
And I shall be but one of all the dead,
Dead, with that child, in a forgotten grave—
I speak for them, and they will keep my word.
Yes, if you harm that child . . . the British. . . . Ah !
                              [*They advance towards her.*
I have one bullet for the child and five

To share between you and myself.
    First Soldier.   Come on!
She can't shoot!   Look at the way she's holding it!
Duck down, and make a rush for it.
    Soldiers.   Come on!
        [*They make a rush.* RADA *steps back into the bed-
            room and shuts the door in their faces.*

Second Soldier. Locked out in the cold.   Come, break
    the damned thing down!
Bettine [*crying within*]. O British!   British!   Come!
    Come quickly, British!
Brander [*trying to interpose*]. She'll keep her word.
    You'll never get 'em alive.
Tarrasch. Never.   I know that kind.   You'd better
    clear out.
First Soldier. Down with the door!
        [*They put their shoulders to it.* BRANDER *makes
            a sign to* TARRASCH. *They try to pull the men
            back.   There is a scuffle and* BRANDER *is knocked
            down.   He rises with the blood running down
            his face, while* TARRASCH *still struggles.   The
            door begins to give.   A shot is heard within.
            The men pause and there is another shot.*
Brander. By God, she's done it!
               [*There is a booming of distant artillery.*
                          Hear!
She was not lying.   That came from the south-west.
It is the British!
          [*A bugle-call sounds in the village street.*
    Tarrasch.   The British!   A night-attack!
        [*They all rush out except* NANKO, *who peers after
            them from the door.   Leaving it open to the night,
            he takes a* marron glacé *from the table, crosses
            the room, and begins to examine the gramophone.
            Confused sounds of men rushing to arms, thin bugle-
            calls in the distance, and the occasional clatter of
            a galloping horse are blown in from the blackness*

framed in the open door.   The deep pulsation of
the British artillery is heard throughout, in a
steady undertone.

Nanko [*calling aloud as he munches*].   Come, Rada, you're
 pretending.   They're all gone.
Rada, these *marrons glacés* are delicious.
It's over now !   Come, I don't think it's right
To spoil a person's pleasure on Christmas Eve.
   [*He tiptoes to the door and peers into the night.*
Come quick, Bettine, rockets are going up !
They are breaking into clusters of green stars !
Oh, there's a red one !   You could see for miles
When that one broke.   The willow-trees jumped out
Like witches ; and, between them, the canal
Dwindled away to a little thread of blood.
And there were lines of men running and falling,
And guns and horses floundering in a ditch.
Oh, Rada ! there's a bonfire by the mill.
They've burned the little cottage.   There's a man
Hanging above the bonfire by his hands,
And heaps of dead all round him.   Come and see !
It's terrible, but it's magnificent,
Like one of Goya's pictures.   That's the way
He painted war.   Well, everybody's gone. . . .
To think *I* was the fittest, after all !
     [*He returns to the gramophone.*
I wonder how this gramophone does work.
He said the tune that he was putting in
Was just the thing for Christmas Eve.   I wonder,
I wonder what it was.   Listen to this !
       [*He reads the title.*
It's a good omen, Rada—*A Christmas carol*
Sung by the Grand Imperial Choir—d' you hear ?—
At midnight in St Petersburg—*Adeste*
Fideles !   Fancy that !   A Christmas carol
Upon the gramophone !
So all the future ages will be sure
To know exactly what religion was.

To think we must not hear it !   Rada, they say
The Angel Gabriel composed that tune
On the first Christmas Eve.   So don't you think
That we might hear it ?
Everybody is gone, except the dead.
It will not wake them. . . .
Come, Rada, you're pretending !   Do not make
The war more dreadful than it really is.

> [*He accidentally sets the gramophone working and*
> *jumps back, a little alarmed.   He runs to the*
> *bedroom door.*

Rada !   I've started it !   Bettine, d' you hear ?
The gramophone's working.

> [*The artillery booms like a thunder-peal in the*
> *distance.   Then the gramophone drowns it with*
> *the massed voices of the Imperial Choir singing :*

ADESTE FIDELES,
LÆTI TRIUMPHANTES,
   ADESTE, ADESTE IN BETHLEHEM !
   NATUM VIDETE
   REGEM ANGELORUM :
   VENITE, ADOREMUS,
   VENITE, ADOREMUS,
   VENITE, ADOREMUS DOMINUM.

> [*NANKO touches the floor under the door of the*
> *bedroom and stares at his hand.*

Nanko.   Something red again ?   Trickling under the
   door ?
Blood, I suppose. . . .

> [*A look of horror comes into his face as he stands*
> *listening to the music.   Then, as if slowly waking*
> *from a dream and almost as if sanity had*
> *returned for a moment, he cries :*

It's true !   It's true !   Rada, I am awake !
I am awake !   And, in the name of Christ,
I accuse, I accuse . . . O God, forgive us all !

[*He falls on his knees by the bedroom door and calls,
    as if to the dead within :*
Awake, and after nineteen hundred years. . . .
Bettine, Bettine ! the British, they are coming !
Rada, you said it—they are coming quickly !
They are coming, with the reign of right and law.
But, O Bettine ! Bettine ! will they remember ?
Are they awake ?   I only hear their guns.
What if they should grow used to it, Bettine,
And fail to wipe this horror from the world ?
God, is there any hope for poor mankind ?
God, are Thy little nations and Thy weak,
Thine innocent, condemned to hell for ever ?
God, will the strong deliverers break the sword
And bring this world at last to Christmas Eve ?

THE IMPERIAL CHOIR.

ÆTERNI PARENTIS
SPLENDOREM ÆTERNUM,
VELATUM SUB CARNE VIDEBIMUS,
DEUM INFANTEM,
PANNIS INVOLUTUM,
VENITE, ADOREMUS,
VENITE, ADOREMUS,
VENITE, ADOREMUS DOMINUM.

Nanko. Will Christ be born, oh, not in Bethlehem,
But in the soul of man, the abode of God ?
There, in that deep, undying soul of man
(I still believe it), that immortal soul,
Will they lift up the cross with Christ upon it,
The Fool of God, whom intellectual fools,
The little fools of dust, in every land,
Grinning their *What is Truth ?* still crucify.
Could they not thrust their hands into His wounds ?
His wounds are these—these dead are all His wounds.
Bettine, Bettine ! the British, they are coming !
But you are silent now, so silent now !

Will they lift up God's poor old broken Fool,
And sleep no more until His kingdom come,
His infinite kingdom come?

Will they remember?

*[He bows his head against the closed door, while the
gramophone lifts the chorus of the Imperial Choir
over the deepening thunder of the guns.*

NUNC CANTET, EXULTANS,
CHORUS ANGELORUM,
CANTET NUNC AULA CELESTIUM,
GLORIA, GLORIA,
IN EXCELSIS DEO!
VENITE, ADOREMUS,
VENITE, ADOREMUS,
VENITE, ADOREMUS DOMINUM.

EPILOGUE.

Intercession.

Now the muttering gun-fire dies,
   Now the night has cloaked the slain,
Now the stars patrol the skies,
   Hear our sleepless prayer again!
They who work their country's will,
Fight and die for Britain still,
Soldiers, but not haters, know
   Thou must pity friend and foe.
      Therefore hear,
Both for foe and friend, our prayer.

Thou whose wounded Hands do reach
   Over every land and sea,
Thoughts too deep for human speech
   Rise from all our souls to Thee;
Deeper than the wrath that burns
Round our hosts when day returns;
Deeper than the peace that fills
All these trenched and waiting hills.
      Hear, O hear!
Both for foe and friend, our prayer.

Pity deeper than the grave
   Sees, beyond the death we wield,
Faces of the young and brave
   Hurled against us in the field.

Cannon-fodder!   They *must* come,
We must slay them, and be dumb,
Slaughter, while we pity, these
Most implacable enemies.
　　　　Master, hear,
Both for foe and friend, our prayer.

They are blind, as we are blind,
　　Urged by duties past reply.
Ours is but the task assigned;
　　Theirs to strike us ere they die.
Who can see his country fall?
Who but answers at her call?
Who has power to pause and think
When she reels upon the brink?
　　　　Hear, O hear,
Both for foe and friend, our prayer.

Shield them from that bitterest lie
　　Laughed by fools who quote their mirth,
When the wings of death go by
　　And their brother shrieks on earth.
Though they clamp their hearts with steel,
Conquering every fear they feel,
There are dreams they dare not tell.
Shield, O shield, their eyes from hell.
　　　　Father, hear,
Both for foe and friend, our prayer.

Where the naked bodies burn,
　　Where the wounded toss at home,
Weep and bleed and laugh in turn,
　　Yes, the masking jest may come.
Let him jest who daily dies.
But O hide his haunted eyes.
Pain alone he might control.
Shield, O shield, his wounded soul.
　　　　Master, hear,
Both for foe and friend, our prayer.

Peace? We steel us to the end.
　Hope betrayed us, long ago.
Duty binds both foe and friend.
　It is ours to break the foe.
Then, O God! that we might break
This red Moloch for Thy sake;
Know that Truth indeed prevails,
And that Justice holds the scales.
　　　Father, hear,
Both for foe and friend, our prayer.

England, could this awful hour,
　Dawning on thy long renown,
Mark the purpose of thy power,
　Crown thee with that mightier crown!
Broadening to that purpose climb
All the blood red wars of Time. . . .
Set the struggling peoples free,
Crown with Law their Liberty!
　　　England, hear,
Both for foe and friend, our prayer!

Speed, O speed what every age
　Writes with a prophetic hand.
Read the midnight's moving page,
　Read the stars and understand:
Out of Chaos ye shall draw
Deepening harmonies of Law
Till around the Eternal Sun
All your peoples move in one.
　　　Christ-God, hear,
Both for foe and friend, our prayer.

A SALUTE FROM THE FLEET

AND OTHER POEMS.

A SALUTE FROM THE FLEET.

I.

OCEAN - MOTHER of England, thine is the crowning
 acclaim !
 Here, in the morning of battle, from over the world and
 beyond,
 Here, by our fleets of steel, silently foam into line
Fleets of our glorious dead, thy shadowy oak-walled ships.
Mother, for O, thy soul must speak thro' our iron lips !
 How should we speak to the ages, unless with a word
 of thine ?
 Utter it, Victory ! Let thy great signal flash thro' the
 flame !
 Answer, *Bellerophon ! Marlborough, Thunderer, Con-
 dor*, respond !

II.

Out of the ages we speak unto you, O ye ages to be !
 Rocks of Sevastopol, echo our thunder-word, bruit it afar !
 Roll it, O Mediterranean, round by Gibraltar again !
Buffet it, Porto Bello, back to the Nile once more !

Answer it, great St Vincent!   Answer it, Elsinore,
  Buffet it back from your crags and roll it over the
    main!
  Heights of Quebec, O hear and re-echo it back to the
    Baltic Sea!
    Answer it, *Camperdown!*   Answer it, answer it,
      Trafalgar!

III.

How should we speak to the ages, if not with a word of
    thine,
  Maker of cloud and harvest, foam and the sea-bird's
    wing,
    Ocean-Mother of England and all things living and
      free?
Deep that wast moved by the Spirit to bloom with the first
    white morn,
Mother of Light and Freedom, mother of hopes unborn,
  Speak, O world-wide welder of nations, O Soul of the
    sea!
  Thine was the watchword that called us of old o'er the
    grey sky-line:
    Lift thy stormy salute!   It is freedom and peace that
      we bring!

IV.

Therefore on thee we call, O Mother, for we are thy sons!
  Speak, with thy world-wide voice, O wake us anew from
    our sleep!
    Speak, for the Light of the world still lives and grows
      on thy face!
Give us the ancient Word once more, the unchangeable
    Word,—
This that Nelson knew, this that Effingham heard,
    This that resounds for ever in all the hearts of our race,
  This that lives for a moment on the iron lips of our guns,
    This—that echoes for ever and ever—the Word of the
      Deep.

V.

How shall a king be saved by the multitude of an host ?
    Was not the answer thine, when fleet upon fleet swept,
        hurled
        Blind thro' the dark North Sea, with all their in-
            vincible ships ?
Thine was the answer, O mother of all men born to be free !
Witness again, Cape Wrath !—O thine, everlastingly,
    Thine as Freedom arose and rolled thy song from
        her lips,
    Thine when she 'stablished her throne in thy sight, on
        our rough rock-coast,
    Thine with thy lustral glory and thunder, washing the
        world !

VI.

O for that ancient cry of the watch at the midnight bell,
    Under the unknown stars, from the decks that Frobisher
        trod !
        Hark, *Before the world ?*—he questions a fleet in the
            dark !
Answer it, friend or foe !   And, ringing from mast to mast,
Mother, hast thou forgotten what counter-cry went past,
        Answering still as he questioned ?   *Before the world ?*
        O, hark,
        Ringing anear, *Before the world ?* . . . *was God !* . . .
        All's well !
        Dying afar . . . *Before the world ?* . . . All's well
        . . . *was God !*

VII.

Raleigh and Grenville heard it, Knights of the Ocean-sea !
    Have we forgotten it only, we with our leagues of steel ?
        Give us our watchword again, O mother, in this great
        hour !
Here, in the morning of battle, here as we gather our
        might,

Here, as the nations of earth in the light of thy freedom
    unite,
  Shake our hearts with thy Word, O 'stablish our peace
    on thy power!
 'Stablish our power on thy peace, thy glory, thy liberty,
  'Stablish on thy deep Word the throne of our Com-
    monweal!

VIII.

They that go down to the sea in ships—they heard it of
    old—
  They shall behold His wonders, alone on the Deep, the
    Deep!
  Have *we* forgotten, we only? O, rend the heavens
    again,
Voice of the Everlasting, shake the great hills with thy
    breath!
Roll the Voice of our God thro' the valleys of doubt and
    death!
  Waken the fog-bound cities with the shout of the
    wind-swept main,
 Inland over the smouldering plains, till the mists unfold,
  Darkness die, and England, England arise from sleep.

IX.

Queen of the North and the South, Queen of our ocean-
    renown,
  England, England, England, O lift thine eyes to the sun!
  Wake, for the hope of the whole world yearns to thee,
    watches and waits!
Now on the full flood-tide of the ages, the supreme hour
Beacons thee onward in might to the purpose and crown of
    thy power!
  Hark, for the whole Atlantic thunders against thy gates,
 Take the Crown of all Time, all might, earth's crowning
    Crown,
  Throne thy children in peace and in freedom together,
    O weld them in one.

X.

Throne them in triumph together.   Thine is the crowning cry!
  Thine the glory for ever in the nation born of thy womb!
    *Thine the Sword and the Shield, and the shout that
      Salamis heard,*
Surging in Æschylean splendour, earth-shaking acclaim!
Ocean-mother of England, thine is the throne of her fame!
  Breaker of many fleets, O thine the victorious word,
    *Thine the Sun and the Freedom, the God and the wind-
      swept sky,*
      *Thine the thunder and thine the lightning, thine the
        doom!*

IN MEMORY OF A BRITISH AVIATOR.

On those young brows that knew no fear
  We lay the Roman athlete's crown,
The laurel of the charioteer,
  The imperial garland of renown,
While those young eyes, beyond the sun,
See Drake, see Raleigh, smile "Well done."

Their desert seas that knew no shore
  To-night with fleets like cities flare;
But, frailer even than theirs of yore,
  His keel a new-found deep would dare:
They watch, with thrice-experienced eyes
What fleets shall follow through the skies.

They would not scoff, though man should set
  To feebler wings a mightier task.
They know what wonders wait us yet.
  Not all things in an hour they ask;
But in each noble failure see
The inevitable victory.

A thousand years have borne us far
  From that dark isle the Saxon swayed,
And star whispers to trembling star
  While Space and Time shrink back afraid,—
"Ten thousand thousand years remain
For man to dare our deep again."

Thou, too, shalt hear across that deep
    Our challenging fleets of thought draw nigh,
Round which the suns and systems sweep
    Like cloven foam from sky to sky,
Till Death himself at last restore
His captives to our eyes once more.

.   .   .   .   .

Feeble the wings, dauntless the soul!
    Take thou the conqueror's laurel crown;
Take—for thy chariot grazed the goal—
    The imperial garland of renown;
While those young eyes, beyond the sun,
See Drake, see Raleigh, smile "Well done."

BEFORE THE WORLD.

(Written in answer to certain statements on the "origin of life.")

I.

In the beginning? . . . Slowly grope we back
    Along the narrowing track,
Back to the deserts of the world's pale prime,
    The mire, the clay, the slime,
And then—what then?—Surely to something *less!*
    Back, back to Nothingness.

II.

You dare not halt upon that dwindling way.
    There is no gulf to stay
Your footsteps to the last. Go back you must.
    Far, far below the dust
Descend, descend. Grade by dissolving grade,
    We follow, unafraid.
Dissolve, dissolve, this moving world of men
    Into thin air. And then?

III.

O pioneers, O warriors of the light,
    In that abysmal night,
Will you have courage, then, to rise and tell
    Earth of this miracle?

Will you have courage, then, to bow the head
        And say, when all is said,—
Out of this Nothingness arose our thought?
        This blank abysmal Nought
Woke, and brought forth that lighted City street,
        Those towers, and that great fleet.

IV.

When you have seen those vacant primal skies
        Beyond the centuries,
Watched the pale mists across their darkness flow
        (As in a lantern show!),
Watched the great hills like clouds arise, and set,
        And one named Olivet;
When you have seen as a shadow passing away
        One child clasp hands and pray;
When you have seen emerge from that dark mire
        One martyr, ringed with fire;
Or from that Nothingness, by special grace,
        One woman's love-lit face. . .

Will you have courage, then, to front that law
        (From which your sophists draw
Their only right to flout one human creed)
        That nothing can proceed
(Not even thought, not even love!) from less
        Than its own nothingness.
The law is yours. But dare you waive your pride,
        And kneel where you denied?
The law is yours. Dare you re-kindle, then,
        One faith for faithless men;
And say you found, on that dark road you trod,
        In the beginning—God?

THE SACRED OAK.

(*A Song of Britain.*)

I.

VOICE of the summer stars that, long ago,
  Sang thro' the old oak-forests of our isle,
Enchanted voice, pure as her falling snow,
  Dark as her storms, bright as her sunniest smile,
Taliessin, voice of Britain, the fierce flow
  Of fourteen hundred years has whelmed not thee!
    Still art thou singing, lavrock of her morn,
Singing to heaven in that first golden glow,
  Singing above her mountains and her sea.
      Not older yet are grown
      Thy four winds in their moan
  For Urien.   Still thy charlock blooms in the billow-
    ing corn.

II.

Thy dew is bright upon this beechen spray.
  Spring wakes thy harp!   I hear—I see—again,
Thy wild steeds foaming thro' the crimson fray,
  The raven on the white breast of thy slain,
The tumult of thy chariots, far away,
  The weeping in the glens, the lustrous hair
    Dishevelled o'er the stricken eagle's fall,
And in thy Druid groves, at fall of day
  One gift that Britain gave her valorous there,
      One gift of lordlier pride
      Than aught—save to have died—
  One spray of the sacred oak, they coveted most
    of all.

III.

I watch thy nested brambles growing green
   O strange, across that misty waste of years,
To glimpse the shadowy thrush that thou hast seen,
   To touch, across the ages, touch with tears
The ferns that hide thee with their fairy screen,
   Or only hear them rustling in the dawn ;
     And—as a dreamer waking—in thy words,
For all the golden clouds that drowse between,
   To feel the veil of centuries withdrawn,
      To feel thy sun re-risen
      Unbuild our shadowy prison
    And hear on thy fresh boughs the carol of waking
    birds.

IV.

O, happy voice, born in that far, clear time,
   Over thy single harp thy simple strain
Attuned all life for Britain to the chime
   Of viking oars and the sea's dark refrain,
And thine own beating heart, and the sublime
   Measure to which the moons and stars revolve
     Untroubled by the storms that, year by year,
In ever-swelling symphonies still climb
   To embrace our growing world and to resolve
      Discords unknown to thee,
      In the infinite harmony
    Which still transcends our strife and leaves us
    darkling here.

V.

For, now, one sings of heaven and one of hell,
   One soars with hope, one plunges to despair.
This, trembling, doubts if aught be ill or well ;
   And that cries "fair is foul and foul is fair" ;

And this cries "forward, though I cannot tell
  Whither, and all too surely all things die";
    And that sighs "rest, then, sleep and take thine ease,"
One sings his country and one rings its knell,
  One hymns mankind, one dwarfs them with the sky!
      O, Britain, let thy soul
      Once more command the whole,
    Once more command the strings of the world-wide
      harmony.

VI.

For hark! One sings *The gods, the gods are dead!*
  Man triumphs! And hark—*Blind Space his funeral*
    urn!
And hark, one whispers with reverted head
  To the old dead gods—*Bring back our heaven, return!*
And hark, one moans—*The ancient order is fled,*
  We are children of blind chance and vacant dreams!
    Heed not mine utterance—that was chance-born too!
And hark, the answer of Science—*All they said,*
  Your fathers, in that old time, lit by gleams
    Of what their hearts could feel,
    The rolling years reveal
  As fragments of one law, one covenant, simply true.

VII.

I find, she cries, *in all this march of time*
  And space, no gulf, no break, nothing that mars
Its unity. I watch the primal slime
  Lift Athens like a flower to greet the stars!
I flash my messages from clime to clime,
  I link the increasing world from depth to height!
    Not yet ye see the wonder that draws nigh,
When at some sudden contact, some sublime
  Touch, as of memory, all this boundless night
    Wherein ye grope entombed
    Shall, by that touch illumed,
  Like one electric City shine from sky to sky.

VIII.

No longer then the memories that ye hold
Dark in your brain shall slumber.   Ye shall see
That City whose gates are more than pearl or gold
And all its towers firm as Eternity.
The stones of the earth have cried to it from of old !
Why will ye turn from Him who reigns above
Because your highest words fall short ?   Kneel—call
On Him whose name—I AM—doth still enfold
Past, present, future, memory, hope and love !
No seed falls fruitless there.
Beyond your Father's care—
The old covenant still holds fast—no bird, no leaf
can fall.

IX.

O Time, thou mask of the ever-living Soul,
    Thou veil to shield us from that blinding Face,
Thou art wearing thin !   We are nearer to the goal
    When man no more shall need thy saving grace,
But all the folded years like one great scroll
    Shall be unrolled in the omnipresent Now,
        And He that saith *I AM* unseal the tomb.
Nearer His thunders and His trumpets roll,
    I catch the gleam that lit thy lifted brow,
        O singer whose wild eyes
        Possess these April skies,
    I touch—I clasp thy hands thro' all the clouds of
    doom.

X.

Teach thou our living choirs amid the sound
    Of their tempestuous chords once more to hear
That harmony wherewith the whole is crowned,
    The singing heavens that sphere by choral sphere
Break open, height o'er height, to the utmost bound

Of passionate thought!   O, as this glorious land,
   This sacred country shining on the sea
Grows mightier, let not her clear voice be drowned
   In the fierce waves of faction.   Let her stand
        A beacon to the blind,
        A signal to mankind!
   A witness to the heavens' profoundest unity.

XI.

Her altars are forgotten and her creeds
   Dust, and her soul foregoes the lesser Cross!
O, point her to the greater!   Her heart bleeds
   Still, where men simply feel some vague deep loss;
Their hands grope earthward, knowing not what she needs.
   We would not call her back in this great hour;
     But, upward, onward, to the heights untrod
Signal us, living voices, by those deeds
   Of all her deathless heroes, by the Power
        That still, still walks her waves,
        Still chastens her, still saves,
   Signal us, not to the dead, but to the living God.

XII.

Signal us with that watchword of the deep,
   The watchword that her boldest seamen gave
The winds of the unknown ocean-sea to keep,
   When round their oaken walls the midnight wave
Heaved and subsided in gigantic sleep,
   And they plunged Westward with her flag unfurled.
   Hark, o'er their cloudy sails and glimmering spars,
The watch cries, as they proudly onward sweep,—
   Before the world . . . All's well! . . . Before the
     world . . .
        From mast to calling mast
        The counter-cry goes past—
   Before the world was God!—it rings against the stars.

XIII.

Signal us o'er the little heavens of gold
     With that heroic signal Nelson knew
When, thro' the thunder and flame that round him rolled
     He pointed to the dream that still held true!
Cry o'er the warring nations, cry as of old
          A little child shall lead them!   They shall be
               One people under the shadow of God's wing!
There shall be no more weeping!   Let it be told
     That Britain set one foot upon the sea,
               One foot on the earth!   Her eyes
               Burned thro' the conquered skies,
     And, as the angel of God, she bade the whole
          world sing.

XIV.

A dream?   Nay, have ye heard or have ye known
     That the everlasting God who made the ends
Of all creation wearieth?   His worlds groan
     Together in travail still.   Still He descends
From heaven.   The increasing worlds are still His throne
     And His creative Calvary and His tomb
          Through which He sinks, dies, triumphs with each
          and all,
And ascends, multitudinous and at one
     With all the hosts of His evolving doom,
               His vast redeeming strife,
               His everlasting life,
          His love, beyond which not one bird, one leaf
          can fall.

XV.

And hark, His whispers thro' creation flow,
     Lovest thou Me?   His nations answer "yea!"
And—*Feed My lambs*, His voice as long ago
     Steals from that highest heaven, how far away!

And yet again saith—*Lovest thou Me?* and "O,
   Thou knowest we love Thee," passionately we cry:
      But, heeding not our tumult, out of the deep
The great grave whisper, pitiful and low,
   Breathes—*Feed My sheep;* and yet once more the sky
         Thrills with that deep strange plea,
            Lovest thou, lovest thou Me?
      And our lips answer "yea"; but our God—*Feed
      My sheep.*

XVI.

O sink not yet beneath the exceeding weight
   Of splendour, thou still single-hearted voice
Of Britain.   Droop not earthward now to freight
   Thy soul with fragments of the song, rejoice
In no faint flights of music that create
   Low heavens o'er-arched by skies without a star,
      Nor sink in the easier gulfs of shallower pain!
Sing thou in the whole majesty of thy fate,
   Teach us thro' joy, thro' grief, thro' peace, thro' war,
            With single heart and soul
            Still, still to seek the goal,
      And thro' our perishing heavens, point us to Heaven
      again.

XVII.

Voice of the summer stars that long ago
   Sang thro' the old oak-forests of our isle,
An ocean-music that thou ne'er couldst know
   Storms Heaven—O, keep us steadfast all the while;
Not idly swayed by tides that ebb and flow,
   But strong to embrace the whole vast symphony
      Wherein no note (no bird, no leaf) can fall
Beyond His care, to enfold it all as though
   Thy single harp were ours, its unity
            In battle like one sword,
            And O, its one reward
      One spray of the sacred oak, still coveted most
      of all.

A KNIGHT OF OLD JAPAN.

MAKE me a stave of song, the Master said,
On yonder cherry-bough, whose white and red
   Hangs in the sunset over those green seas.
The young knight looked upon his untried blade,
Then shrugged his wings of gold and blue brocade:
   How should a warrior play with thoughts like these?

Fresh from the battle, in that self-same hour,
A mail-clad warrior watched each delicate flower
   Close in that cloud of beauty against the West.
Drinking the last deep light, he watched it long.
He raised his face as if to pray.   *The strong*,
   The Master whispered, *are the tenderest.*

ON THE EMBANKMENT.

WITHIN, it was colour and laughter, warmth and wine.
  Without, it was darkness, hunger and bitter cold,
Where those white globes on the wet Embankment shine,
  Greasing the Thames with gold.

And was it a bundle of fog in the dark drew nigh?
  A bundle of rags and bones it crept to the light,—
A monstrous thing that coughed as it shuffled by,
  A shape of the shapeless night,

Spawned as brown things that mimic their mothering earth,
  Green creeping things that the grass lifts to the sun,
Out of its wrongs the City had brought to the birth
  The shape of those wrongs, in one.

A woman, a woman whose lips had once been kissed,
  (It was Christmas Eve, and the bells began their chime!)
She sank to a seat like a coughing bundle of mist
  Exhaled from the river-slime.

Bells for the birth of Christ! She heard, and she thought—
  Vacantly—of her man, that was long since dead,
The smell of the Christmas food, and the drink they had
      bought
  Together, the year they were wed.

She thought of their one-room home, and the night-long
      sigh
  Recalled, as he slept, of his breath in her loosened hair.
He slept. She opened her haggard eyes with a cry.
  But only the night was there.

Then, out of the formless night, at her furtive glance,
   Crouched at the end of her cold wet bench, there grew
A bundle of fog, a bundle of rags that, perchance,
   Once was a woman, too.

A huddled shape, a fungus of foul grey mist
   Spawned of the river, in peace and much goodwill,
And even the woman whose lips had once been kissed
   Wondered, it crouched so still.

No breath, no shadow of breath in the lamplight smoked,
   It crouched so still—that bunch at the bench's end.
She stretched her neck like a crow, then leaned and
      croaked
   "A Merry Christmas, friend!"

She rose, and peered, peered at its vacant eyes.
   Touched its cold claws.   Its arms of knotted bone
Were wands of ice; like iron rods the thighs;
   The left breast—like a stone.

Far, far along the rows of warmth and light
   The Christmas waits, with cornet and bassoon,
Carolled "While shepherds watched their flocks by night."
   The bells pealed to the moon.

A bundle of rags and bones, a bundle of mist,
   And never a hell or heaven to hear or see,
The woman, the woman whose lips had once been kissed,
   Knelt down feverishly.

She plucked the shawl out of that frozen clutch.
   The dead are dead.   Why should the living freeze?
She touched the cold flesh that she feared to touch,
   Kneeling upon her knees.

Her palsied hands unlaced the shoes—good shoes!—
    She tore them quick from the crooked yellow feet.
If Death be generous, why should Life refuse
    To take, and pawn, and eat?

A heavy step drew nearer thro' the mist.
    She bundled them into the shawl.   Her eyes were bright.
The woman, the woman whose lips had once been kissed,
    Slunk, chuckling, thro' the night.

THE IRON CROWN.

Not memory of a vanished bliss,
  But suddenly to know,
I had forgotten !   This, O this
  With iron crowned my woe :

To know that on some midnight sea
  Whence none could lift the pall,
A drowning hand was waved to me,
  Then—swept beyond recall.

ENCELADUS.

In the Black Country, from a little window,
Before I slept, across the haggard wastes
Of dust and ashes, I saw Titanic shafts
Like shadowy columns of wan-hope arise
To waste, on the blear sky, their slow sad wreaths
Of smoke, their infinitely sad slow prayers.
Then, as night deepened, the blast-furnaces,
Red smears upon the sulphurous blackness, turned
All that sad region to a City of Dis,
Where naked sweating giants all night long
Bowed their strong necks, melted flesh, blood and bone,
To brim the dry ducts of the gods of gloom
With terrible rivers, branches of living gold.
O, like some tragic gesture of great souls
In agony, those awful columns towered
Against the clouds, that city of ash and slag
Assumed the stature of some direr Thebes
Arising to the death-chant of those gods,
A dreadful Order climbing from the dark
Of Chaos and Corruption, threatening to take
Heaven with its vast slow storm.

I slept, and dreamed.
And like the slow beats of some Titan heart
Buried beneath immeasurable woes,
The huge trip-hammers thudded through the dream :—

Huge on a fallen tree,
Lost in the darkness of primæval woods,
Enceladus, earth-born Enceladus,

The naked giant, brooded all alone.
Born of the lower earth, he knew not how,
Born of the mire and clay, he knew not when,
Brought forth in darkness, and he knew not why!

Thus, like a wind, went by a thousand years.

Anhungered, yet no comrade of the wolf,
And cold, but with no power upon the sun,
A master of this world that mastered him!

Thus, like a cloud, went by a thousand years.

Who chained this other giant in his heart
That heaved and burned like Etna?   Heavily
He bent his brows and wondered and was dumb.

And, like one wave, a thousand years went by.

He raised his matted head and scanned the stars!
He stood erect!   He lifted his uncouth arms!
With inarticulate sounds his uncouth lips
Wrestled and strove—*I am full-fed, and yet
I hunger!
Who set this fiercer famine in my maw?
Can I eat moons, gorge on the Milky Way,
Swill sunsets down, or sup the wash of the dawn
Out of the rolling swine-troughs of the sea?
Can I drink oceans, lie beneath the mountains,
And nuzzle their heavy boulders like a cub
Sucking the dark teats of the tigress?   Who,
Who set this deeper hunger in my heart?*
And the dark forest echoed—*Who? Ah, who?*

"*I hunger!*"
And the night-wind answered him,
"Hunt, then, for food!"

" *I hunger !* "
And the sleek gorged lioness
Drew nigh him, dripping freshly from the kill,
Redder her lolling tongue, whiter her fangs,
And gazed with ignorant eyes of golden flame.

" *I hunger !* "
Like a breaking sea his cry
Swept through the night !   Against his swarthy knees
She rubbed the red wet velvet of her ears
With mellow thunders of unweeting bliss,
Purring,—*Ah, seek, and you shall find !*
Ah, seek, and you shall slaughter, gorge—ah, seek,
Seek, seek, you shall feed full—ah seek, ah seek !

Enceladus, earth-born Enceladus,
Bewildered like a desert-pilgrim, saw
A rosy City, opening in the clouds,
The hunger-born mirage of his own heart,
Far, far above the world, a home of gods,
Where One, a goddess, veiled in the sleek waves
Of her deep hair, yet glimmering golden through,
Lifted, with radiant arms, ambrosial food
For hunger such as this !   Up the dark hills
He rushed, a thunder-cloud,
Urged by the famine of his heart !   He stood
High on the topmost crags, he hailed the gods
In thunder, and the clouds re-echoed it !
He hailed the gods !
And like a sea of thunder round their thrones
Washing, a midnight sea, his earth-born voice
Besieged the halls of heaven !   He hailed the gods !
They laughed, he heard them laugh !
With echo and re-echo, far and wide,
A golden sea of mockery, they laughed !

Enceladus, earth-born Enceladus,
Laid hold upon the rosy gates of heaven,

And shook them with gigantic sooty hands,
Asking he knew not what, but not for alms ;
And the gates opened, opened as in jest ;
And, like a sooty Jest, he stumbled in !

Round him the gods, the young and scornful gods,
Clustered and laughed to mark the ravaged face,
The brutal brows, the deep and dog-like eyes,
The blunt black nails, and back with burdens bowed.
And, when they laughed, he snarled with uncouth lips
And made them laugh again.

"Whence comest thou ?"

He could not speak !
How should he speak whose heart within him heaved
And burned like Etna ? Through his mouth there came
A sound of ice-bergs in a frozen sea
Of tears, a sullen region of black ice
Rending and breaking, very far away.
They laughed !
He stared at them, bewildered, and they laughed
Again, *"Whence comest thou ?"*
He could not speak !
But through his mouth a moan of midnight woods,
Where wild beasts lay in wait to slaughter and gorge,
A moan of forest-caverns where the wolf
Brought forth her litter, a moan of the wild earth
In travail with strange shapes of mire and clay,
Creatures of clay, clay images of the gods,
That hungered like the gods, the most high gods,
But found no food, and perished like the beasts.
And the gods laughed,—
Art thou, then, such a God? And, like a leaf
Unfolding in dark woods, in his deep brain
A sudden memory woke ; and like an ape
He nodded, and all heaven with laughter rocked,
While Artemis cried out with scornful lips,—
Perchance He is the Maker of you all !

Then, piteously outstretching calloused hands,
He sank upon his knees, his huge gnarled knees,
And echoed, falteringly, with slow harsh tongue,—
Perchance, perchance, the Maker of you all!

They wept with laughter! And Aphrodite, she,
With keener mockery than white Artemis
Who smiled aloof, drew nigh him unabashed
In all her blinding beauty. Carelessly
As o'er the brute brows of a stallèd ox
Across that sooty muzzle and brawny breast,
Contemptuously, she swept her golden hair
In one deep wave, a many-millioned scourge
Intolerable and beautiful as fire;
Then turned and left him, reeling, gasping, dumb,
While heaven re-echoed and re-echoed, *See,*
Perchance, perchance, the Maker of us all!

Enceladus, earth-born Enceladus,
Rose to his feet, and with one terrible cry
"*I hunger*," rushed upon the scornful gods,
And strove to seize and hold them with his hands!
And still the laughter deepened as they rolled
Their clouds around them, baffling him. But once,
Once with a shout, in his gigantic arms
He crushed a slippery splendour on his breast
And felt on his harsh skin the cool smooth peaks
Of Aphrodite's bosom. One black hand
Slid down the naked snow of her long side
And bruised it where he held her. Then, like snow
Vanishing in a furnace, out of his arms
The splendour suddenly melted, and a roll
Of thunder split the dream, and head-long down
He fell, from heaven to earth; while, overhead
The young and scornful gods—he heard them laugh!—
Toppled the crags down after him. He lay
Supine. They plucked up Etna by the roots

And buried him beneath it.   His broad breast
Heaved, like that other giant in his heart,
And through the crater burst his fiery breath,
But could not burst his bonds.

                      And so he lay
Breathing in agony thrice a thousand years.

Then came a Voice, he knew not whence, "Arise,
Enceladus!"   And from his heart a crag
Fell, and one arm was free, and one thought free,
And suddenly he awoke, and stood upright,
Shaking the mountains from him like a dream;
And the tremendous light and awful truth
Smote, like the dawn, upon his blinded eyes,
That out of his first wonder at the world,
Out of his own heart's deep humility
And simple worship, he had fashioned gods
Of cloud, and heaven out of a hollow shell.
And groping now no more in the empty space
Outward, but inward in his own deep heart,
He suddenly felt the secret gates of heaven
Open, and from the infinite heavens of hope
Inward, a voice, from the innermost courts of Love,
Rang—*Thou shalt have none other gods but Me !*

Enceladus, the foul Enceladus,
When the clear light out of that inward heaven
Whose gates are only inward in the soul,
Showed him that one true Kingdom, said

                        "I will stretch
My hands out once again !   And, as the God
That made me is the Heart within my heart,
So shall my heart be to this dust and earth
A god and a creator.   I will strive
With mountains, fires and seas, wrestle and strive,
Fashion and make, and that which I have made
In anguish I shall love as God loves me.

In the Black Country, from a little window,
Waking at dawn, I saw those giant Shafts
—O great dark word out of our elder speech,
Long since the poor man's kingly heritage—
The Shapings, the dim Sceptres of Creation,
The Shafts like columns of wan-hope arise
To waste, on the blear sky, their slow sad wreaths
Of smoke, their infinitely sad slow prayers.
Then, as the dawn crimsoned, the sordid clouds,
The puddling furnaces, the mounds of slag,
The cinders, and the sand-beds and the rows
Of wretched roofs, assumed a majesty
Beyond all majesties of earth or air ;
Beauty beyond all beauty, as of a child
In rags, upraised thro' the still gold of heaven,
With wasted arms and hungering eyes, to bring
The armoured seraphim down upon their knees
And teach eternal God humility ;
The solemn beauty of the unfulfilled
Moving towards fulfilment on a height
Beyond all heights ; the dreadful beauty of hope ;
The naked wrestler struggling from the rock
Under the sculptor's chisel, the rough mass
Of clay more glorious for the poor blind face
And bosom that half emerge into the light,
More glorious and august, even in defeat,
Than that too cold dominion God forswore
To bear this passionate universal load,
This Calvary of Creation, with mankind.

IN MEMORIAM

SAMUEL COLERIDGE-TAYLOR.

FAREWELL! The soft mists of the sunset-sky
  Slowly enfold his fading birch-canoe.
Farewell! His dark, his desolate forests cry,
  Moved to their vast, their sorrowful depths anew.

Fading? Nay, freed from all the shores of night,
  His proud sails brightening thro' that crimson flame,
Another Hiawatha, clothed with light,
  Home to Ponemah takes his youthful fame.

Generous as a child, so wholly free
  From all base pride that fools forgot his crown,
He adored Beauty, in pure ecstasy,
  And waived the mere rewards of his renown.

The spark that falls from heaven not oft on earth
  To human hearts this vital splendour gives.
His was the simple, true, immortal birth.
  Scholars compose; but *this man's music lives!*

Greater than England or than Earth discerned,
  He never paltered with his art for gain:
When many a vaunted crown to dust is turned,
  This uncrowned king shall take his throne and reign.

Far distant years shall hear his forests moan ;
    And throngs unborn shall hear his winds lament,
Hear the strange grief that deepened through his own,
    The vast cry of a buried continent.

Through him, his race a moment lifted up
    Forests of hands to Beauty as in prayer ;
Touched through his lips the sacramental Cup,
    And then sank back—benumbed in our bleak air.

Through him, through him, a lost world hailed the light,
    The tragedy of that triumph none can tell,—
So great, so brief, so quickly snatched from sight ;
    Yet, Hiawatha, hail, and not farewell !

INSCRIPTION.

(For the Grave of Coleridge-Taylor.)

SLEEP, crowned with fame; fearless of change or time,
    Sleep, like remembered music in the soul,
Silent, immortal; while our discords climb
    To that great chord which shall resolve the whole.

Silent with Mozart on that solemn shore;
    Secure, where neither waves nor hearts can break;
Sleep—till the Master of the World, once more,
    Touch the remembered strings, and bid thee wake . . .

Touch the remembered strings, and bid thee wake.

THE TORCH.

(Sussex Landscape.)

Is it your watch-fire, elves, where the down with its darken-
　　ing shoulder
　Lifts on the death of the sun, out of the valley of thyme?
Dropt on the broad chalk path, and cresting the ridge of
　　it, smoulder
　　Crimson as blood on the white, halting my feet as they
　　　climb,

Clusters of clover-bloom, spilled from what negligent arms
　　in the tender
　Dusk of the great grey world, last of the tints of the day,
Beautiful, sorrowful, strange, last stain of that perishing
　　splendour.
　　Elves, from what torn white feet, trickled that red on the
　　　way?

No—from the sunburnt hands of what lovers that fade in
　　the distance?
　　Here—was it here that they paused?　Here that the
　　　legend was told?
Even a kiss would be heard in this hush; but, with mock-
　　ing insistence,
　　Now thro' the valley resound—only the bells of the fold.

Dropt from the hands of what beautiful throng? Did they
    cry "*Follow after*,"
  Dancing into the West, leaving this token for me,—
Memory dead on the path, and the sunset to bury their
    laughter?
    Youth? Is it youth that has flown? Darkness covers
    the sea.

Darkness covers the earth. But the path is here. I
    assay it.
  Let the bloom fall like a flake, dropt from the torch of
    a friend.
Beautiful revellers, happy companions, I see and obey it;
  Follow your torch in the night, follow your path to the
    end.

THE WORLD'S WEDDING.

"Et quid curae nobis de generibus et speciebus? Ex uno Verbo omnia, et unum loquuntur omnia. Cui omnia unum sunt, quique ad unum omnia trahit et omnia in uno videt, potest stabilis corde esse."—THOMAS À KEMPIS.

I.

WHEN poppies fired the nut-brown wheat,
  My love went by with sun-stained feet :
I followed her laughter, followed her, followed her, all a
    summer's morn !
    But O, from an elfin palace of air,
    A wild bird sang a song so rare,
    I stayed to listen and—lost my Fair,
      And walked the world forlorn.

II.

When chalk shone white between the sheaves,
  My love went by as one that grieves ;
I followed her weeping, followed her, followed her, all an
    autumn noon !
    The sunset flamed so fierce a red
    From North to South—I turned my head
    To wonder—and my Fair was fled
      Beyond the dawning moon.

III.

When bare black boughs were choked with snow,
    My love went by, as long ago ;
I followed her, dreaming, followed her, followed her, all a
        winter's night !
    But O, along that snow-white track
    With thorny shadows printed black,
    I saw three kings come riding back,
        And—lost my life's delight.

IV.

    They are so many, and she but One ;
    And I and she, like moon and sun
So separate ever ! Ah yet, I follow her, follow her, faint
        and far ;
    For what if all this diverse bliss
    Should run together in one kiss !
    Swift, Spring, with the sweet clue I miss
    Between these several instances,—
        The kings, that inn, that star.

V.

Between the hawk's and the wood-dove's wing,
    My love, my love flashed by like Spring !
    The year had finished its golden ring !
    Earth, the Gipsy, and Heaven, the King,
    Were married like notes in the song I sing,
And O, I followed her, followed her, followed her over
        the hills of Time,
    Never to lose her now I know
    For whom the sun was clasped in snow,
    The heights linked to the depths below,
    The rose's flush to the planet's glow,
    Death the friend to life the foe,
    The Winter's joy to the Spring's woe,
        And the world made one in a rhyme.

THE GREAT NORTH ROAD.

Just as the moon was rising, I met a ghostly pedlar
  Singing for company beneath his ghostly load,—
Once, there were velvet lads with vizards on their faces,
  Riding up to rob me on the great North Road.

Now, my pack is heavy, and my pocket full of guineas
  Chimes like a wedding-peal, but little I enjoy
Roads that never echo to the chirrup of their canter,—
  The gay Golden Farmer and the Hereford Boy.

Rogues were they all, but their raid was from Elf-land!
  Shod with elfin silver were the steeds they bestrode.
Merlin buckled on the spurs that wheeled thro' the wet fern
  Bright as Jack-o'-Lanthorns off the great North Road.

Tales were told in country inns when Turpin rode to
    Rippleside!
  Puck tuned the fiddle-strings, and country maids grew
    coy,
Tavern doors grew magical when Colonel Jack might tap
    at them,
  The gay Golden Farmer and the Hereford Boy.

What are you seeking, then?   I asked this honest pedlar.
  —O, Mulled Sack or Natty Hawes might ease me of
    my load !—
Where are they flown then?—Flown where I follow ;
  They are all gone for ever up the great North Road.

Rogues were they all ; but the white dust assoils 'em !
  Paradise without a spice of deviltry would cloy.
Heavy is my pack till I meet with Jerry Abershaw,
  The gay Golden Farmer and the Hereford Boy.

THE OUTLAW.

Deep in the greenwood of my heart
　　My wild hounds race.
I cloak my soul at feast and mart,
　　I mask my face ;

Outlawed, but not alone, for Truth
　　Is outlawed too.
Proud world, you cannot banish us.
　　We banish *you*.

Go by, go by, with all your din,
　　Your dust, your greed, your guile,
Proud world, your thrones can never win—
　　From Her—one smile.

She sings to me in a lonely place,
　　She takes my hand.
I look into her lovely face
　　And understand . . .

Outlawed, but not alone, for Love
　　Is outlawed too.
You cannot banish us, proud world.
　　We banish *you*.

Now, which is outlawed, which alone?
   Around us fall and rise
Murmurs of leaf and fern, the moan
   Of Paradise.

Outlawed?   Then hills and woods and streams
   Are outlawed too!
Proud world, from our immortal dreams,
   We banish you.

THE HEDGE-ROSE OPENS.

How passionately it opens after rain,
      And O, how like a prayer
To those great shining skies!   Do they disdain
      A bride so small and fair?
See the imploring petals, how they part
      And utterly lay bare
The perishing treasures of that piteous heart
      In wild surrender there.
What?   Would'st *thou*, too, drink up the Eternal bliss,
      Ecstatically dare,
O, little bride of God, to invoke *His* kiss?—
      But O, how like a prayer!

AT EDEN GATES.

To Eden Garden—so the sign-post said ;
    I could not see the road ;
But, where the Sussex clover blossomed red
    Its runaway blisses flowed.

I traced them back for many a night and day,
    —The way she, too, had gone !—
Till lo, the terrible Angel in the way
    Inexorably shone.

Up to the Gates, a fearless fool I came ;
    Between the lily and rose
Fluttering these evil rags of sordid shame,
    A thing to scare the crows.

"And hath the Master given thee, then, no word ? "
    The scornful Angel smiled :
Only two souls may pass my Flaming Sword,—
    The Lover and the Child.

I raised my head,—" Now let all hell make mirth,
    Where Love went, I go, too ! "
His eyes met mine. The sword sank to the earth,
    And let her lover through.

LAMPS.

IMMENSE and silent night,
　Over the lonely downs I go ;
And the deep gloom is pricked with points of light
　Above me and below.

I cannot break the bars
　Of Time and Fate ; and, if I scan the sky,
There comes to me, questioning those cold stars,
　No signal, no reply.

Yet are they less than these——
　These village-lights, which I do scan
Below me, or far out on darkling seas
　Those messages from man ?

Round me the darkness rolls.
　Out of the depth, each lance of light
Shoots from lost lanthorns, thrills from living souls
　And shall I doubt the height ?

No signal ?　No reply ?
　As through the deepening night I roam,
Hope opens all her casements in the sky
　And lights the lamps of home.

PARACLETE.

TONGUE hath not told it,
 Heart hath not known ;
Yet shall the bough swing
 When it hath flown.

Dreams have denied it,
 Fools forsworn :
Yet it hath comforted
 Each man born.

Once and again it is
 Blown to me,
Sweet from the wild thyme,
 Salt from the sea ;

Blown thro' the ferns
 Faint from the sky ;
Shadowed in water,
 Yet clear as a cry.

Light on a face,
 Or touch of a hand,
Making my still heart
 Understand.

Earth hath not seen it,
　Nor heaven above.
Yet shall the wild bough
　Bend with the Dove.

Yea, tho' the bloom fall
　Under Thy feet,
Veni, Creator,
　Paraclete!

THE DEATH OF A GREAT MAN.

No—not that he is dead.   The pang's not there,
  Nor in the City's many-coloured bloom
Of swift black-lettered posters, which the throng
  Passes with bovine stare,
To say *He is dead* and *Is it going to rain?*
  Or hum stray snatches of a rag-time song.
Nor is it in that falsest shibboleth
(Which orators toss to the dumb scorn of death)
  That all the world stands weeping at his tomb.
London is dining, dancing, through it all.
  And, in the unchecked smiles along the street
Where men, that slightly knew him, lightly meet,
  With all the old indifferent grimaces,
There is no jot of grief, no tittle of pain.
  No.   No.   For nearer things do most tears fall.
Grief is for near and little things.   But pride,
  O, pride was to be found by two or three,
And glory in his great battling memory,
  Prouder and purer than the loud world knows,
In one more dreadful sign, the day he died—
  The dreadful light upon a thousand faces,
The peace upon the faces of his foes.

THE INNER PASSION.

THERE is a Master in my heart
  To whom, though oft against my will,
I bring the songs I sing apart
  And strive to think that they fulfil
His silent law, within my heart.

But He is blind to my desires,
  And deaf to all that I would plead :
He tests my truth at purer fires
  And shames my purple with His need.
He claims my deeds, not my desires.

And often when my comrades praise,
  I sadden, for He turns from me.
But, sometimes, when they blame, I raise
  Mine eyes to His, and in them see
A tenderness too deep for praise.

He is not to be bought with gold,
  Or lured by thornless crowns of fame ;
But when some rebel thought hath sold
  Him to dishonour and to shame,
And my heart's Pilate cries " Behold,"

" Behold the Man," I know Him then ;
  And all those wild thronged clamours die
In my heart's judgment hall again,
  Or if it ring with " Crucify ! "
Some few are faithful even then.

Some few sad thoughts,—one bears His cross,
  To that dark Calvary of my pride ;
One stands far off and mourns His loss,
  And one poor thief on either side
Hangs on his own unworthy cross.

And one—O, truth in ancient guise !—
  Rails, and one bids him cease alway,
And the God turns His hungering eyes
  On that poor thought with " Thou, this day,
Shalt sing, shalt sing, in Paradise."

VALUES.

THE moon that sways the rhythmic seas,
   The wheeling earth, the marching sky,—
     I ask not whence the order came
      That moves them all as one.

These are your chariots.   Nor shall these
   Appal me with immensity;
     I know they carry one heart of flame
      More precious than the sun.

A COUNTRY LANE IN HEAVEN.

THE exceeding weight of glory bowed
   My head, in that pure clime :
I found a road that ran through cloud
   Along the coasts of Time . . .

Out of that mist of years there came
   A cross-barred gate of wood.
I clutched, I kissed the unheavenly frame
   So hard, it trickled blood.

My head upon the iron lay.
   I slobbered blood and foam.
Yea, like a dog, I knew the way,
   A hundred yards from home.

Iron and blood and wood !   They knew
   The secret of that cry
When the Eternal Passion drew
   Their Maker through——to die.

I knew each little hawthorn-cloud
   Along my misty lane,
Then my heart burst. She sobbed aloud,
   Between my arms again.

THE *TITANIC*.

If in the noon they doubted, in the night
    They never swerved.   Death had no power to appal.
There was one Way, one Truth, one Life, one Light,
    One Love that shone triumphant over all.

If in the noon they doubted, at the last
    There was no Way to part, no Way but One
That rolled the waves of Nature back and cast
    In ancient days a shadow across the sun.

If in the noon they doubted, their last breath
    Saluted once again the eternal goal,
Chanted a love-song in the face of Death
    And rent the veil of darkness from the soul.

If in the noon they doubted, in the night
    They waved the shadowy world of strife aside,
Flooded high heaven with an immortal light,
    And taught the deep how its Creator died.

TO THE DESTROYERS.

Yes.   You have shattered many an ancient wrong,
  And we were with you, heart and mind and soul,
  But there are fools who cast away control
In life and thought and art ; because the strong
We dare to say it—have now destroyed so long,
  That reckless minds forget the unchanging goal—
  The nobler order which shall make us whole,
The service which is freedom, beauty, song.

We shall be stoned as traitors to your cause
  While the real traitors that you did not know,
    Chaos and Vice, trumpet themselves as free.
Pray God that, loyal to the eternal laws,
  A little remnant, mauled by friend and foe,
    Save you through Truth, and bring you Liberty.

THE ROMAN WAY.

He that has loyally served the State
 Whereof he found himself a part,
Or spent his life-blood to create
 A kingdom's treasure in his art;

Who sees the enemies of his land
 Applauded, by her sects and schools;
And the high thought they scarce had scanned
 Derided and belied by fools;

—Better to know it soon than late!—
 Struggling, he wins a meed of praise;
Achieving, he is dogged by hate
 Or stung by malice all his days.

O, Emperor of the Stoic clan,
 Enfold him, then, with nobler pride.
Teach him that nought can hurt a man
 Who will not turn or stoop to chide.

Can falsehood kindle or bedim
 One bay-leaf in his quiet crown?
Ten thousand Lies may pluck at him,
 But only Truth can tear him down.

Why should he heed the thing they say?
    They never asked if it were true.
Why brush one scribbler's tale away
    For others to invent a new?

No, let him search his heart, secure
    —If Truth be there—from tongue or pen;
And teach us, Emperor, to endure,
    To think like Romans and like men.

ASTRID.

(*An Experiment in Initial Rhymes.*)

WHITE-ARMED Astrid,—ah, but she was beautiful!—
Nightly wandered weeping thro' the ferns in the moon,
Slowly, weaving her strange garland in the forest,
Crowned with white violets,
Gowned in green.
Holy was that glen where she glided,
Making her wild garland as Merlin had bidden her,
Breaking off the milk-white horns of the honeysuckle,
Sweetly dripped the dew upon her small white
Feet.

White-throated Astrid,—ah, but she was beautiful!—
Nightly sought the answer to that riddle in the moon.
She must weave her garland, ere she save her soul.
Three long years she has wandered there in vain.
Always, always, the blossom that would finish it
Falls to her feet, and the garland breaks and vanishes,
Breaks like a dream in the dawn when the dreamer
Wakes.

White-bosomed Astrid,—ah, but she was beautiful!—
Nightly tastes the sorrow of the world in the moon.
Will it be this little white miracle, she wonders.
How shall she know it, the star that will save her?
Still, ah still, in the moonlight she crouches
Bowing her head, for the garland has crumbled!
All the wild petals for the thousand and second time
Fall.

White-footed Astrid,—ah, but she is beautiful!—
Nightly seeks the secret of the world in the moon.
She will find the secret.   She will find the golden
Key to the riddle, on the night when she has numbered
        them,
Marshalled all her wild flowers, ordered them as music,
Star by star, note by note, changing them and ranging
        them,
Suddenly, as at a kiss, all will flash together,
Flooding like the dawn thro' the arches of the woodland,
Fern and thyme and violet, maiden-hair and primrose
Turn to the Rose of the World, and He shall fold her,
Kiss her on the mouth, saying, all the world is one now,
This is the secret of the music that the soul hears,—
This.

THE INIMITABLE LOVERS.

THEY tell this proud tale of the Queen — Cleopatra,
    Subtlest of women that the world has ever seen,
How that, on the night when she parted with her lover
    Anthony, tearless, dry-throated, and sick-hearted,
A strange thing befell them in the darkness where they
        stood.

    Bitter as blood was that darkness.
And they stood in a deep window, looking to the west.
    Her white breast was brighter than the moon upon
        the sea,
And it moved in her agony (because it was the end !)
    Like a deep sea, where many had been drowned.
Proud ships that were crowned with an Emperor's eagles
    Were sunken there forgotten, with their emeralds and
        gold.
They had drunken of that glory, and their tale was told,
        utterly,
    Told.

There, as they parted, heart from heart, mouth from mouth,
    They stared upon each other.   They listened.
        For the South-wind
Brought them a rumour from afar ; and she said,
    Lifting her head, too beautiful for anguish,
        Too proud for pity,—
It is the gods that leave the City !   O, Anthony,
    Anthony, the gods have forsaken us ;
Because it is the end !   They leave us to our doom.

Hear it!   And unshaken in the darkness,
Dull as dropping earth upon a tomb in the distance,
   They heard, as when across a wood a low wind comes,
A muttering of drums, drawing nearer,
   Then louder and clearer, as when a trumpet sings
To battle, it came rushing on the wings of the wind,
   A sound of sacked cities, a sound of lamentation,
A cry of desolation, as when a conquered nation
   Is weeping in the darkness, because its tale is told ;
And then—a sound of chariots that rolled thro' that sorrow
   Trampled like a storm of wild stallions, tossing nearer,
Trampled louder, clearer, triumphantly as music
   Till lo ! in that great darkness, along that vacant street,
A red light beat like a furnace on the walls,
   Then—like the blast when the North-wind calls to battle
Blaring thro' the blood-red tumult and the flame,
   Shaking the proud City as they came, an hundred
      elephants,
Cream-white and bronze, and splashed with bitter crimson,
   Trumpeting for battle as they trod, an hundred elephants,
Bronze and cream-white, and trapped with gold and purple,
   Towered like tuskéd castles, every thunder-laden footfall
Dreadful as the shattering of a City.   Yet they trod,
   Rocking like an earthquake, to a great triumphant music,
And, swinging like the stars, black planets, white moons,
   Thro' the stream of the torches, they brought the red
      chariot,
The chariot of the battle-god—Mars.
   While the tall spears of Sparta tossed clashing in his train,
And a host of ghostly warriors cried aloud
   All hail! to those twain, and went rushing to the darkness
Like a pageantry of cloud, for their tale was told—utterly—
   Told.

And following, in the fury of the vine, rushing down
   Like a many-visaged torrent, with ivy-rod and thyrse,
And many a wild and foaming crown of roses,
   Crowded the Bacchanals, the brown-limbed shepherds,

The red-tongued leopards, and the glory of the god!
  Iacchus! Iacchus! without dance, without song,
They cried and swept along to the darkness.
  Only for a breath when the tumult of their torches
Crimsoned the deep window where that dark warrior stood
  With the blood upon his mail, and the Queen—Cleopatra,
Frozen to white marble—the Mænads raised their timbrels,
  Tossed their white arms, with a clash—*All hail!*
Like wild swimmers, pale, in a sea of blood and wine,
  All hail! All hail! Then they swept into the darkness
And the darkness buried them. Their tale was told—
  utterly—
  Told.

And following them, O softer than the moon upon the sea,
  Aphrodite, implacably, shone.
Like a furnace of white roses, Aphrodite and her train
  Lifted their white arms to those twain in the silence
Once, and were gone into the darkness;
  Once, and away into the darkness they were swept
Like a pageantry of cloud, without praise, without pity.
  Then the dark City slept. And the Queen—Cleopatra—
Subtlest of women that this earth has ever seen,
  Turning to her lover in the darkness where he stood,
With the blood upon his mail,
  Bowing her head upon that iron in the darkness,
  Wept.

A SONG OF HOPE.

Not in those eyes, too kind for truth,
   Which dare not note how beauties wane;
Nor in that crueller joy of youth
   Which turns from sorrow with disdain;
      No—no—not there,
   Abides the hope that answers our despair.

Lie where they hid thy dead away.
   Knock on that unrelenting door;
Then break, O desolate heart, and say
   Farewell, farewell, for evermore . . .
      There, only there,
   Abides the hope that conquers all despair.

The silence that refused to bless
   Till grief had turned the heart to stone . . .
What soul compact of nothingness
   Could hear so fierce a trumpet blown?
      Then hear, O hear,
   The dreadful hope that equals all despair.

There, till the deep atoning Might
   Shall answer all that each can pray,
The very boundlessness of night
   Proclaims—and waits—an equal day.
      There, only there,
—*But O, sing low, sweet strings, lest hope take*
    wing!—
   Abides the hope that answers all despair.

OLDER THAN THE HILLS.

OLDER than the hills, older than the sea,
  Older than the heart of the Spring,
O, what is this that breaks
From the blind shell, wakes,
  Wakes, and is gone like a wing?

Older than the sea, older than the moon,
  Older than the heart of the May,
What is this blind refrain
Of a song that shall remain
  When the singer is long gone away?

Older than the moon, older than the stars,
  Older than the wind in the night,—
Though the young dews are sweet
On the heather at our feet
  And the blue hills laughing back the light,—

Till the stars grow young, till the hills grow young,
  O, Love, we shall walk through Time,
Till we round the world at last,
And the future be the past,
  And the winds of Eden greet us from the prime.

FOUR SONGS.

(*After Verlaine.*)

I. RAIN.

My heart is full of the rain
    As it weeps on the dim grey town.
O, what is this endless pain
    That weeps in my heart with the rain?

The grey sky breaks into tears
    On the brown earth and grey roofs.
O, heart, after all these years,
    Are you heavy with tears?

It rains without reason to-night
    In a heart that is numbed with pain,
A world without hope of the light
    Grieves without reason to-night.

Ah, the one grief keener than all
    Is to wonder—when grief is fled—
Why the tears of the old time fall
    In a heart grown tired of it all.

II. AUTUMN.

Touch the dark strings.
Pale Autumn sings.
    Wet winds creep
The bare boughs through . . .
O, woods we knew,
    I, too, weep.

Stifled and blind
I call to mind
  Dreams long lost,
Dreams all astray
In that dead May,
  With Love's ghost.

Then I, too, go,
As the winds blow,
  Grey with grief,
Hither, thither,
I know not whither,—
  A dead leaf.

III. AT NOON.

The sky is blue above the roof,
 So calm, so blue,
One rustling bough above the roof,
 Rocks, the noon through.

The bell-tower in the sky, aloof,
 Tenderly rings !
A bird upon the bough, aloof,
 Sorrows and sings.

My God, my God, and life is here
 So simple and still !
Far off, the murmuring town I hear
 At the wind's will. . . .

What hast thou done, thou, weeping there ?
 O quick, the truth !
What hast thou done, thou, weeping there,
 With thy lost youth ?

IV. SHADOWS.

The mirrored trees in that nocturnal stream
  Drown like a cloudy dream.
The bird upon the green bough, looking down,
  Sees his own shadow drown.

He thinks it is his true love drowning there ;
  And moans in his despair.
Ah, many a heart on high among green leaves,
  Grieves, as that sweet fool grieves.

A SKY-SONG.

The Devil has launched his great grey craft
　　To voyage in the sky ;
But Life puts out with a thousand wings,
　　To rake His Majesty fore and aft
　　　　And prove that Wrong must die.

So has it been since time began,—
　　When Death would mount and fly,
A swifter fleet, with sharper stings,
　　Round him in lightning circles ran
　　　　And proved that Death must die.

Invincible, he came of old.
　　His galleons towered on high ;
But Drake and his companions bold,
　　And this proud sea that laughs and sings
　　　　Declared that Death must die.

So all these four free winds declare
　　And these pure realms of sky ;
And these new admirals of the air,
　　Ay, Life with all her radiant wings
　　　　Declares that Death must die.

THE CAROL OF THE FIR-TREE.

QUOTH the Fir-tree, "Orange and vine"
  Sing 'Nowell, Nowell, Nowell'!
"Have their honour : I have mine!"
  In Excelsis Gloria!
"I am kin to the great king's house,"
  Ring 'Nowell, Nowell, Nowell'!
"And Lebanon whispers in my boughs."
  In Excelsis Gloria!

Apple and cherry, pear and plum,
  Winds of Autumn, sigh 'Nowell'!
All the trees like mages come
  Bending low with 'Gloria'!
Holding out on every hand
  Summer pilgrims to Nowell!
Gorgeous gifts from Elfin-land.
  And the May saith 'Gloria'!

Out of the darkness—who shall say
  Gold and myrrh for this Nowell!
How they win their wizard way?
  Out of the East with 'Gloria'!
Men that eat of the sun and dew,
  Angels laugh and sing, 'Nowell'
Call it "fruit," and say it "grew"!
  Into the West with 'Gloria'!

"Leaves that fall," whispered the Fir
  Through the forest sing 'Nowell'!
"I am winter's minister."
  In Excelsis Gloria!
Summer friends may come and go,
  Up the mountain sing 'Nowell.'
Love abides thro' storm and snow.
  Down the valley, 'Gloria'!

"On my boughs, on mine, on mine,"
  Father and mother, sing 'Nowell'!
"All the fruits of the earth shall twine."
  Bending low with 'Gloria.'
"Sword of wood and doll of wax"
  Little children, sing 'Nowell.'
"Swing on the stem was cleft with the axe!"
  Craftsmen all, a 'Gloria.'

"Hear! I have looked on the other side."
  Out of the East, O sing 'Nowell'!
"Because to live this night I died!"
  Into the West with 'Gloria.'
"Hear! In this lighted room I have found"
  Ye that seek, O sing 'Nowell'!
"The spell that worketh underground."
  Ye that doubt, a 'Gloria.'

"I have found it, even I,"
  Ye that are lowly, sing 'Nowell'!
"The secret of this alchemy!"
  Ye that are poor, a 'Gloria.'
"Look, your tinsel turneth to gold."
  Sing 'Nowell! Nowell! Nowell!'
"Your dust to a hand for love to hold!"
  In Excelsis Gloria.

"Lay the axe at my young stem now!"
Woodman, woodman, sing 'Nowell.'
"Set a star on every bough!"
In Excelsis Gloria.
"Hall and cot shall see me stand,"
Rich and poor man, sing 'Nowell'!
"Giver of gifts from Elfin-land."
Oberon, answer 'Gloria.'

"Hung by the hilt on your Christmas-tree"
Little children, sing 'Nowell'!
"Your wooden sword is a cross for me."
Emperors, a 'Gloria.'
"I have found that fabulous stone"
Ocean-worthies, cry 'Nowell.'
"Which turneth all things into one."
Wise men all, a 'Gloria.'

"It is not ruby nor anything"
Jeweller, jeweller, sing 'Nowell'!
"Fit for the crown of an earthly king."
In Excelsis Gloria!
"It is not here!   It is not there!"
Traveller, rest and cry 'Nowell'!
"It is one thing and everywhere!"
Heaven and Earth sing 'Gloria.'

"It is the earth, the moon, the sun,"
Mote in the sunbeam, sing 'Nowell'!
"And all the stars that march as one."
In Excelsis Gloria!
"Here, by the touch of it, I can see"
Sing, O Life, a sweet Nowell!
"The world's King die on a Christmas-tree."
Answer, Death, with "Gloria."

"Here, not set in a realm apart,"
   East and West are one 'Nowell'!
"Holy Land is in your Heart!"
   North and South one 'Gloria'!
"Death is a birth, birth is a death,"
   Love is all, O sing 'Nowell'!
"And London one with Nazareth."
   And all the World a 'Gloria.'

"And angels over your heart's roof sing"
   Birds of God, O pour 'Nowell'!
"That a poor man's son is the Son of a King!"
   Out of your heart this 'Gloria'!
"Round the world you'll not away"
   In your own soul, they sing 'Nowell'!
"From Holy Land this Christmas Day!"
   In your own soul, this 'Gloria.'

END OF VOL. III.

PRINTED BY WILLIAM BLACKWOOD AND SONS.